# HANDCRAFTING JEWELRY

## designs & techniques

William E. Garrison
*and*
Merle E. Dowd

nry Regnery Company
CHICAGO

Copyright © 1972 by William E. Garrison and Merle E. Dowd.
All rights reserved.
Published by Henry Regnery Company
180 North Michigan Avenue, Chicago, Illinois 60601
Manufactured in the United States of America
Library of Congress Catalog Card Number: 71-183815
International Standard Book Number: 0-8092-8851-6


Published simultaneously in Canada by
Fitzhenry & Whiteside Limited
150 Lesmill Road
Don Mills, Ontario M3B 2T5
Canada

# contents

*William E. Garrison*
*Merle E. Dowd*

# introduction

HANDCRAFTING JEWELRY can be fun and profitable. More and more, individuals are rebelling against the wearing of mass-produced, look-alike jewelry. Buyers and craftsmen alike appreciate the authentic, honest look of one-of-a-kind handcrafted earrings, cuff links, pendants, pins, medallions, tie-bars, rings, and other body adornments. Learning metal crafting and casting skills and making your own handcrafted jewelry can be tremendously satisfying. Wearing the products of your own skill and presenting gifts you have made with your hands are far more satisfying experiences than either wearing or giving mass-produced jewelry.

Jewelry crafting is gaining popularity among hobbyists, artists, and practicing craftsmen for two primary reasons:

First, learning jewelry craft skills can be as challenging as you choose. Once you've mastered one technique, there is always another one waiting to be conquered. Although many skills used in making jewelry have been developed and refined over centuries, new methods and techniques continue to be developed as new materials and innovative equipment become available. The true jewelry craftsman learns the skills of joining metals with heat, of shaping metals and gems into unique designs, and of combining materials in new and unusual ways. A craftsman never really learns all there is to know about jewelry silversmithing, goldsmithing, and casting.

The second reason for the increased interest in jewelry crafting is that the products created are worn and used. The unlimited array of earrings, rings, pendants, and the many other pieces coming from the jewelry handcrafter's bench are functional as well as being eye-appealing and often works of art in their own right.

*Handcrafting Jewelry: Designs and Techniques* will help you apply your creative abilities to jewelry design while you simultaneously learn the procedures and techniques necessary to complete a specific project. The techniques and methods detailed in the following chapters are basic to all jewelry metalcrafting and casting. These methods start with projects that call for basic materials. There are no simple stick-together kits of premanufactured pieces in these pages.

In the following chapters you are introduced to one or more basic techniques through the step-by-step process of actually crafting a piece of jewelry. Mastery of these techniques will lead you into your own creative designs. Along with the step-by-step approach, each chapter offers a wide variety of finished designs to stimulate your own creativity and to widen the range of your thinking. In the early chapters step-by-step techniques are more detailed to help you master such basic skills as soldering, sawing, and fusing. Later chapters emphasize variations of basic techniques and help you to continue building a repertoire of skills.

*Handcrafting Jewelry* does not attempt to teach the novice craftsman every possible technique. These chapters aim to help you develop complementary skills to carry you one step further in turning gemstones, crystals, polished stones, and metals into strikingly original jewelry.

This book is a basic book. It assumes no prior knowledge of jewelry crafting techniques or jewelry materials and tools. However, it is not just a beginner's book. Every practicing craftsman can learn new approaches to old techniques and new techniques not found elsewhere. One of the major contributions offered is an introduction to innovative tools for both metalcrafting and casting that permit the craftsman to accomplish difficult techniques more easily or to accomplish specific techniques, such as prong bending, in a completely new way.

1

As the reader develops and practices the basic skills in a logical sequence, he or she will be encouraged to strike out alone, to apply confidently the techniques learned in creating unique designs.

Along with the step-by-step approach to learning techniques and creating your own jewelry, later chapters provide a wealth of essential information on tools and materials along with a workable list of sources. As you become more experienced in making jewelry, you may find that assembling exactly the kind of materials and tools you need may become a frustrating experience because all supplies are not readily available from one source. But you will find that the tools necessary to get started and to make a remarkable variety of jewelry can be acquired for less than almost any other major craft. Hand tools for getting started in jewelry crafting can be bought at retail prices ranging from $50-$75. Of course, if you buy power buffs, electric pickle pots, and other desirable but expensive alternatives to basic tools and equipment, the price can triple — or more.

Materials for jewelry making range from inexpensive brass and copper to more expensive sterling silver and gold. In the beginning you probably will want to start with less expensive metals, graduating to gold and silver when you have gained confidence in your skills. Jewelry crafted in the more economical brass, copper, and German silver is stunning and eye catching. You will find that it is the skill and artistry applied to the material that makes for an outstanding piece of jewelry and not the quality of the metal itself.

We wish to thank all of the artists and craftsmen who have contributed examples of their work to this book. Their names are credited along with the illustrations of their jewelry.

# rings without stones

*Joint Soldering Techniques*

*Sterling silver band ring stamped and pierced. Anne Gries, Flushing, New York.*

RINGS CAN BE AS INDIVIDUAL as a fingerprint. They can be plain, decorated, small, enormous, with or without stones, narrow or wide. In this chapter you will begin learning jewelry metalcrafting techniques with the most basic of jewelry forms, the simple band ring. By using your own creativity and the techniques of flame soldering, which you will learn in the following pages, you can design and make a band ring.

## BAND RING PROJECT

The best way to learn to make jewelry is simply to begin. However, if you feel that you need to learn something about the tools and materials that you will be using so that you can purchase the necessary equipment, then read Chapters 15 and 16 before starting the band ring project to be completed in this chapter.

### Metal Characteristics

Chapter 18 includes a glossary of terms that should be useful to you as you learn jewelry handcrafting. But to fully understand why metals react as they do and to familiarize yourself with some of their basic characteristics, experiment with scrap pieces of metal to study the following properties before beginning any project.

1. Heat conductivity — the rate or speed at which a metal transmits heat. Silver conducts heat readily; so does copper. Iron and steel are poor conductors. Heat conductivity is important for successful soldering and annealing. To test the heat conductivity of various metals, hold a wire of steel, brass, and sterling, one at a time, in the blue flame cone of the propane torch. Note the differences in time before the wires become uncomfortably hot to the touch. You might want to keep a written record of these times for reference.

2. Malleability — the ability of a metal to be bent, rolled, or shaped. Soft metals, particularly silver and gold, exhibit excellent malleability. Steel is less malleable, and copper and brass fall in a middle range.

3. Work hardening — the characteristic of most metals to become hard and finally break or crack when bent, hammered, or shaped repeatedly. To demonstrate the rate at which different metals become work-hardened bend a ¼-inch strip of soft 16-gauge copper between your fingers. Note how easily it bends. Now hammer the copper over the full surface with the 2-ounce hammer. Try bending the strip and notice how much harder it is to bend. Continue bending the strip back and forth until it becomes so work-hardened that it no longer bends easily or begins cracking at an edge. Try this same experiment with various other metals.

4. Annealing — a method of softening work-hardened metal. Annealing consists of heating work-hardened metal and allowing it to cool. Place the copper work-hard-

3

ened strip on a heating block. Heat the strip evenly, keeping the blue cone of the flame constantly moving around the entire piece. Heat the strip until it becomes visibly red, about 1200° F. The red glow of the metal will be more visible in a partially dark room. Set the strip aside to cool in the air or dunk it in plain water. Now try bending the strip; you will find that it is soft and workable. Most jewelry metals can be annealed in this manner.

5. Oxidation — a metallic reaction with oxygen, such as common rust on steel. Copper, sterling, brass, and other jewelry metals also oxidize. Gold oxidizes very little, although the other metal(s) in gold alloys may oxidize selectively. You should recognize oxidation and learn to prevent it because oxidation is the single most common reason for poor soldering.

6. Flux action — the chemical method for preventing oxidation during heating. Two kinds of flux are commonly used: self-pickling and borax flux. Self-pickling flux helps to clean metal while preventing it from oxidizing during heating. Borax flux does no cleaning, but borax resists heat longer than self-pickling flux. (See Chapter 16 for more information on fluxes.) Oxidation and flux action can be demonstrated together. Note that the black on the annealed copper strip is oxidized copper. Coat half of a strip of clean copper with flux. Adjust the torch to a low heat and dry the flux slowly. Note that the flux first dries to a grainy white powder. With the torch at medium heat, continue heating the strip. The flux first bubbles and finally melts to a clear liquid, indicating the metal is approaching soldering temperature. Allow the strip to cool. Note the difference between the fluxed and unfluxed portions of the strip. The unfluxed portion will be oxidized black, while the fluxed portion will remain clean of oxidation.

7. Pickling or cleaning oxidation from jewelry metals. Oxidation and other contamination must be cleaned from metals before solder will bond. When cleaning is

4

*Fig. 1-1. - The correct ring size can be found with a ring-size gauge. Numbers for ring sizes normally range from 0 through 13 1/2 by half-sizes.*

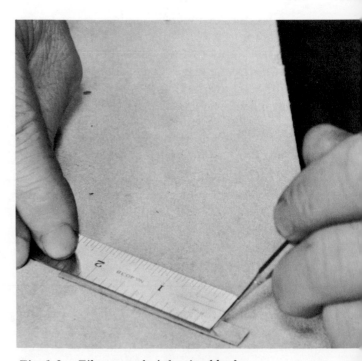

*Fig. 1-2. - File one end of the ring blank square and decide the proper length for the ring you are making by consulting Table 18E in Chapter 18. Align the edge of the ruler with the ring blank and scribe the correct length across the metal.*

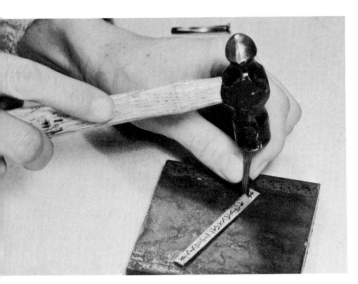

Fig. 1-3. - When stamping designs, place the ring blank on a metal block. Strike the stamp (nail) with one sharp blow. If a mark is too light, don't try to deepen it—just consider a light mark as part of your design. Don't allow the sharp edge of the steel stamp to extend over the edge of the ring blank.

chemical, it is known as pickling. Filing, silicon carbide paper sanding, or grinding with power equipment mechanically cleans metal surfaces.

In making a band ring there is one thing you should know before cutting a strip of metal that when joined and rounded has to fit a specific finger. A narrow band can be smaller than a wide band and still fit the same finger. There are several reasons for this, and you will probably discover most of them through trial and error. But to start with, let's just say there are no rigid rules governing the way different rings are going to fit.

Using a ring gauge (Fig. 1-1), determine the size of the ring you are going to make. Then consult Table 18E in Chapter 18 to determine the length of the metal strip that will round to the size you have selected. For example, if your ring is to be size 9½, you'll see that the blank should be cut to 2.50 or 2½ inches.

Select a metal blank from 16- or 18-gauge sterling silver, or use brass if you prefer to practice with an inexpensive material. A ¼-inch width is a handy strip with which to start. Until you learn sawing techniques, select a blank already trimmed to an even ¼-inch width. Trim or file one end of the strip square. Then, using a metal scale, measure off 2½ inches as shown in Fig. 1-2. Trim along the scored mark with metal shears.

Any decorating that is to be done to the ring should be completed before the ends of the metal strip are joined. Decorating the band ring can take many forms. One of the simplest ways is to stamp a random or repetitive design onto the surface with a straight or curved edge stamp — or a combination of both. Concrete nails with their edges shaped on a grinder make ideal metal stamps for decorating jewelry metals (Fig. 1-3). You can buy these nails with different shaped points or grind them yourself (see Chapter 15). Odd-shaped ends can be ground on stamps to achieve the results shown in Fig. 1-4. One caution: don't allow the cutting edge of a stamp to extend over the edge of the metal strip being decorated.

Edge treatment (Fig. 1-5) is another way of adding design variety to rings. Later, in Chapter 6, you will learn how to saw designs by piercing (Fig. 1-6). When you have mastered the techniques of sweat soldering metal overlays (see Chapter 3), you can add raised designs in metals with contrasting colors (Fig. 1-7).

After stamping your design, recheck the length of the ring blank because the stamping may have stretched it. The ends of the blank should be square, and it probably will be necessary to hand file (Fig. 1-8) or square them with a powered grinding tool.

The next step after squaring the ends of the blank is to bend the ends together in position to be soldered. But before doing this, let's learn the fundamentals of joint soldering.

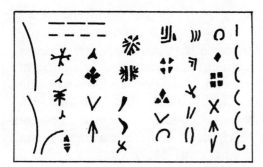

Fig. 1-4. - These interesting shapes can be ground from scrap pieces of tool steel or concrete nails to form stamps that can be used to extend design possibilities.

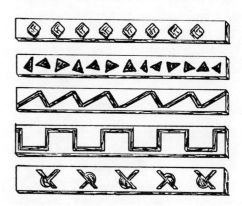

Fig. 1-7. - Overlays of thin metal may be sawed to shape and sweat soldered to a band before the metal is bent. Overlays add depth and varied colors plus variety of design. See Chapter 3 for sweat soldering techniques. Try sterling overlays on a brass or copper base, or sweat solder 14K gold overlays onto a sterling band.

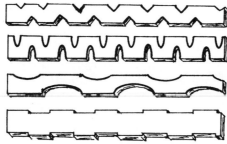

Fig. 1-5. - Edge treatment adds a sculptural effect to band rings. Small indentations may simply be filed into the metal. Larger effects have to be sawed and edges filed smooth. The inside edges should be polished.

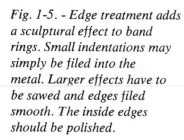

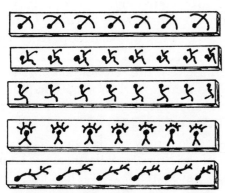

Fig. 1-6. - Pierced designs are sawed through the depth of the metal band before it is bent and soldered. The tiny round dot in each design is a drilled hole in which the saw is inserted for piercing. See Chapter 6 for more complete details on piercing techniques.

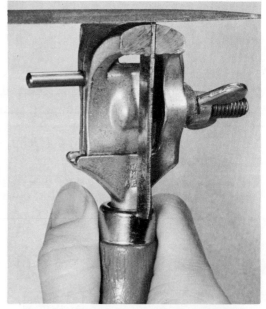

Fig. 1-8. - The ends of a blank should be filed square and flat. Filing will also remove fire scale and oxidation resulting from annealing. Note how the ends of ring blank are tapered after shearing.

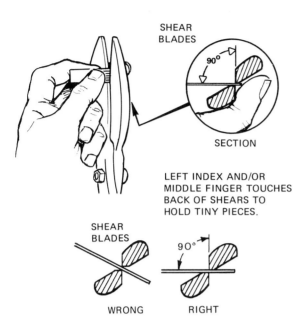

Fig. 1-9. - Sheets of silver solder first should be sliced into narrow strips 1/32 to 1/16 inch wide. Squares, or bits (paillons), are then cut off across the strips. When cutting keep jaws of the shears at right angles to the sheet. By keeping your thumb or finger along the outer edge of the strip, you will prevent the tiny solder bits from flying off in all directions.

Fig. 1-10. - Chemical cleaning, or pickling, removes oxidation quickly and easily. (See Chapter 16 for proportions and mixing.) An improvised heating stand can be cut from a coffee can. (See Chapter 15 for mesh top and tripod stand.) Keep the pickle in a Pyrex glass beaker to allow for repeated boiling. Hot annealed or soldered pieces may be dropped immediately into the pickling solution for quick cleaning. They also can be left in a cool pickle overnight, but a heated pickle solution works faster. After cleaning, rinse the work in cool, plain water and continue working on it immediately.

## Flame Soldering

Silver solder is one of the "hard" solders, which means that it melts at a much higher temperature than does common tin-lead "soft" solders. Silver solder is available in five melting temperatures, or "melts," as shown in Fig. 16-7, Chapter 16. Silver solder is available in sheet form and must be cut into tiny squares or strips (paillons) as shown in Fig. 1-9. Most jewelry soldering calls for an easy melt solder that melts at around 1325° F. Remember these important facts about soldering:

1. Silver solder will not span or bridge a gap between two pieces to be joined. The ends or surfaces to be soldered must actually touch.

2. Silver solder will not bond to dirty metal. "Dirt" may be any contaminant, but the most common form is oxidation. Surfaces to be soldered may be cleaned mechanically by filing or wire brushing, but the simplest and quickest way is to clean the surfaces chemically (Fig. 1-10). If the solder balls up but does not flow, the metal is dirty.

7

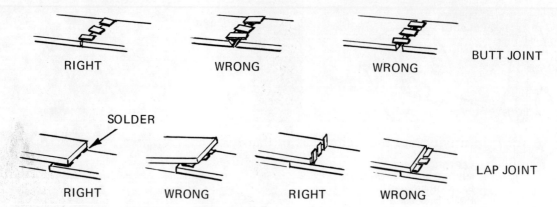

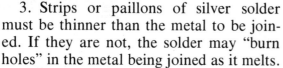

Fig. 1-11. - *When placing solder bits for butt joints, make sure no V joint or gap exists. For lap joints, solder bits may separate the work pieces as long as the surfaces to be joined remain parallel. When soldering lap joints, bits may be placed on end across the edge of the upper work piece. Molten solder is drawn between the work pieces by capillary attraction.*

Fig. 1-12. - *By cradling the torch and propane fuel cylinder along your left arm, you support the weight of the cylinder and leave your right hand free for other work. (If you are left-handed, support the tank in your right arm.) Note the position of the left hand on gas-flow valve.*

3. Strips or paillons of silver solder must be thinner than the metal to be joined. If they are not, the solder may "burn holes" in the metal being joined as it melts.

4. Silver solder melts before it "runs" or flows, but it must flow to effect a bond between surfaces being joined. Flowing or "running" means that the solder melts and the liquid metal is drawn into the joint by heat and capillary attraction. Only a very little solder is necessary to form a strong joint. When conditions are right, the silver solder is attracted to the work surfaces. Correct soldering technique involves setting up the right conditions. These conditions are discussed in the following pages.

5. Work to be soldered must be "dead soft" — annealed. Otherwise, when the work is heated, stresses in the metal may open the gap to be joined or distort the metal.

Two types of joints cover most of the work in jewelry crafting — butt joint and lap joint. In a butt joint, the two ends of the work touch in the same plane. In a lap joint, the two ends are not in the same plane, but the pieces joined must be parallel. Fig. 1-11 shows the right and wrong positioning of solder bits when joining pieces with either butt or lap joints.

Common jewelry materials — gold, silver, brass, copper, and others — are easily soldered with the 2000° F. heat available with a common propane torch (Fig. 1-12). Whether the fuel is supplied from its own tank or a hose is immaterial, although a flexible hose supply is much less tiring than cradling a tank in your arm. Learn to light the propane torch with a flint lighter (Fig. 1-13). Practice controlling the heat

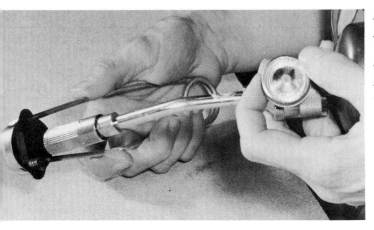

*Fig. 1-13. - To light the torch of the propane fuel cylinder, hold the flint lighter about 1 inch away from the end. Open the valve only slightly, as too much gas will blow the flame out after it is ignited. Snap the spring arm of the lighter briskly to generate sparks.*

*Fig. 1-14. - Adjust the flame by turning the control valve slowly and gently. The torch tip automatically mixes air with the gas. Note the cone of blue flame that begins at the end of the torch tip. The length of the blue cone and the hiss and roar of the flame determine the amount of heat being generated.*

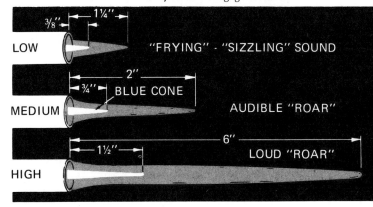

from the flame by adjusting the flame to low, medium, and high levels as noted in Fig. 1-14. The blue cone at the center is the hottest part of the flame. You can further control the heat of the torch by adjusting the distance of the flame from the work.

To practice soldering, cut two small pieces of ¼-inch wide, 16-gauge brass sheet metal. File the ends square and remove the oxidation from the metal by boiling the pieces in a pickling solution (Fig. 1-10). Butt the ends of the pieces on a small heating block, and coat the surface and ends of the pieces with flux (Fig. 1-15). Flux keeps the surfaces of the metal from oxidizing when the heat from the torch contacts them during soldering. Without flux the oxidized surfaces would prevent the solder from bonding. (See Chapter 16 for an explanation of various fluxes.)

Using the same brush as you used for applying the flux, pick up the solder bits and place them at the joint as shown in Fig. 1-16. About three 1/16-inch square bits of "easy" solder will join the two pieces of brass.

Now you're ready to solder. Light the torch and adjust the flame tip to a medium heat (refer to Fig. 1-14). Warm the metal slowly with the flame cone at least 1 inch away from the work to allow the flux to dry. If the flux bubbles, you're heating the metal too fast. Keep the flame moving. Each "pass" with the torch heats the solder a little hotter.

*Fig. 1-15. - Practice soldering with 2 pieces of brass or copper. The ends of the pieces must be filed square and parallel. With the ends in contact and the pieces laying on an asbestos heating block, apply the flux and solder bits.*

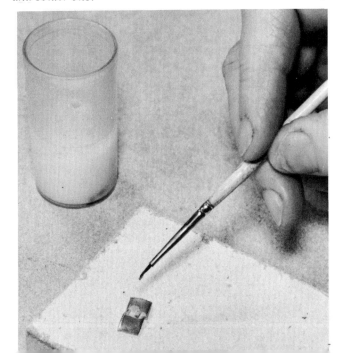

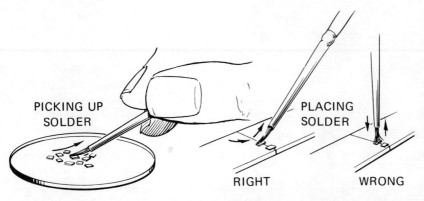

PICKING UP SOLDER

PLACING SOLDER

RIGHT

WRONG

Fig. 1-16. - Pick up the tiny solder bits with a wet flux brush. With the side of the brush tip, touch the bits in a sweeping motion rather than a poking one. Wipe the bits off the brush over the joint.

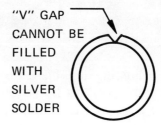

"V" GAP CANNOT BE FILLED WITH SILVER SOLDER

Fig. 1-17. - Bending the ends of the band in a circle leaves a V gap. The V gap may be cut away, leaving the ends parallel.

The metal along both edges of the butt joint must reach soldering temperature at the same time as the solder melts. Suddenly the solder will "run" in a flash and flow into the joint. Remember, the solder must run into the joint and not just melt into a raised puddle on the surface of the metal.

Until you develop confidence in your soldering techniques, you may hesitate to apply enough heat to bring the work and solder up to temperature quickly after the flux dries. Applying heat over a long period burns the flux away and oxidizes the surfaces of the work. If this happens, the solder will not run, and you must start all over again by pickling the pieces to remove the oxidation. Most often solder balls up and refuses to flow because the surfaces of the work are dirty — usually from oxidation. Practice soldering until you develop skill in controlling the heat. Once you get the hang of it, you will have learned one of the most useful skills in crafting jewelry.

Now returning to the ring band that you have stamped or decorated: faces of the ends of the metal strip must be touching for an invisible joint. One way to get the faces of the ends to touch is to round the band until just the inner edges touch, leaving a V-gap (Fig. 1-17). You can remove the V-gap by cutting the triangular bits out with a jeweler's saw. Hold the round shape on a bench pin while sawing (see Chapter 3). Or, with a flexible shaft or powered hand tool, cut the material out with a silicon carbide separating disc or other thin abrasive. Realign the ends after sawing and filing. In the round shape, the ring band may pull apart during soldering

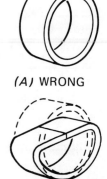

Fig. 1-18. - A quick way to bend ends together for contact across the full face of the joint is shown in B. Note how the contact surfaces fit square and parallel when the ends are in line.

(A) WRONG

(B) RIGHT

due to residual stress in the band. You can prevent this by tying the ends tightly together with binding wire, preferably light stainless steel rather than copper or iron wire.

A faster technique for bringing the faces of the two edges of the metal strip together rather than sawing, filing, and tying with binding wire is to bend the two ends to be joined together into a butt joint (Fig. 1-18). Bend the ends together with two pliers as shown in Fig. 1-19. You can protect the ring band from scratches by taping the pliers' jaws with plastic tape. Again, as with learning any procedure, practice helps; so try forming the band in cheap

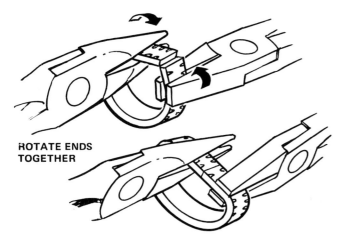

ROTATE ENDS
TOGETHER

Fig. 1-19. - Bend the ends of the metal strip together until the inside edges of the butt joint are touching (left). Then rotate the ends around until the end surfaces are aligned (right). Adjust the alignment of the ring blank ends so that they come in contact across the full face. If more than one or two bending attempts are necessary, anneal and pickle the blank before final bending.

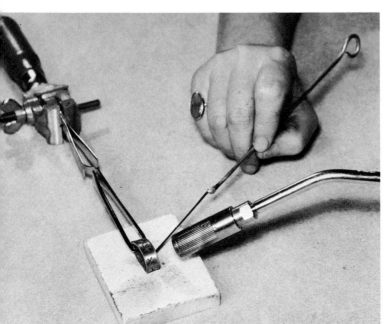

Fig. 1-20. - To set up for soldering a band ring, use self-locking tweezers in a hand vise to hold the ring blank. The butt joint should be laying flat on the heating block. This set-up leaves one hand free to handle the torch and the other free to manipulate the poker. The poker is used to move the solder bits over the joint or to "tease" the molten solder across the full width of the joint.

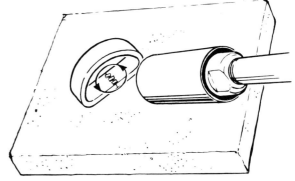

Fig. 1-21. - With the flame of the torch set to a low temperature, warm the ring to dry the flux. Keep the tip of the torch moving about 1 inch from the joint. When the flux is dry, increase the heat to medium and keep the flame moving. As the metal heats, the flux first "balls up," or swells; when it melts to a clear liquid, and the solder bits settle in the joint, you know the work is approaching soldering temperature. Now move in closer until the blue cone of flame brushes the joint area. Keep the flame moving in a small circle. When the solder bits begin to melt at the corners and edges of the work, move in closer and slow the circling motion. Within seconds, the solder should run into the joint.

scrap before working on the real thing. If bending and rebending cause the metal to work-harden, anneal the band. After soldering the edges, the ring will be worked into a round shape.

Two different procedures for soldering the butt joint in the ring can be used. One procedure employs liquid flux, the other uses powdered flux. When using liquid flux, place the bent ring face down on a heating block (Fig. 1-20). Apply flux and place three or four bits of solder across the joint as in Fig. 1-21. Apply heat from the torch with a circular motion, holding the tip of the flame about 1 inch from the

11

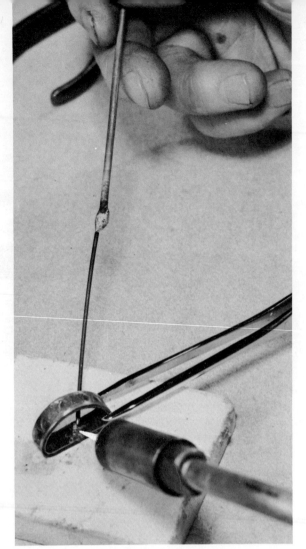

Fig. 1-22. - If solder refuses to run or if it remains on the surface of the joint, tease it with a poker. A poker with a titanium alloy tip remains strong even when red hot, and the solder will not stick to it. Scratch the area near the joint with the poker, moving it in and out of the molten solder to break its surface tension. The poker is used to push the solder where you want it and to move the bits back into position if drying or melting flux shifts them away from the joint.

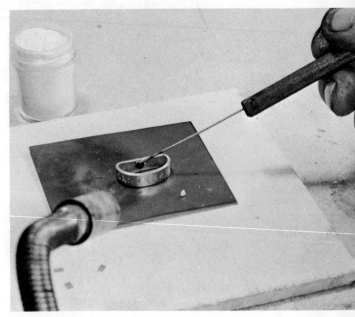

Fig. 1-23. - As an alternative, dry rather than wet flux can be applied to a piece before soldering. Heat the applicator before dipping it into the dry flux. Heat the flux on the applicator until it melts and runs down to cover the joint. Immediately pick up the solder bit with the sticky flux. Place the solder over the joint. Apply heat from inside the ring until the solder runs.

joint (Fig. 1-22). When the solder runs to the joint, dunk the work in plain water to cool. When using this system, use a minimum of solder. Any excess solder may flow through the joint and solidify on the face of the ring as it lies against the heating block.

An alternative soldering technique completely eliminates any problem of solder on the outside of the joint. The ring is laid on its side, and the heat is applied to the inside. As an alternative to liquid flux, a flux applicator is heated and dipped into dry powdered flux. With the flux adhering to the applicator, melt the flux with the torch, and when it is liquid, touch it to the joint. Immediately pick up a chunk of silver solder with the solder wand (see Chapter 15), touch the solder to the joint, and continue heating until the solder runs (Fig. 1-23). Cool the ring immediately in plain water. Dry powdered flux applies more working chemical to the surface of the metal than does liquid flux and practically eliminates oxidation.

**Finishing Techniques**

Round the soldered ring by forcing it

with your fingers onto the ring mandrel as far as possible. Use a 2-ounce metal hammer to shape the ring (Fig. 1-24). Strike the ring with the full face of the hammer — not the edge. You can use more force with a soft-faced hammer without fear of damaging the design. Reverse the band frequently to avoid building in a taper. On the mandrel, check the ring size on both edges to make sure the ring is the same size from all sides.

After rounding the ring, pickle it in a hot solution of *Sparex No. 2* or other pickle. Or simply heat the ring and drop it into the pickle solution while it is still hot.

By using a contrasting color in the stamped areas of the ring, you can accentuate the design. Experiment with this technique by practicing with a brass blank. An easy way to simulate antiquing is to coat the outside of the ring design with a felt marker. Then polish the surface, leaving the color in the recesses of the design. If your ring is sterling, you can antique the ring by any of the three methods detailed in Chapter 17, which also includes other methods for coloring metals.

To smooth the inside of the ring, wrap the ring mandrel with silicon carbide paper with the abrasive side out and work the ring over the paper (Fig. 1-25). Another, quicker method for smoothing the inside of the ring is to chuck a length of ½-inch wooden dowel into an electric drill and fit wet-dry silicon carbide paper in the drill slots. Wrap the silicon carbide paper in the direction of the drill rotation. Dampen the paper to assure a very smooth finish. Smooth the edges of the ring with a file and a silicon carbide block (Fig. 1-26). Or use a small vertical face plate with wet-dry silicon carbide paper. Always work with wet silicon carbide paper for a finer finish. Finally, smooth the face of the ring by using the silicon carbide block or a vertical lap followed by polishing buffs. Stroke the wet surface of the silicon carbide board against the ring "face." Handle the board

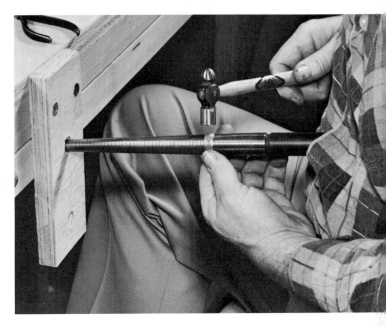

Fig. 1-24. - *Rounding the ring begins by first forcing the soldered half-moon band over the small end of the ring mandrel as far as it will go. Begin shaping with a 2-ounce hammer or one of the soft-faced hammers. Note the working position in the photograph. The small end of the mandrel is inserted in a hole board attached to the bench, the big end is held against the person. This position leaves both hands free.*

much as you would a file, always moving the board around the circle of the ring. If you don't move the file around the ring, you may polish a succession of "flats" on the surface.

Polishing is faster and gives better results when you use powered equipment. Buff your ring first with tripoli and finally with red jeweler's rouge (Fig. 1-27).

Before going on to Chapter 2, try your hand at a number of different designs for band rings — possibly crafted in a variety of metals. In addition to having completed a number of rings in this chapter, you will have learned two basic jewelry crafting skills — soldering and shaping with the hammer.

Fig. 1-25. - Polishing begins inside the ring. Wrap a loose piece of wet-dry silicon-carbide paper on the ring mandrel, with the grit side out. Keep the abrasive wet during polishing for a smoother finish. Turn the ring against the abrasive and reverse the band frequently to counter the effects of the tapered ring mandrel.

Fig. 1-26. - After filing the rough edges of the ring smooth, finish the edges of the ring by sliding them over a wet silicon-carbide block—first on the 240-grit side, finally on the 400-grit side.

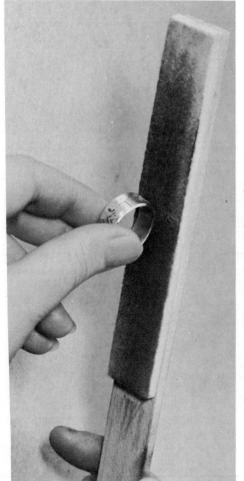

Fig. 1-27. - Powered buffing wheels speed final polishing. But, if you use hand buffs, begin with tripoli, a very light abrasive that brings the surface of the piece to a high sheen. Wash the ring thoroughly in a 1:1 mixture of household ammonia and water. Polish again with a second buff and red (jeweler's) rouge. The rouge brightens the surface even more. Finally, wash the ring again with the ammonia-water mixture.

*Sterling and brass rings with stamped designs. Dr. D. L. Marchbanks, Salina, Kansas.*

*Sterling band rings with stamped and edge—sculptured designs. W. Merrill Snyder, Eden, North Carolina.*

*Sterling band with dimpled, stamped design. Dr. D. L. Marchbanks, Salina, Kansas.*

15

*Gold band antiqued with free-form fused design. William E. Garrison.*

*Antiqued sterling band with sterling designs fused to surface. Mrs. Taft Mitchell, Eugene, Oregon.*

*Sterling ring band with fused sterling wire design. Leigh Garrison.*

*Fused gold ring. William E. Garrison.*

Band earrings constructed in brass. Dr. D. L. Marchbanks, Salina, Kansas.

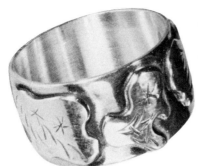

Sterling band with stamped appliqués sweat soldered before rounding. William E. Garrison.

Sterling ring band with stamped designs and fused appliqués. Anne Gries, Flushing, New York.

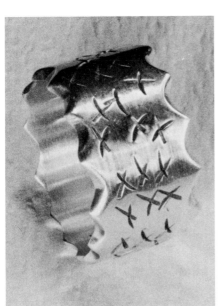

Sterling band featuring stamped designs and scalloped edges. William E. Garrison.

# earrings
*Using Wire, Beads, and Baubles*

DANGLING, BRIGHT, AND AS MODERN AS day after tomorrow, earrings are eye-catching and a joy to make. Start simply — with a single-loop earring.

One design limitation you need to learn about before you begin is weight. Some women will wear heavier earrings than others, but a practical limit is 2½ penny-weight (⅛-ounce troy) for any metal. Simple wire earrings seldom reach that limit unless you add beads or stone danglers.

Begin by consulting Table 18F in Chapter 18 for the length of wire needed to form the loop. The maximum practical size you can round on a normal ring mandrel has a ⅞-inch diameter. Measure the length of 14-gauge wire that you will need and cut two lengths exactly the same size. Anneal and file the ends square so they can be butt-joint soldered. A hand vise or other gripper holds the wire so the tapered ends left by the nippers can be filed away. The wire ends must be flat and "square" with the axis of the wire.

To prepare ends for soldering, bend both wire blanks around the ring mandrel into a U shape. With your fingers or two pliers, bend the ends of the wire together so that they form a butt joint (Fig. 2-1). Solder the ends as detailed in Fig. 2-2. Resolder the joint in air to assure that the solder is redistributed properly for a strong joint (Fig. 2-3).

When you get the hang of soldering the wire loop, you can dispense with the first step of soldering on a heating block and solder the joints directly in air. But before soldering in the air, apply thick flux to the joint. While holding the loop in the tweezers, add one piece of solder to the joint on the top. The thick flux holds the solder bit in place during soldering. Direct medium heat at joint from underneath. For the soldering to work, the wire must reach soldering temperature at the same time the solder melts. Wire joints soldered in air are smoother and stronger than those soldered on a heating block because capillary

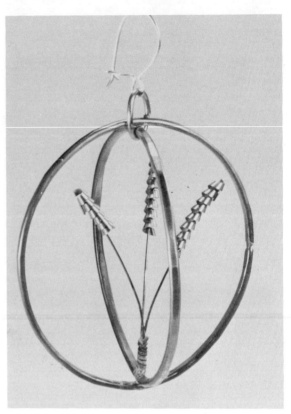

*Double loop brass earring soldered to form a sphere. William E. Garrison.*

attraction holds the solder all across the contact face of the wire ends. Only one tiny bit of solder is needed for air soldering.

After soldering, round the wire loops into circles using the technique shown in Fig. 1-25. After rounding, the loops may end up circular but not flat. To flatten a loop, hammer it between a flattening plate and a block (Fig. 2-4).

There are many ways of forging designs around wire loops. In Fig. 2-5 several techniques for decorating are given. Forging, or hammering, the end of a wire flattens or thins it and also lengthens the wire (Fig. 2-6). Different surface textures can be

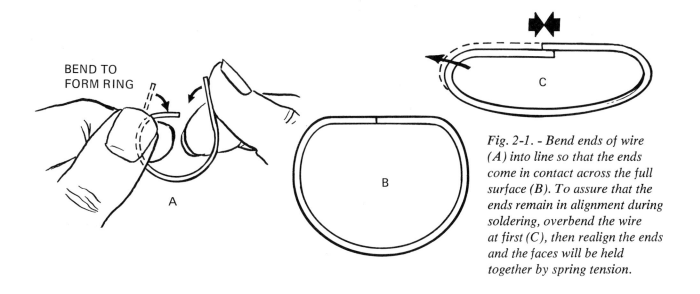

BEND TO
FORM RING

A

B

C

*Fig. 2-1. - Bend ends of wire (A) into line so that the ends come in contact across the full surface (B). To assure that the ends remain in alignment during soldering, overbend the wire at first (C), then realign the ends and the faces will be held together by spring tension.*

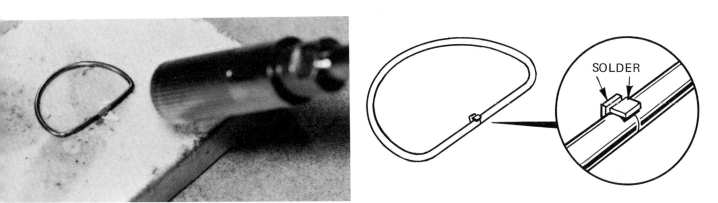

SOLDER

*Fig. 2-2. - To solder, set the torch at medium, and heat the entire loop, keeping the flame moving. At the first sign of the solder balling or melting, move in quickly. The solder should run immediately. The illustration (right) shows the placement of the solder bits behind and on top of the joint. Heating from the near side of the joint will pull the solder in.*

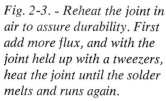

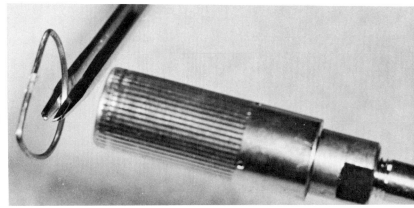

*Fig. 2-3. - Reheat the joint in air to assure durability. First add more flux, and with the joint held up with a tweezers, heat the joint until the solder melts and runs again.*

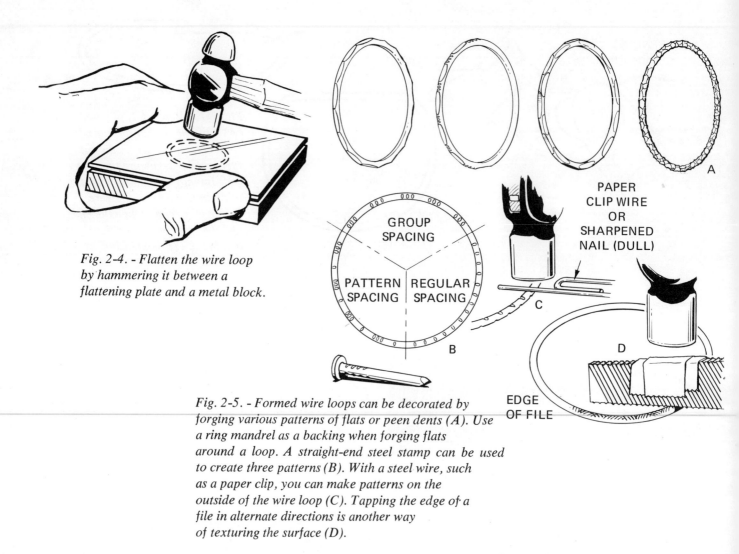

Fig. 2-4. - *Flatten the wire loop by hammering it between a flattening plate and a metal block.*

Fig. 2-5. - *Formed wire loops can be decorated by forging various patterns of flats or peen dents (A). Use a ring mandrel as a backing when forging flats around a loop. A straight-end steel stamp can be used to create three patterns (B). With a steel wire, such as a paper clip, you can make patterns on the outside of the wire loop (C). Tapping the edge of a file in alternate directions is another way of texturing the surface (D).*

achieved by forging with different hammer strokes (Fig. 2-7). Hammered "flats" around the wire can be used as a decorative element.

After forging the loops, pickle them to remove oxidation and then polish to a gleaming finish with metal-cleaning polish and a soft cloth. The loops now are ready for assembly with attachment fittings you make yourself.

## ATTACHMENT FITTINGS

Before making the specific attachment that you will need to fasten the wire loops to the ear-screws (or ear-wires if you are making earrings for pierced ears), you should practice making an eye-pin. Forming an eye-pin allows you to exercise a series of techniques that will be useful in working with wire, and is necessary for assembling loop earrings. Crafting wire jewelry calls for making all kinds of bends. Sharp corners in wire are bent with flat-nose pliers (Fig. 2-8). Rounded, large-radius bends can be formed by using the ring mandrel, the horn of an anvil, or other rounded surface, such as a pipe or rolling pin. Small-diameter bends are easily formed with round-nose pliers (Fig. 2-9).

*Fig. 2-6. - Try different kinds of wire to develop a feel for the amount of forging needed to flatten various metals and diameters of wires.*

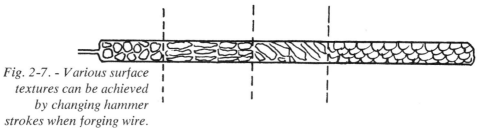

*Fig. 2-7. - Various surface textures can be achieved by changing hammer strokes when forging wire.*

*Figs. 2-8 and 2-9. - The sharp corners in the wire are bent with a flat-nose pliers (left). The tapered jaws of a round-nose pliers form small circles. For larger circles, bend the wire around a ring mandrel, an anvil horn, or other round object.*

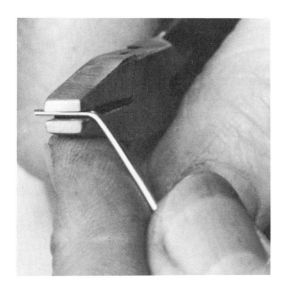

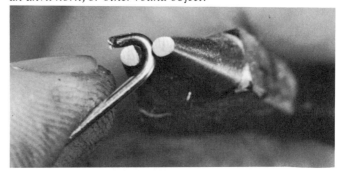

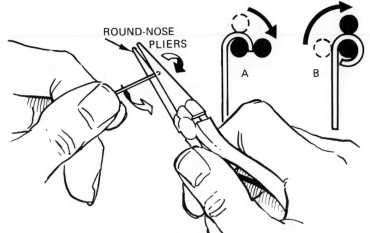

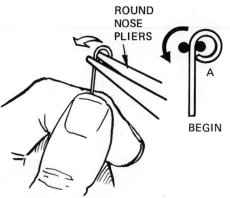

Fig. 2-10. - *Practice bending an eye-pin, using 16-gauge brass wire. Shift the jaws of the pliers in a series of turns (A) to make a full circle at the end of the wire (B). Begin with a 1/8- or 3/16-inch inside diameter.*

Fig. 2-11. - *Complete the eye-pin by grasping the wire at the beginning of the circle (A). Bend the wire loop back until the straight section of the wire aligns with the center of the loop (B). Practice with 20- and 24-gauge wire and bend tiny loops. These are useful for adding danglers inside loops.*

To make the eye-pin, begin with any length of 16-gauge brass wire. Using a round-nose pliers, bend the end of the wire into a loop as shown in the series of steps detailed in Fig. 2-10. When the loop is complete, bend it back about one-eighth of a turn until the straight shank of the wire aligns with the center of the formed circle (Fig. 2-11). You might want to repeat this exercise with 20- and 24-gauge wire until you can form tiny eyes at the head of straight pins, which are useful in assembling beads for danglers.

Opening the eye-pin (illustrated in Fig. 2-12) is a basic technique that is important to know because you will use it when connecting chains or jump rings for different pieces of jewelry. To open a loop, bend one end away from the pin stem — never attempt to unbend the loop.

Loops can be attached to ear-screws or ear-wires in several ways. (Ear-screws and ear-wires are one of the findings you usually buy rather than make.) But a simple connection is an unsoldered oval jump ring or a figure-8 link (Fig. 2-13). (Forming and soldering the more complicated circular jump rings, which also can be used

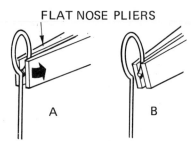

Fig. 2-12. - *You will often have to open and close loops. The correct technique for opening an eye-pin or other unsoldered loop is to grasp the end of the wire with flat-jaw pliers (A). Bend the loop to the side with a 1/8 to 1/4 turn (B). Never attempt to open a loop by "unbending" the circle.*

Fig. 2-13. - *A figure-8 link is used to join wire loops to an ear-screw or ear-wire without solder. The ends of the loop meet near the center so they won't pull the loops open.*

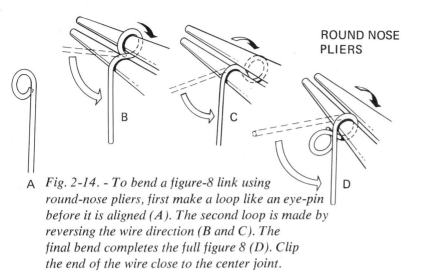

ROUND NOSE
PLIERS

A  *Fig. 2-14. - To bend a figure-8 link using round-nose pliers, first make a loop like an eye-pin before it is aligned (A). The second loop is made by reversing the wire direction (B and C). The final bend completes the full figure 8 (D). Clip the end of the wire close to the center joint.*

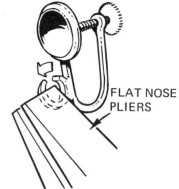

FLAT NOSE
PLIERS

*Fig. 2-15. - The first step in assembling single-loop earrings is to open the attachment loop of the ear-screw with flat-nose pliers. (See Fig. 2-12.)*

for attaching loops and ear-screws, is detailed in Chapter 5.)

To form a figure-8 link, polish a 2-inch length of 20-gauge wire to match your loops. You'll find it easier to polish the wire with metal-cleaning polish before forming the links than afterward. Form the figure-8 links with the series of bends shown in Fig. 2-14.

Now you're ready to assemble the single loop, the figure-8 link, and ear-screw, which should match the metal used for the loop and figure-8 link. Open the attachment loop on the ear-screw as shown in Fig. 2-15. (This is the same action you practiced by opening the eye-pin.) Slip the upper loop of the figure-8 link through the loop of the ear-screw and close the ear-screw loop. Open the bottom loop of the figure-8 link, slip the finished earring loop through the opening, and close the bottom link. You may wish to twist the figure-8 link in such a way that the loop hangs parallel to the side of the face or at right angles to it.

Do not hang earring loops directly from ear-wires. Always use a figure-8 link or jump ring for the connection, because the movement of the loop will have less pull on the ear this way.

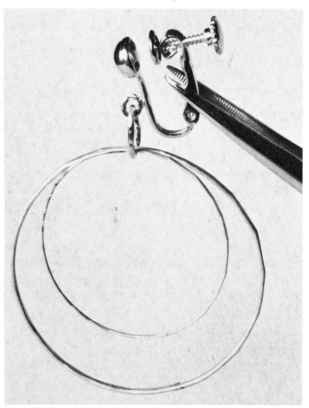

*Fig. 2-16. - The danglers of an earring should hang from an oval jump ring and the loop of an ear-screw.*

23

*Fig. 2-17. - To round a large loop you can use an improvised circular anvil. A junk bearing case, obtained from an auto-wrecking yard, is mounted on the rounded end of a square stick. A wedge driven into the slotted end holds the bearing in place.*

## CRAFTING DOUBLE-LOOP EARRINGS

A dangling inner loop of wire adds an interesting dimension to loop earrings (Fig. 2-16). The lengths of wire blanks needed for large loops are listed in Table 18F in Chapter 18. An inner loop having a 1½-inch diameter and an outer loop 2⅛ inches in diameter in copper, brass, or sterling look pleasing and in proportion. For the inner loops, cut two lengths of 18-gauge wire 4 15/16 inches long. When rounded and soldered, this length will make a loop having a 1½-inch diameter. Anneal and pickle the wire before soldering each loop, preferably in air.

You can improvise a circular mandrel for rounding the loops (Fig. 2-17). Other objects, such as a pipe, baseball bat, or rolling pin, also may be used as a mandrel. Almost anything circular will work as long as the surface is hard enough so the wire can be rounded as you tap it lightly and directly at right angles to the mandrel. Flatten the loop as shown in Fig. 2-4. You may want to forge, file, or texture surface designs around the perimeter of the loops similar to the designs used for the single-loop earrings.

For the large outer loops, cut two pieces of wire 6⅞ inches long. Follow the same procedure that you used for making the smaller loops. You may want to use the same design on the outer loops as you used on the inner loops, or you may want to leave the larger loops plain. Finally, pickle the loops and polish them to a bright fin-ish with metal-cleaning polish and a cloth.

Two loops do not dangle freely from an ear-screw when attached with a figure-8 link. They need to be attached with an oval jump ring (Fig. 2-16). To form oval jump rings, polish a 6- or 8-inch length of 20-gauge wire that matches the earring. Wrap the wire around a mandrel of 2 3/32-inch diameter rods chucked in a hand drill (see Fig. 5-5, Chapter 5). After making a continuous coil of jump rings, cut the individual rings apart as shown in Fig. 5-7, Chapter 5.

To assemble the double-loop earrings, open the oval link as you did the eye-pin and slip it through the attachment loop of the ear-screw or onto the ear-wire. Slip both loop earrings through the same opening of the oval link and close the jump ring, but do not solder. The loops will hang from the link with the smaller loop inside the larger one.

## DESIGN VARIATIONS

Single- and double-loop earrings are only the beginning of the kinds of earrings that can be achieved with loops. Besides adding forged or textured designs around the loops themselves, other elements can be added to create an unlimited variety of designs. For some idea starters see Figs. 2-18, 2-19, 2-20, 2-21, and 2-22. Let your imagination soar in devising combinations of these and other ideas to produce a wide variety of eye-catching, dangling earrings.

Fig. 2-18. - When suspended from the same jump ring as the loop itself, danglers swing and sway inside a single loop. Glass beads or painted wood baubles alone or in combination can be suspended on 24- or 28-gauge wire eye-pins.

Fig. 2-20. - Outside danglers on a jump ring or hanging from jump rings soldered symmetrically to the outside of the loop slide around the loop.

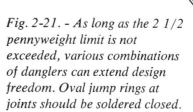

Fig. 2-21. - As long as the 2 1/2 pennyweight limit is not exceeded, various combinations of danglers can extend design freedom. Oval jump rings at joints should be soldered closed.

Fig. 2-19. - Side-mounted, internal danglers can be hung from jump rings soldered inside the single loop. Chains, eye-pins, beads, and baubles mounted in this way offer a great variety of creative designs.

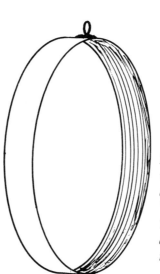

Fig. 2-22. - A striking variation of wire loops is a circular band of very light-gauge sheet metal. The jump ring for the attachment is soldered at the butt joint.

25

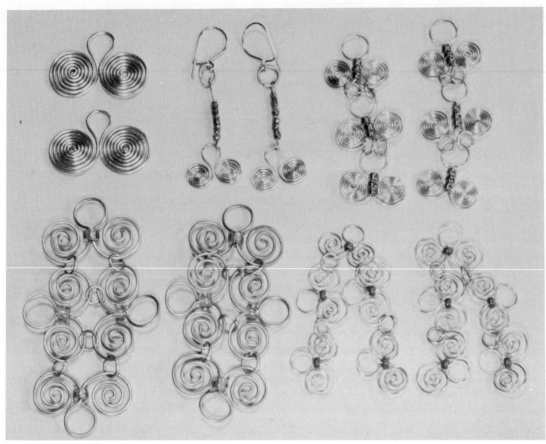

*Wire swirls in brass and steel wire. David Graham, Seattle, Washington.*

*Spider webs in brass and black iron wire. William E. Garrison.*

*Double loop brass spheres with flower centers. William E. Garrison.*

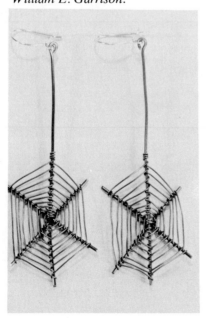

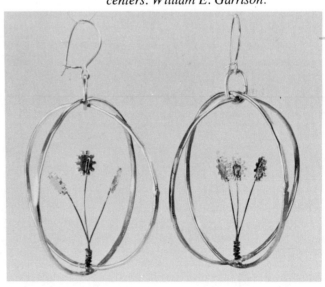

*Double loop earrings in polished brass with stamped design. Gordon Longley, Downers Grove, Illinois.*

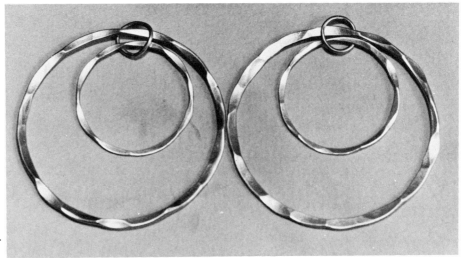

*Double loops with forged flats. Leigh Garrison.*

*Twisted and forged single sterling loops. Dr. R. A. Cunningham, Defiance, Ohio.*

# cuff links
## *Sweat Soldering and Sawing*

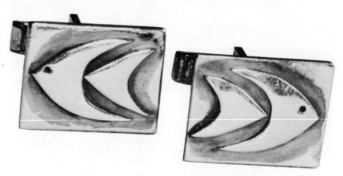

*Brass overlays sweat soldered to copper base. W. Merrill Snyder, Eden, North Carolina.*

HANDCRAFTED CUFF LINKS CAN BE real eye-catchers, and they offer their wearers an excellent opportunity for dressing more distinctively. Design possibilities for cuff links are not limited by weight as they are with earrings, so you can be far more flexible with your creativity.

In this chapter you will craft a pair of cuff links while you learn the technique of sweat soldering one metal to another — not as a joint but as an appliqué or face-to-face joining. Sawing with a jeweler's saw is another way of cutting metal besides the cutting techniques you have already learned. It is a skill that is developed with practice, so once learned, do not hesitate to use it.

## CRAFTING A PAIR OF CUFF LINKS

In making your first pair of cuff links, begin with a simple design. Once you have mastered the technique of sweat soldering, you can advance to more spectacular pieces. The double-triangle design (Fig. 3-1) is clean and simple and is especially good for learning and practice.

### Metal Sawing

You will need to cut two ⅝-by-1-inch rectangular base pieces from 16-gauge metal. You could cut these rectangular pieces with shears, but you should use the jeweler's saw to keep the surfaces flat.

The jeweler's saw looks much like the coping saw used by carpenters and hobbyists. An adjustable U-shaped frame holds the very thin blade. But you should recognize one important difference between the two: the jeweler's saw cuts on the pull stroke rather than the push stroke, as is common with a coping saw. For most sawing you'll be using the jeweler's saw with a bench pin (Fig. 3-2). Insert a 2-0 blade (see Chapter 15 for the range of blade sizes) with the teeth outward and the points toward the handle. Since blade tension affects saw action, learn to adjust the blades properly from the beginning. With the blade tightly fastened at the bow end,

push against the handle end to spring the frame (Fig. 3-3).

Tensioning the blade of the jeweler's saw is a trick you learn with experience. A loose blade wanders when sawing, but a blade tensioned too tightly may break. When correctly tensioned, the blade "sings" when strummed. Loosen the wing nut near the handle of the saw to release the blade tension each time you finish sawing.

Hold the saw lightly, as shown in Fig. 3-4. In cutting, the blade should move up and down almost vertically with only *light* pressure against the metal. Rubbing the blade with paraffin or beeswax extends its life.

After marking the metal area to be cut with a felt-tip marking pen and scratching the lines with a scribe, start a cut by first sawing two or three strokes into the wood of the bench pin. The slight cut into the wood controls and steadies the blade as it begins to engage the edge of the metal. Slide the metal into contact with the blade and cut into the metal along the marked line with several strokes. When the metal is cut deeply enough to hold the blade, move the work away from the bench pin

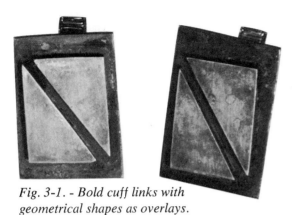

Fig. 3-1. - Bold cuff links with
geometrical shapes as overlays.

Fig. 3-2. - The bench pin is the clamped
wooden piece that has a V opening
(not visible in photo). The metal is
held over it with one hand, while the
saw is pulled vertically to cut the metal.
For comfort and precise eye control
during sawing, sit low at the bench on a
stool about four inches shorter
than you would normally sit.

Fig. 3-3. - Clamp the blade in the bow end first;
then adjust blade tension by springing the
frame of the jeweler's saw. Note how the frame
is braced in the V of the bench pin for sure
control during blade tensioning. Leaning against
the handle to spring the frame leaves both
hands free to hold and fasten the blade.

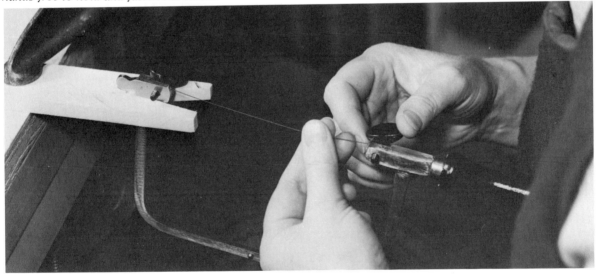

Fig. 3-4. - Practice holding the jeweler's
saw with only three fingers to concentrate
on vertical stroking. To apply only
very light pressure against the metal during
sawing, think of the saw as a violin
bow. Imagine how you might stroke the
bow evenly and with almost no pressure
over the strings. Later, to guide the
blade around curves or corners, you can
hold the saw with the full handle as
shown in Fig. 3-2.

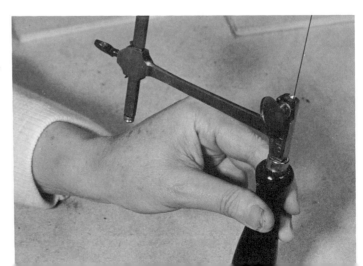

29

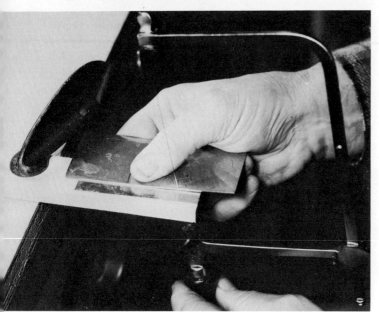

Fig. 3-5. - *Use a metal straightedge as a guide for learning to saw a straight line.*

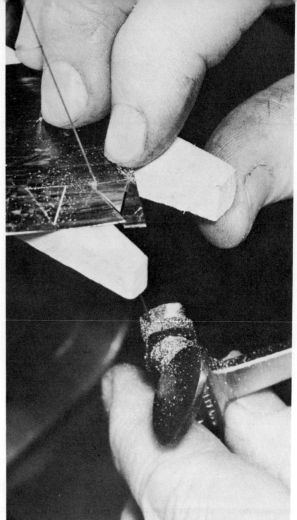

Fig. 3-7. - *Support the work close to the edges or V of the bench pin. Practice cutting small overlays from the metal sheet. Overlays should be sawed rather than sheared to insure flatness. Small pieces are difficult to flatten for all-over contact with a base once they've been cut with shears.*

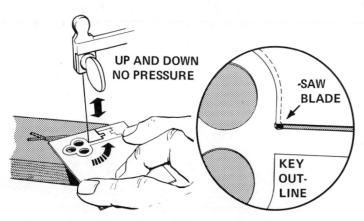

UP AND DOWN
NO PRESSURE

-SAW
BLADE

KEY
OUT-
LINE

Fig. 3-6. - *When sawing around curves, direct the work into the blade rather than turning the blade into the work. In a tight corner, saw out the circle by turning the work as you continue to move the blade up and down, but with no forward cutting pressure.*

If you allow the metal to move, the blade can bind or catch in the cut and it may break. If the blade tends to wander off the marked line, it may be tensioned too loosely.

Sawing straight may be more difficult at first than sawing curves, so try using a straightedge to guide the saw in straight-line cutting (Fig. 3-5). When sawing curves, turn the work and keep it moving into the blade. To saw a sharp angle, cut toward the corner from both directions. Or saw around a corner by turning the blade while continuing to stroke the saw (Fig. 3-6).

Choose the blade for a job according to the thickness of the metal and the kind of shape to be sawed. Jeweler's saw blades are numbered in reverse order; that is, a

slightly so the blade no longer runs into the wood. Continue stroking, cutting near the V-opening of the bench pin or along one side of it, using long, even strokes. Support the metal solidly at the cutting point.

30

small number, such as 2-0, indicates a larger, heavier blade than 8-0. Generally, use a 2-0 blade for 18-gauge and heavier metal. For ordinary cutting, a 4-0 blade works best on 20-gauge and thinner metal. An 8-0 blade should be used only for narrow cuts in very thin metal or to achieve special effects, such as pierced designs.

Cut the triangular or other shape overlays that will be soldered to the rectangular base of the cuff link. Mark the shape with a felt-tip marking pen and scribe. Saw the overlays from sheet metal as shown in Fig. 3-7. Use tweezers to help you control the tiny shapes as you cut them out of the sheet.

### Sweat Soldering

The technique for joining metal overlays is termed "sweat soldering" — meaning where one piece of metal is soldered to another along the flat surfaces. Overlays are not only sweat soldered when making cuff links, but they may also be sweat soldered to band rings.

Steps to be followed in sweat soldering with hard solder are:

1. The piece to be overlaid is turned upside down and the backside, or side to be joined, is fluxed.

2. Bits of solder are placed on the piece with a wet flux brush and heated until the solder runs over the surface.

3. The base shape is cleaned and fluxed over the entire surface.

4. The overlay is placed right side up (solder side down) in position on the base.

5. Base and overlay are heated from beneath on a heating frame until the solder begins to melt. When the overlay begins to sink down into the solder, quickly bring the torch up from beneath the two pieces to heat the work from the top.

6. The solder will run to bond the overlay to the base.

7. Allow the work to cool.

There are two reasons for heating the work from underneath. First, you must keep the small overlay from heating too fast. Ordinarily, the base will be heavier

Fig. 3-8. - Triangular overlays for cuff links and base are placed on a heating frame after solder has been applied to the back of the overlays and new flux has been applied to all pieces.

and more massive, so heating the work from the bottom brings the assembly to soldering temperature at roughly the same time. If the overlay reaches soldering temperature before the base, the solder may bond to the overlay but not to the base. Second, overlays tend to be small. Depending on their design, they may have narrow sections or sharp points. If the overlay is heated from the top, these small parts or points may melt and soften or flow, particularly if the overlay is sterling.

Practice the technique of sweat soldering with scrap pieces of metal before attempting it with the pieces you have cut for the cuff links. Select two small triangular pieces of metal, possibly left over from your sawing practice, for overlays. Flux the

31

Fig. 3-9. - From underneath the three-pound coffee can heat the overlay-base sandwich from the bottom with a medium to hot flame.

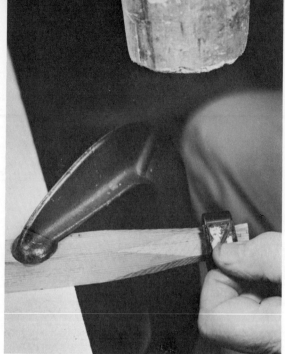

Fig. 3-10. - After sweat soldering, cuff-link designs may be curved slightly by using a soft-face hammer on a circular anvil (see Chapter 2).

back side of the pieces of metal, apply solder bits, and heat from the top with a low flame to dry the flux. Then bring the torch closer and melt the solder until it flows to cover the entire surface of the overlays. As you gain experience, you will heat the work only enough to melt the solder until it slumps and runs. When the solder melts and flows as a liquid over the hot metal, you can judge whether you have placed too much or too little solder. Use just enough solder to cover the surfaces and no more. When working with brass, stop heating immediately when the solder flows; otherwise the brass will absorb the solder by amalgamation.

Select a larger piece of clean 16-gauge sheet scrap as a base. Flux the base and the cooled overlays. Turn the overlays over and place the soldered surfaces down on the base. Place the base piece with the overlays in position on a heating frame.

The usual heating frame is a steel mesh on a tripod (Fig. 3-8). However, a three-pound coffee can with holes punched in the top and a square cut out of the side may be used instead (Fig. 3-9). Using a medium to hot flame, heat the pieces from the bottom. Observe the action of the solder. The base piece will reach a bright red color before the solder melts. If you applied too much solder to the back side of the overlay, molten solder will flow beyond the overlay edges. Excessive solder may flow to cover the entire surface of the base and this can cause problems in polishing. Also, if you intend to "antique" sterling, the sulfur will react differently with the solder than with base sterling, and you may end up with a spotted piece. One aim of the practice piece is to develop judgment for the amount of solder needed to sweat solder an appliqué to a base. If just the right amount of solder has been used, the overlay will visibly sink into the base as the solder runs. At this point you can adjust the position of the overlay, if necessary, with a poker while the solder is molten.

32

Fig. 3-11. - Attaching a cuff-link finding to the back of a face piece is another two-step process. Begin by heating soft solder in the shallow cup of the attachment disk. Direct the heat away from the spring mechanism and use tweezers to shield the mechanism from heat to prevent damaging it. The cup of the attachment should be level full with solder. By heating the solder in the cup of the finding in the air, you will prevent the solder from spreading over the back of the attachment.

After practicing soldering until you feel you've got the hang of it, take the pieces you've cut and follow the same procedure that you did in the practice session(s). By this time you know how much solder to use and how much heat to apply, so you shouldn't have any trouble.

After soldering the cuff links and allowing them to cool, clean the assembly in a pickle.

If you wish to antique the cuff links, refer to Chapter 17 for the details. To achieve highlights after antiquing, place the face of each piece down on the 240-grit side of a *wet* silicon carbide board and rub until the overlays are bright and even. Repeat the procedure on the 400-grit side for semi-polish.

Cuff links may be curved for design purposes after they are sweat soldered and before the findings are attached. Use a soft-face hammer on a circular anvil to shape the assembly face (Fig. 3-10).

To attach cuff-link findings to the back side of the base and overlay, use the soft solder procedure described in the following section.

## Soft Soldering

Readily available soft solders are various alloys of tin and lead with a range of melting temperatures (see Table 18G in Chapter 18). Compared to silver solder, all soft solders are brittle and weak. You will be using soft solder only when the high temperatures needed for melting hard solders would damage gemstones or soften the springs in cuff links and ear-clips.

Practice soft soldering by first flattening a piece of soft solder wire until it is about as thick as 20-gauge sheet metal. Cut this flattened wire into square bits about 1/16 inch to 1/8 inch square. With the tweezers, touch each bit of soft solder in soft-solder flux (see Chapter 16). Use very little flux, as the more you use, the more clean-up will be necessary. Don't attempt to use the acid- or resin-core soft solder sold in hardware stores. Acid- and resin-core solders are used for soldering everything from rain gutters to a radio chassis — acid for most metals and resin for electronic wiring. When soft soldering jewelry, so little of either of these solders is needed that the flux (acid or resin) in the core would be insufficient to keep the joining surface free of oxidation. To use these core solders with a separate flux could void the cleansing action. Jewelry soft solders are purer and more compatible with silver, brass, and copper than acid- or resin-core solders. However, you could use either of these solders in an emergency, but only then. It is important that you apply the special soft-solder flux yourself to maintain close control. Practice heating the soft-solder bit on a piece of clean scrap brass to develop a feel for the heat required to melt the solder.

In preparation for attaching the face assemblies of the cuff links to findings, first hold a finding "upside down" in the air with tweezers. Place fluxed chunks of soft solder in the shallow cap of the finding. Melt the soft solder in the cup as shown in Fig. 3-11. Repeat the same procedure for the second finding and allow both pieces to cool. Apply more soft-solder flux to the

33

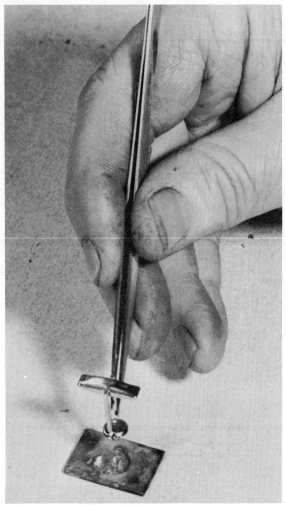

Fig. 3-12. - Position the cuff-link finding over a cleaned and fluxed spot on the back side of the face piece.

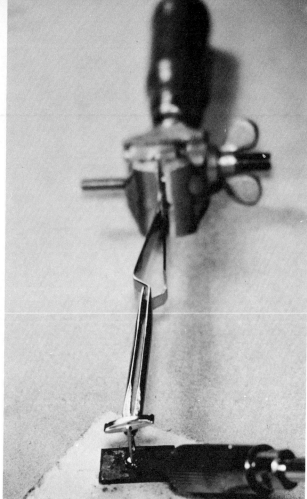

Fig. 3-13. - Support the finding in position with a third-hand or tweezers clamped in a hand vise. Adjust the torch to a low flame and reheat the attachment cup and the back until the solder runs. The finding should sink into place. Be careful to direct the heat toward the base of the design piece and away from the finding linkage.

exposed solder in the finding cups. A neat job of applying the flux to the finding can be done with a sliver of wood.

Clean the back side of the cuff link where the finding will be attached. With the assembly-face side of the cuff link down on a heating block, position the finding on the cleaned spot on the back of the assembly face (Fig. 3-12). Use a third-hand or tweezers held in a hand vise to support the finding in position (Fig. 3-13). Heat the cup and back until solder runs, and repeat the procedure for the second assembly. Soft solder must be allowed to cool before an assembly can be moved.

Finally polish the face pieces with household metal polish to bring out the full luster of the overlays.

Design possibilities are almost endless for cuff links. In addition to triangle overlays, other design ideas are shown in Figs. 3-14 and 3-15. Using contrasting colors for overlay and base metals is another way to achieve design variations. Initials sweat soldered onto the base personalize cuff links for gifts (Fig. 3-16). Not shown here but detailed in Chapter 6 are pierced designs with portions of the overlay or base cut out to achieve a three-dimensional effect.

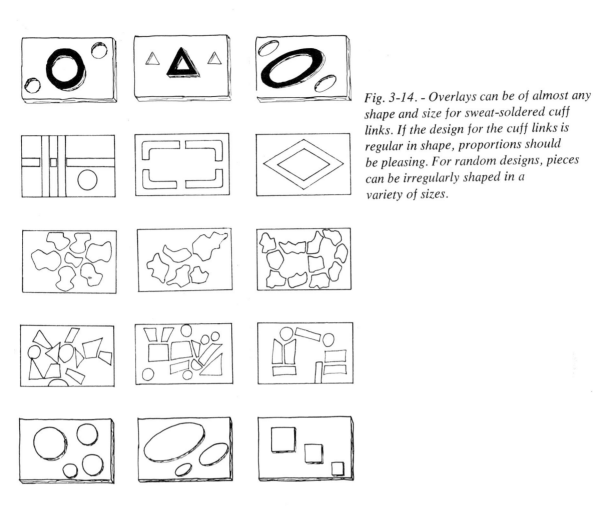

Fig. 3-14. - Overlays can be of almost any shape and size for sweat-soldered cuff links. If the design for the cuff links is regular in shape, proportions should be pleasing. For random designs, pieces can be irregularly shaped in a variety of sizes.

Fig. 3-15. - Sculptured edge treatments add another design dimension to cuff links. The edges on the back side of the cuff links should be smooth to prevent wearing the cuff fabric.

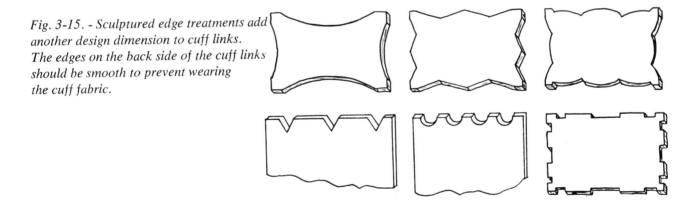

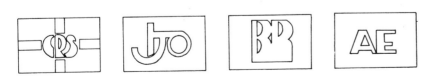

Fig. 3-16. - Initialed overlays, sweat soldered to the face of the cuff links, personalize designs and are particularly appropriate for gifts.

35

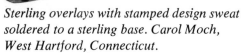

*Sterling overlays with stamped design sweat soldered to a sterling base. Carol Moch, West Hartford, Connecticut.*

*Sterling sweat soldered to textured sterling base. Anne Gries, Flushing, New York.*

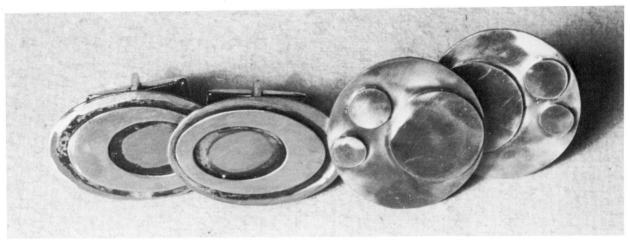

*Practice cuff links in brass and copper. William E. Garrison.*

*Sterling cuff link textured by stamping. William E. Garrison.*

*Sterling overlays sweat soldered to antiqued sterling base.*
*W. Merrill Snyder,*
*Eden, North Carolina.*

FREE-FORM, STRAIGHT-SIDED, CABOCHON stone rings offer the rockhound and lapidary creative opportunities for mounting favorite stones. With the free-form technique all sizes and shapes of stones can be mounted with a minimum of cutting and shaping — thereby preserving the unique shape of the stones. Free-form gemstones with all sides straight can be massive and square or rectangular or slim, dainty, and restrained. Because of their individuality, you'll find few free-form stones available commercially.

## SOLDERED-STRIP TECHNIQUE

A thin-gauge strip soldered around a base cut to fit a gemstone holds the stone in place. A ring-shank soldered to the back of the base completes a simple ring assembly (Fig. 4-1). Important in this technique is that the ring mount is shaped to fit the stone — rather than the stone cut to fit the base. Before tackling a finished ring, you should practice the soldered-strip technique.

Being able to hold the strip against the side of a base is critical in this technique. A special soldering fixture with a weight is used to hold the thin edge (bezel) against the base during the soldering operation (Fig. 4-2).

For practice in soldering the bezel to a base, cut a piece of 20-gauge metal ½ inch wide and long enough to cut several pieces ½ inch to 1 inch long. After cutting these base pieces, set them aside for a moment. To assure straight cutting of the very thin edge material (26-30-gauge metal) to be used for the bezel, coat the surface of a piece approximately 3 inches long (the width can vary) with a felt-tip marker. Scribe parallel lines 3/32 inch apart lengthwise on the surface (Fig. 4-3). Shear the strips straight and exactly on the lines; otherwise, gaps may show when the strip is soldered to the base.

Assemble the strip against the edge of a base ½ inch square, as shown in Fig. 4-4. Apply flux along the joint between the

*Chapter Four*

# rings with stones

*Soldered-Strip Technique*

*Unbalanced diamond-shaped cabochon with a wide ring shank. William E. Garrison.*

bezel-strip and base. While the flux brush is still wet, apply bits of hard solder at the joint (Fig. 4-5). Warm the pieces slowly with the torch at low heat to dry the flux, then proceed with the soldering as shown in Fig. 4-6.

Remove the weight from the hot assembly and allow it to cool. Snip off the excess length of bezel-strip. Clean the base with fine silicon carbide paper and examine the joint carefully, preferably with the aid of a magnifying glass. Look to see if the solder joins the bezel-strip to the base along the full length of the joint. If gaps appear, determine if you used too little solder, if the joint surfaces may have been oxidized, or if the bezel-strip was not firmly in contact along the full length of the edge. Repeat the soldering practice, using longer base pieces each time until you develop confidence. Determine the amount of hard

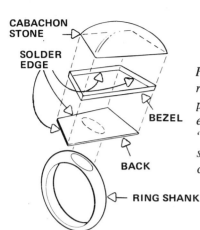

CABACHON
STONE

SOLDER
EDGE

BEZEL

BACK

RING SHANK

Fig. 4-1. - Parts for assembling a free-form ring are the shank, metal back, or base, plate, bezel-strip soldered around the edge of the back, and the gemstone. This "soldered-strip" technique can be used for straight-sided or curved-edge cabochon gemstones.

Fig. 4-2. - The soldering fixture holds the bezel-strip in contact with the edge of the base while the joint is being soldered. To make a soldering fixture, drive stainless steel pins into a block of asbestos or asbestos board glued to a plywood backing. If you can't locate stainless steel pins, use 1/2- or 3/4-inch brads with the heads clipped. However, stainless steel pins of about the same diameter as brads are preferred, because the solder will not easily bond to them. The weight to hold the base in place may be a chunk of firebrick or a stone, such as serpentine, that will not fracture from heat. The weight is shoved against the base to hold the joint along the pin line together.

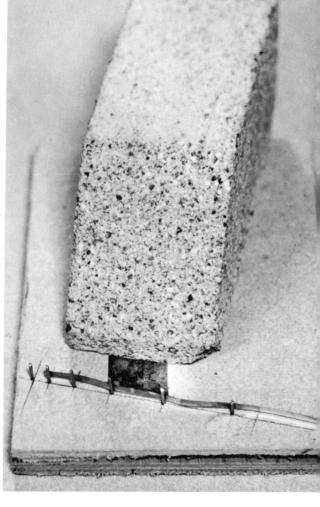

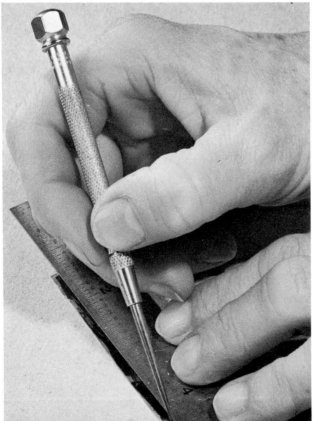

Fig. 4-3. - To make the bezel-strip, scribe thin material for shearing to the height required for the bezel. Accuracy in scribing and shearing is important.

Fig. 4-4. - The bezel-strip is positioned on edge against the pins. The opposite side of the strip bears against the edge of the back. Position the weight so the pieces are held together firmly. Use a magnifying glass if necessary to make sure the thin bezel-strip touches the asbestos surface along the strip's full length.

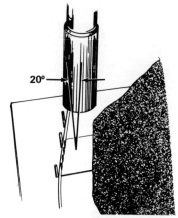

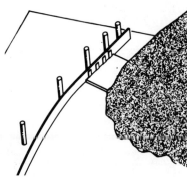

Fig. 4-5. - Solder bits must contact the vertical bezel-strip, otherwise the solder will not flow along the strip-base joint. Judge the amount of solder needed from experience and practice. Cutting hard solder bits in rectangles distinguishes them from easy melt bits.

Fig 4-6 - With the torch set at medium, direct the flame almost straight down toward the middle of the base—never at the bezel-strip. Keep the torch moving with the tip of the blue cone within about 1/2 inch of the surface of the base. If you hold the torch at a low angle, you will direct excessive heat at the bezel-strip and may melt it. The bezel-strip will certainly reach soldering temperature before the back even if it doesn't melt. Holding the torch at an angle of about 20 degrees is about right; holding it vertical may blow out the flame.

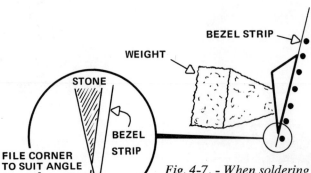

Fig. 4-7. - When soldering bezel-strips at sharp corners, solder one side first. Then, file off the face of the bezel-strip to match the angle of the base; otherwise, the corner will have a bump or exhibit a rounded look.

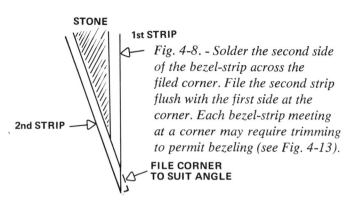

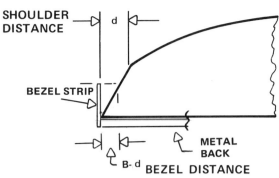

STONE

1st STRIP

2nd STRIP

FILE CORNER TO SUIT ANGLE

Fig. 4-8. - Solder the second side of the bezel-strip across the filed corner. File the second strip flush with the first side at the corner. Each bezel-strip meeting at a corner may require trimming to permit bezeling (see Fig. 4-13).

SHOULDER DISTANCE

d

BEZEL STRIP

METAL BACK

B-d BEZEL DISTANCE

Fig. 4-10. - Distances from inside the bezel-strip to the stone are important for smooth, secure bezeling. Only when the bezel-strip is exactly the same height as the break of the shoulder will "d" equal bezel distance, "B-d"—the distance the strip must be bezeled to contact the stone. B-d should be about 1/32 inch. If B-d is as much as 1/16 inch or more, crimping the strip around the stone will be difficult or impossible. Since the bezel-strip is seldom straight or absolutely vertical, measure B-d at several points.

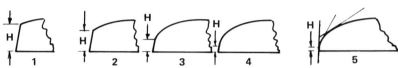

H 1    H 2    H 3    H 4    H 5

Fig. 4-9. - Stones 1 through 4 display a clear break point for measuring "H," the height of the shoulder. Stone 5, however, curves continuously from the base plane and does not have an obvious break. One way to simulate H for stone 5 is to treat the curve as a series of straight lines drawn tangent to the curve. Such stones are normally bezeled with a strip designed for a low bezel height.

solder needed from your examination of the first joint and adjust the quantity needed with each practice piece until you have the correct amount of solder.

## GEMSTONE BEZEL-STRIP MOUNTS

When selecting the gemstone to be mounted, recognize that the design of the mount depends on the number of sides, sharpness of corners, and the shoulder shape of the cabochon stone. When mounting symmetrical, straight-sided stones (triangles, squares, rectangles, diamonds, or regular polygons), each side must be as nearly straight as possible. The slightest deviation from perfect straightness appears obvious. Irregular gemstones may be mounted as easily as symmetrical shapes.

The important factors influencing the design and the selection of a starting point for the soldered strip to mount free-form, straight-sided shapes are:

1. *Sharpness of angle* — It is easy to bend bezel-strips around angles of 90° or more. When corners include sharp angles less than 90°, remember one general rule — the sharper the angle, the more accurate the work required. Corners with angles less than 45° require "perfect" marking and cutting of the base plus accurate strip soldering. *Do not attempt to bend the bezel-strip around angles less than 90°.* Plan to solder strips in two operations around sharp angles, as shown in Figs. 4-7 and 4-8.

2. *Curve of the shoulder* — Cabochon stones may be ground to the same thickness but may have varying shoulders, as shown in Fig. 4-9. The bezel height must *never* exceed the straight shoulder height, "H" in Fig. 4-9. The height, "H," is the point at which the curve of the stone breaks away from the shoulder.

3. *Bezeling distance* — After the bezel-strip has been soldered to the back, you will want to check the stone in the mount and accurately measure the shoulder *distance* (Fig. 4-10). Shoulder distance "d,"

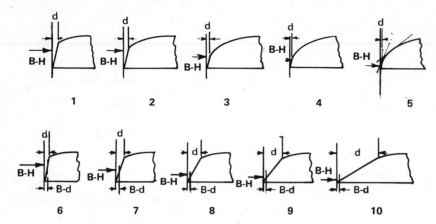

Fig. 4-11. - *Bezel height, that is, the height of the bezel-strip on the stone's shoulder, should be no higher than the arrow labeled B-H.*

Fig. 4-12. - *Bezel height may relate directly to bezel distance, as detailed on typical stones. Generally, the flatter the angle of the shoulder, the shorter the bezel height. Otherwise, B-d becomes excessive.*

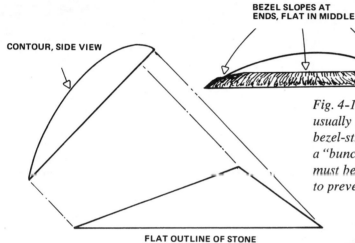

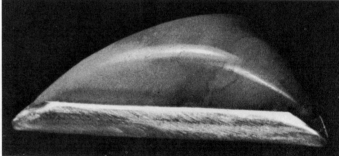

Fig. 4-13. - *Stones with sharp corners usually require that the height of the bezel-strip at the corners be lower to prevent a "bunching up" of metal. The bezel-strip must be cut back from sharp corners to prevent an overlap.*

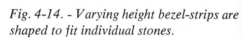

Fig. 4-14. - *Varying height bezel-strips are shaped to fit individual stones.*

is the distance from the break of the shoulder to a line perpendicular from the base. The bezel distance, "B-d," is the distance from the shoulder to the bezel-strip at the height of the bezel-strip. Good design calls for a bezel distance of 1/32 inch, because with that bezel distance the stone is held securely.

4. *Bezel height* — One way to adjust the bezel distance, "B-d" in Fig. 4-10, is to vary

the bezel height. If "B-d" is greater than 1/32 inch, reduce the height of the bezel, "B-H" in Fig. 4-11. Note the varying shapes of cabochon stones and how bezel height and the bezel distance are measured. Typical shoulder angles, bezel heights, and bezel distances for straight-sided and curved stones are shown in Fig. 4-12.

5. *Varying bezel height* — When shaping stones with sharp angles, the lapidary

42

work usually determines the contour of the stone. A typical triangular stone is shown in Fig. 4-13. Bezeled corners may appear like those in Fig. 4-14 with the corners shaped to suit the stone.

## CRAFTING A FREE-FORM RING

Begin construction of the base piece for your ring by numbering a four-sided stone with the same sequence shown in Fig. 4-15 for easy reference during the succeeding steps. Although the stone used in these steps is four-sided, and it probably would be easier if you used a four-sided stone for the first ring, you may use other shapes of stones by setting up a similar numbering scheme.

Place the stone on a piece of 20-gauge metal that has been colored with a felt marker. Scribe around the edges of the stone *precisely*, following the techniques shown in Figs. 4-16 and 4-17. Unless you mark the exact shape of the stone's base with the scribe, the bezeled mount will not fit the stone properly. Using a 4-0 blade in the jeweler's saw and with a straightedge for a guide, cut out the base exactly to the marked shape. Check the cut back against the stone (Fig. 4-18).

Cut a bezel-strip from 26-30-gauge metal to match the base similar to the way in which you cut practice strips (Fig. 4-3). The height of the bezel-strip is determined by the shape of the stone. Refer to Figs. 4-9 through 4-12 to determine the height of the bezel-strip. Measure the distance around the perimeter of the stone and cut the bezel-strip long enough to fit all the way around.

Soldering the bezel-strip to the base should start with a side similar to No. 4 in Fig. 4-15. Assemble the base, *felt pen marked side up,* and bezel-strip on the soldering fixture as shown in Fig. 4-19. Apply flux and hard solder bits to the joint, making sure the bits touch the vertical surface of the bezel-strip. Determine how many bits of solder are needed from your previous practice with straight joints. Your

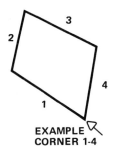

Fig. 4-15. - The numbering system indicated on the illustration will be followed throughout this section to simplify instructions. If you are working with a stone having more than four sides, simply follow the same procedure.

Fig. 4-16. - When marking around a stone on a colored metal base, hold the stone stationary with a notched pencil eraser. Hold the scribe vertically when marking around the stone.

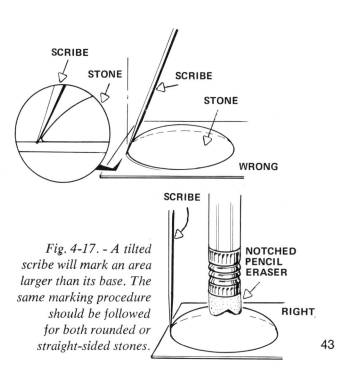

Fig. 4-17. - A tilted scribe will mark an area larger than its base. The same marking procedure should be followed for both rounded or straight-sided stones.

43

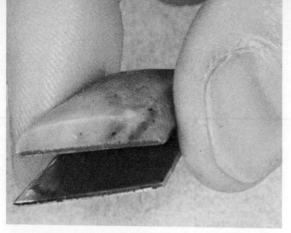

Fig. 4-18. - *After cutting check the fit of the base against the gemstone. A base cut oversize can be sawed or filed to fit. A base that is undersize must be redone.*

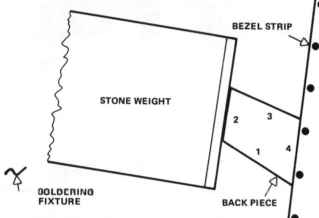

Fig. 4-19. - *Start soldering the bezel-strip to a side next to a corner with an included angle greater than 90°, such as corner 4-3 in the illustration.*

judgment concerning the amount of solder needed develops through practice and by examining the results. Solder the joint as shown in Fig. 4-6. Allow the assembly to cool in air or dunk it in water.

Bend the bezel-strip around corner No. 4-3 (Fig. 4-20). If side No. 3 and the bezel-strip appear to be oxidized, pickle the metal to assure a clean joint. Solder side No. 3 of the bezel-strip to the base as you soldered side No. 4. The weight has to be moved up against side No. 1.

Since corner No. 3-2 is less than 90°, do not attempt to bend the bezel-strip around the corner as you did for No. 4-3. Instead, trim and file the bezel-strip flush with side No. 2 at the No. 3-2 corner (Fig. 4-21). Overlap the bezel-strip at the No. 3-2

corner and continue soldering along side No. 2. When side No. 2 is soldered, bend the bezel-strip around the No. 2-1 corner with a flat-nose pliers.

Trim off only enough of the bezel-strip at the No. 1-4 corner with the shears to permit you to file a sharp corner parallel with side No. 1. Solder side No. 1. On a long side, such as side No. 1, you may need to use a poker to hold the thin bezel-strip in close contact with the base piece during the soldering operation (Fig. 4-22). Set the base and bezel-strip assembly aside while you construct the ring shank.

**Fitting the Ring Shank**

Steps in fitting and soldering a band-type ring shank for attachment to the back of the bezeled mount follow generally the same procedure as that used for simple band rings (see Chapter 1). For a ring with a stone, construct a ring shank from 1/8-inch to 1/4-inch metal. After completing the ring shank (band), grind a flat surface on the shank at least 1/4 inch wide with the 240-grit side of the silicon carbide board. Make sure the flat spot is even across the full width of the band. When you become thoroughly familiar with soldering, place the ring shank joint at the attachment point for the ring back. This location hides the ring shank joint. However, unless the ring shank is dead soft, the joint of the shank may open up during soldering and leave a gap where it is attached to the back.

To attach the ring shank, begin by cleaning the area of the bezeled back where you plan to attach the ring shank with silicon carbide paper. Position the ring shank over the cleaned spot, apply flux, and solder the shank to the back of the bezeled base as shown in Fig. 4-23.

Cool the joint and test it with your fingers. Use considerable force during this test to assure the joint is securely soldered. The shank will break off from the back if the solder melted but did not bond properly to both joining surfaces. If the shank should break off the back during this test,

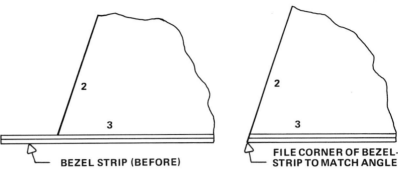

BEZEL STRIP (BEFORE)

FILE CORNER OF BEZEL-STRIP TO MATCH ANGLE

Fig. 4-21. At corners with included angles less than 90°, trim the end of the bezel-strip and file the corner flush with the next side.

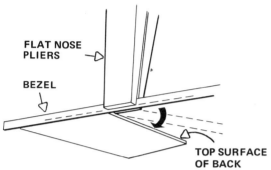

FLAT NOSE PLIERS

BEZEL

TOP SURFACE OF BACK

Fig. 4-20. - Use flat-nose pliers to bend the bezel-strip around obtuse corners. Note that the ends of the flat-jaw pliers are flush with the upper surface of the base.

Fig. 4-23. - To begin soldering the shank to the ring base, place the solder bits on the base over the cleaned spot and hold the ring shank in position on the base with a tweezers from a third-hand or a tweezers held in a hand vise. Adjust the tweezers loosely to allow the ring shank to move down into the base when the solder melts, but don't allow the shank to move to either side. Direct medium flame from the torch base, allowing only a minimum heat to hit the shank. As the solder melts, brush the tip of the blue flame along the joint between the base and shank. As the solder melts, the ring shank should sink down into it.

Fig. 4-22. - The bezel-edge must contact the base along its full length. On long sides, use the poker as necessary to assure continuous contact at the base-strip joint.

45

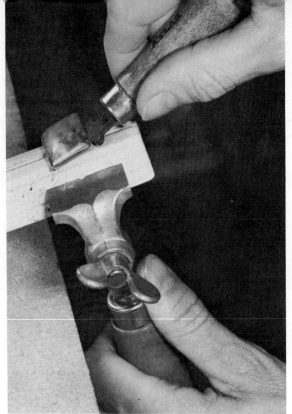

Fig. 4-24. - Soft wood in the jaws of a hand vise protects the ring shank during bezeling. Note the position of the rocker at the start of bezeling. First bezel all corners to restrain the stone. Rock the tool back and forth to force the top edge of the bezel strip toward the stone. Work around the perimeter of the stone with the rocker at about a 45° angle at first. Next, work around the stone with the rocker at about a 20-25° angle from vertical. This increased angle crimps the bezel edge tighter against the stone. Finally, work around the perimeter again with the bezel tool almost vertical. This last step locks the stone tightly in place.

Fig. 4-25. - When using a bent-tip bezeling tool, you tap it with a hammer instead of using brute force to crimp the bezel-strip against the stone. The edge of a bent-tip bezeling tool is rounded and polished so that it leaves no marks on the strip.

file or sand the joining surfaces clean and solder the joint again. To assure solder bonding to both surfaces, bring the ring shank and mount back to soldering temperature at the same time.

Remove any rough spots around the back with a file; you can feel these spots with your finger. When shank and back are firmly joined, clean the entire assembly by pickling. Polish the parts, first with tripoli and finally with jeweler's rouge.

**Bezeling the Stone**

To bezel the stone, or push the top of

the bezel closer to the stone, clamp the ring between two strips of soft pine or other soft material that have been gripped between the jaws of the hand vise (Fig. 4-24). Using the rocker-type bezeling tool, begin to crimp the bezel inward against the stone at the sharp No. 1-4 corner. Work around the stone in the same order as soldering. Smooth any marks left on the bezel during the crimping operation with a file. Polish the bezel again, first with tripoli and finally with rouge. Wash the ring thoroughly with plain water.

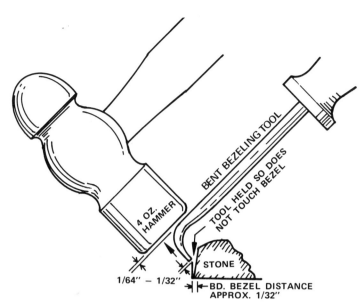

*Fig. 4-26. - Hold the bent-tip bezeling tool in one hand and rest it against the vise with the face at an angle of about 45° from vertical and about 1/64 to 1/32 inch from the strip. Tap the back of the bent-tip tool with the hammer to bend the bezel-strip into position. Your fingers on the tool act as a "spring." Do not hammer the tool while it is resting against the bezel-strip; otherwise you run the risk of fracturing the stone.*

*Fig. 4-27. - Twisted wire soldered around a piece decorates a plain mount and is less difficult to apply than soldering individual balls or shot.*

In an alternative bezeling method you use a special tool (Fig. 4-25). Many craftsmen, particularly women, find that bezeling a stone in a soldered mount is the single most difficult technique in jewelry metalcrafting. Considerable physical force is required to move the metal strip into contact with the stone and to crimp it tightly. An alternative method is to use a special bent-tip bezeling tool and a bench vise. The bent-tip bezeling tool used with a vise allows you to substitute a light hammer for your own physical force to do the *work* of bezeling. With the ring clamped in a soft-jaw vise, follow step by step the procedure detailed in Fig. 4-26. Smooth the bezel with a file and polish with tripoli and rouge.

**DESIGN IDEAS**

A simple bezel-strip mount emphasizes the individuality of a stone. But you may also embellish the plain bezel in several ways. Silver or gold "shot" made by melting bits of metal may be soldered around the edge of a mount to add a look of elegance. Solder individual shots with one bit of solder. Other design ideas are shown in Fig. 4-27. You may also attach "fancy" wires to the bezel near the base.

Beaded, *Cellini,* or other designs of fancy wires are rolled to shape and may be severely work-hardened. You may have difficulty in annealing such fancy wires to a dead-soft condition for soldering, and some breakage may occur as you bend these wires around the corners of the mount. Use the soldering fixture for holding the wires in close contact with the bezel as shown in Fig. 4-28. You may also add a border of shaped, round, or square wires around the mount as shown in Fig. 4-29. Simply cut the shapes and solder their ends to the edge of the bezel.

The base sheet metal may be made to extend beyond the free-form bezel by sweat soldering the bezel back to a larger base piece. Refer to the techniques for sweat soldering overlays in Chapter 3.

47

*Fig. 4-28. - To make twisted wire that can be soldered to a mount, wind 18- or 20-gauge wire together with a hand drill. Bend a single wire in half and clamp the loose ends in a vise. Hook the loop at the opposite end of the wire over an angled wire chucked into a hand drill. Pull the wire taut as you twist it. You must solder the twists together before attaching the twisted wire to a mount. Otherwise, the many points of contact between the twisted wire will "soak up" the solder by capillary attraction. With the twisted wire laying flat on a heating block, place one bit of hard solder at each joint. Heat each joint of wire in turn until the solder runs and bonds the wires together. With the wire soldered at each twist, hold the twisted wire against the mount on the soldering fixture as shown in the photo. Apply flux and use easy solder to avoid remelting the joint between bezel-strip and base.*

*Fig. 4-29. - Half squares or half circles soldered individually around the edge of a mount mark the workmanship of an accomplished jewelry metalcrafter. A tiny bit of easy solder attaches the end of each wire to the mount.*

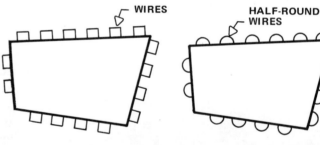

This larger piece, extending out from the base, may be treated in various ways. The edges may be pierced (see Chapter 6) or overlays may be sweat soldered onto the extended area. Sweat solder the overlay designs onto the extended sheet, using hard solder before the extended sheet is sweat soldered to the bezeled back with easy solder. The extended edge of the large back may be stamped with a combination of straight and curved lines (see Chapter 1) or with other special stamps you make yourself. Patterning the extended area by filing or sawing an edge design adds another range of creative designs. Adapt the design ideas discussed for the cuff links made in Chapter 3. To create a three-dimensional effect, use round-nose pliers to roll the sharp points of the edges in and up. The rolled-up pieces will add a new dimension of depth to the design of the ring mount.

*Diamond-shaped gemstone
ring plus flat-top gemstones
for earrings mounted
in sterling.
William E. Garrison.*

*Straight-sided free-form
cabochon gemstones
mounted with
soldered-strip technique.
William E. Garrison*

*Two distinctively designed rings and a
key fob fabricated with soldered-strip
technique in sterling.
Felice Isreeli, Mamaroneck, New York.*

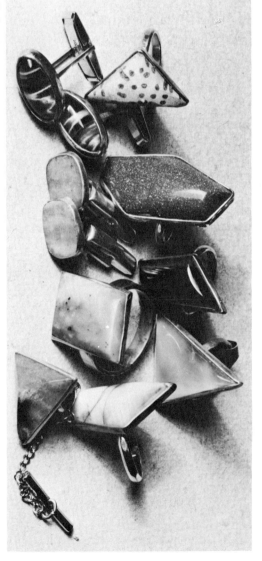

49

MOUNTING OVAL AND ROUND CABOCHON stones calls for a different technique than the one-side-at-a-time method used for straight-sided stones in Chapter 4. Oval and round gemstones may be mounted for rings when relatively small. Larger cabochons may be mounted as pendants or pins. Details for crafting chains for hanging pendants are given in Chapter 7.

## CRAFTING A GEMSTONE PENDANT

Select a large gemstone for this project. Lay the gemstone on 20-gauge metal sheet that has been colored with a felt pen. Scribe around the stone precisely following the techniques detailed in Figs. 4-16 and 4-17 of Chapter 4. Cut around the scribed mark with a 4-0 blade in the jeweler's saw. When sawing around the back, leave the scribed mark, but allow no metal to remain outside of the scribed line. Smooth any rough edges left on the back with a file. Check the back piece against the base of the gemstone for size. If the back is too small, cut another. If the back is too big, saw and/or file the edge until the back fits the stone precisely.

Refer to Figs. 4-9 through 4-12 in Chapter 4 for details on how to design the bezel-strip to be soldered around the back. The shoulder height and shape of the gemstone determines the design of the bezel-strip.

Cut a single strip of 26-28-gauge metal to the bezel height. Cut the strip about ¾ inch longer than the perimeter of the stone. Anneal and pickle the bezel-strip before proceeding.

About ¼ inch from one end of the bezel-strip, bend a sharp 90° corner, using flat-jaw pliers. Beginning with this 90° corner, wrap the bezel-strip around the back plate, keeping it as snugly against the edge as possible. With the flat-jaw pliers, bend another 90° corner on the opposite end of the bezel-strip. Grip both end corners of the bezel-strip with the flat-jaw pliers and pull the bezel-strip tightly around the back (Fig. 5-1). While holding the bezel-strip with pliers, examine the joint around the

# pendants and pins

*Mounting Round and Oval Gemstones*

*Forged and sculptured sterling wire soldered to edge of pendant mounting. Catherine Kramer, West Lafayette, Indiana.*

perimeter. If shallow gaps show between the back and the bezel-strip, bend the strip slightly until it contacts the back. If any concave areas are too deep to eliminate gaps by local bending, you may need to loosen the bezel-strip and file down the shoulders that cause the gaps. Check the back again to make sure the gemstone will fit when the bezeled mount is complete.

Fig. 5-1. - The bezel-strip is drawn tightly around the base to pull the metal close to the edge. Note the 90° corners made at the joint for easy gripping with pliers. Hold the assembly in this same position in the air when soldering and apply heat from the back.

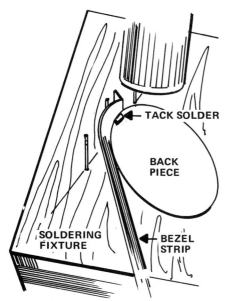

Fig. 5-2. - A single bit of solder is used to tack one corner of the bezel-strip to the base to aid in keeping bezel-strip in place during soldering. Use soldering fixture to hold the strip in position against the base when tack soldering. The joint in the bezel-strip should be located at what is to be the top or bottom of the base.

With pliers holding the bezel-strip around the back, make sure the surface of the back is flush all around with the bottom edge of the bezel-strip. Flux the joint between the bezel-strip and base and place bits of hard solder equally around the perimeter. Judge the number and placement of solder bits from your experience in soldering the straight-sided mount in Chapter 4.

Hold the back and bezel-strip in the air with pliers so that the torch can be directed to the *back* of the work. After applying the flux, warm and dry it with low heat. When the flux has dried, adjust the torch flame to medium heat. Check the solder bits when the flux melts to a clear liquid; if any bits have moved away from contact with the bezel-strip, reposition them with the poker. Direct most of the heat toward the center of the back with the blue cone of flame about 1 inch from the work. Heat all edges and the back evenly until solder flows all around the joint.

An alternative technique for holding the bezel-strip around the base while soldering may simplify this operation for beginners. Some craftsmen find that holding the bezel-strip around the back with pliers is tiring and tricky, so try this gimmick. Before grasping the bezel-strip with the pliers, tack-solder one end of the strip to the back as shown in Fig. 5-2. Another aid is to wind rubber bands around the handles of the pliers to convert them to self-locking pliers that hold the tips closed on the ends of the bezel-strip during the soldering.

Soldering the butt joint at the ends of the bezel-strip is accomplished in two steps. First cut off one end of the bezel-strip straight and square with the back. Pickle the partial assembly. Hold the end of the bezel-strip in contact with the back on the soldering fixture. Add flux, hard solder, and heat the joint until the solder runs.

Scribe the second end of the bezel-edge

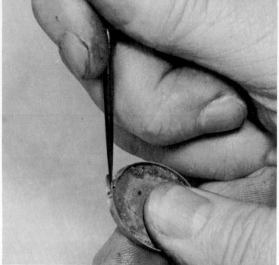

Fig. 5-3. - Mark the end of the bezel-strip slightly longer than exact length for "interference fit." Hammering with a 2-ounce hammer closes the joint so it is practically invisible after soldering.

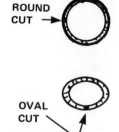

ROUND CUT →

OVAL CUT ↙

Fig. 5-4. - When assembled, the cut in an oval jump ring should be at the side with the pull at the ends. The joint in round jump rings must be soldered; otherwise, the joint will move to top or bottom and pull may open it.

a shade longer than the gap (Fig. 5-3) and cut it at the scribed point. Hammer the edge into position so that it creates a butt joint with the other edge. Solder the end in place as you did the first end for an "invisible" joint.

Adding a mounting ring for a pendant requires jump rings. Jump rings may be oval or round. Oval jump rings are stronger than circular rings for joining pieces, because the pieces always stay toward the narrow ends of the ovals rather than slipping around the entire ring as in the case with the circular ones. The joint of an oval jump ring does not require soldering because the cut is on one side where there is little stress (Fig. 5-4). If you use the same wire gauge, the smaller the diameter of a round jump ring, the stronger it is. In addition to joining pieces and chains, round jump rings are used for decorating larger pieces or to reinforce soldered joints.

Jump rings suitable for a pendant stone of 1¼ to 1½ inches should be about 3/16 inch in diameter. You can make your own by winding wire on a mandrel and cutting the individual rings apart. Smooth and polish the wire before winding it on to a mandrel to simplify clean-up. Chuck a 4- or 5-inch length of a 3/16-inch rod in a hand drill as a mandrel and wind on 16-gauge wire (Fig. 5-5). To form oval jump rings

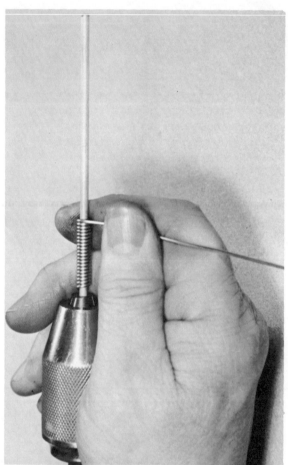

Fig. 5-5. - Winding wire onto a mandrel with the aid of a hand drill forms one continuous metal coil. Fasten one end of the wire in the drill chuck. Support the unattached end of the mandrel in a hole-board on a workbench to aid winding. Rotate the mandrel while feeding on the wire and keep the wire tight against each preceding coil. As you approach the end of the coil, allow at least 2 1/2 inches of wire uncoiled. You will have wound a rather powerful spring during the coiling. You may lose control of a short end, and the wire could cut your hand.

1/8" DIA. MANDRELS

*Fig. 5-6. - To wind oval jump rings chuck two-wire mandrels into a hand drill with one wire off-center. Do not wind more than about 20 coils or you may experience difficulty removing the coil from the mandrels.*

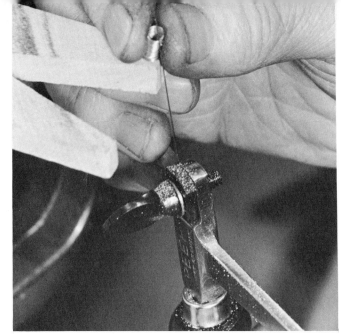

*Fig. 5-8. - An alternative, faster method for cutting jump rings is to hold the coil on a corner of the bench pin and cut through the entire winding at one time. Practice to avoid cutting your fingers.*

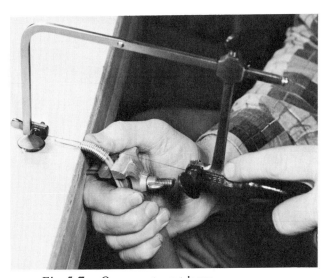

*Fig. 5-7. - One way to cut jump rings apart is to insert a soft metal mandrel into the coil and bend the coil into a curve so that one winding at a time is exposed to the saw. Hold the mandrel in a hand vise and begin sawing at the top.*

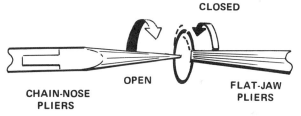

CLOSED

CHAIN-NOSE PLIERS    OPEN    FLAT-JAW PLIERS

*Fig. 5-9. - To open and close jump rings with two pliers, turn the ends of the jump ring past each other. Do not attempt to "unbend" the circle or oval. (Refer also to Figs. 6-14, 6-15, and 6-16 in Chapter 6 for directions on opening and closing jump rings.)*

follow the same procedure, except chuck two rods in the hand drill instead of just one to make the ovals (Fig. 5-6).

If you have made small jump rings, sawing them apart from the wound wire can be difficult. One way to saw them is to insert a soft metal mandrel through the coils and curve it enough to expose one or two windings at a time to the saw blade (Fig. 5-7). A second method is shown in Fig. 5-8.

To open and close jump rings, bend one end of the ring past the other as you did with the eye-pin (see Chapter 2). You'll need two pliers — one to hold each side of the joint (Fig. 5-9).

To solder the joint of jump rings, follow the steps detailed in Fig. 5-10. To solder one ring enclosing another, close a jump ring on a previously soldered jump ring. You can solder one ring closed with one or more soldered jump rings hanging at the bottom (Fig. 5-11).

To make an attachment ring on a pendant mount, place one soldered jump ring

53

*pendants and pins*

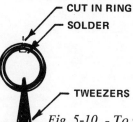

CUT IN RING
SOLDER
TWEEZERS

*Fig. 5-10. - To solder jump rings in the air, hold the ring with tweezers at the bottom opposite the joint. A single bit of solder is held in place on the underside of the joint with flux paste. If flux will not hold the solder to the underside of the joint, the bit can be placed on top. But, the joint will draw the solder better if bit is placed on the underside. Make sure ends of joint touch across full face. Heat the joint from underneath.*

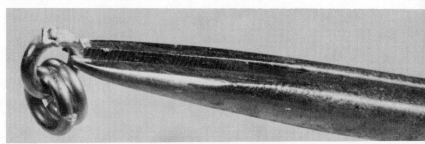

*Fig. 5-11. - Soldering a jump ring to enclose two other rings calls for close heat control. Place the solder bit on top and hold the ring at the side with tweezers to keep the enclosed jump rings as far as possible away from the heated joint. Apply heat quickly and remove it the instant the solder runs.*

*Fig. 5-12. - To solder a center and two reinforcing jump rings to the top of a pendant back, use a steel injector razor blade as a heat shield. Note the dried flux and solder bits at each contact point.*

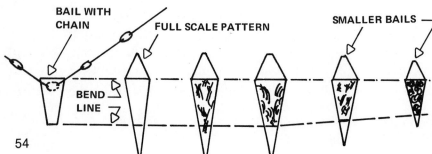

BAIL WITH CHAIN
FULL SCALE PATTERN
SMALLER BAILS
BEND LINE

*Fig. 5-13. - Cut a simple bail for joining a pendant to chain in a flat pattern. Stamp designs or sweat solder appliqués on the center portion of the bail before bending it.*

54

*Fig. 5-14. - A copper back was forged for texture. It has turned-up edges and a self bail for attaching a leather thong. Beth Gilbert, Edmonds, Washington.*

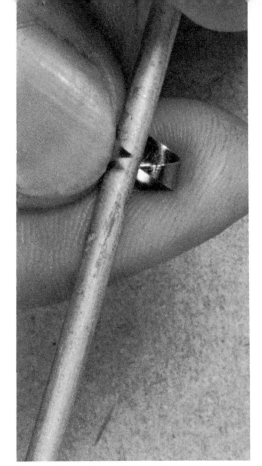

*Fig. 5-15. - Control the radius of the bend for the ends of a bail by bending the bail over a wire mandrel. Leave a smooth, open space for inserting the chain at the top of the bail.*

at the exact center and top of the back to allow the pendant to hang vertically. With only one small joint between the ring and back, the pendant could easily break off if it is heavy enough. To reinforce this joint while adding a decorative touch, solder smaller jump rings at each side of the large jump ring and to the back (Fig. 5-12). Pickle the assembly and polish the outer surface of the bezel and the back.

### Constructing a Bail

A bail is a custom-made finding used with a pendant to keep the pendant hanging straight and to allow the chain to be removed easily. A simple bail has a bend along the top and at the bottom. In a flat pattern, a simple bail looks like the one at the left in Fig. 5-13. A variety of stamps or appliquéd designs may be used to decorate the bail before it is bent. The bail should be designed in scale with the pendant — a large bail for a large pendant and a small bail for a small pendant. Some backs are designed with a self-bail (Fig. 5-14). Cut a shape similar to one of the patterns shown in Fig. 5-13 from fairly thin sheet metal to match the pendant. File any sharp points on the flaps before

bending so they won't snag clothing. Bend the lower tab of the bail up first, because the upper flap should overlay the lower bend (Fig. 5-15). There is no soldering required to hold the flaps of the bail together. Just make sure the flaps fit snugly against one another.

### Bezeling the Stone

Except for the manner of restraint, bezeling an oval or round stone in a mount with a soldered bezel-strip follows the same steps as bezeling the stone in a ring mount (see Figs. 4-24 and 4-25 in Chapter 4). Without an attached rink shank for support, make a V-shaped holding fixture for the pendant (Fig. 5-16). Either the rocker-type or bent-tip bezeling tool may be used with a hammer to bezel the stone (see Fig. 4-26 in Chapter 4).

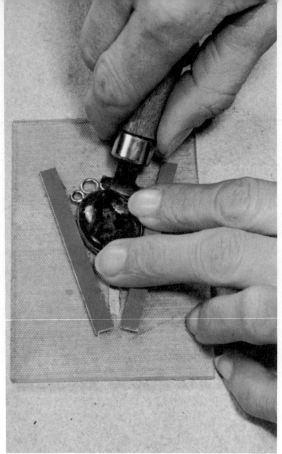

*Fig. 5-16. - A V-shaped holding fixture will help you retain firm control of the mount and stone during bezeling. Hard plastic strips cemented to a plastic back comprise the fixture, which can be easily made. A slot down the center of the backing provides clearance for pin clasps, which must be soldered to the back before the stone is bezeled. If plastic is not available, thin plywood strips may be glued to a plywood backing to create the same design.*

*Fig. 5-17. - A finished pendant with three jump rings at the top hangs from a hand-forged chain.*

To finish the pendant, smooth any marks left during the bezeling with a file. Polish the bezel again, first with tripoli and finally with rouge. Wash the entire assembly in a 1:1 ammonia-water mixture.

For the final step, assemble all the parts. Slip the mounting ring of the pendant into the bail. Slip a chain through the upper part of the bail. A hand-forged chain maintains the handcrafted look of a gemstone pendant. (See Chapter 7 for various designs for chains.) The chain shown with the pendant in Fig. 5-17 was forged from wire and assembled with one unsoldered oval jump ring at each link.

## ALTERNATIVE DESIGNS

Many of the design alternatives applicable to a pendant have already been detailed for rings and free-form gemstones. Note the variety of bails, chains, and attachments shown in the accompanying photographs. An under sheet sweat soldered to the back and rolled, stamped, or edge-contoured adds interest to the design. Round and oval gemstones mounted with soldered bezel-strips may also be adapted for rings and pins. See Chapter 7 for details on how to make pin backs and catches to add to the backs of gemstone mounts.

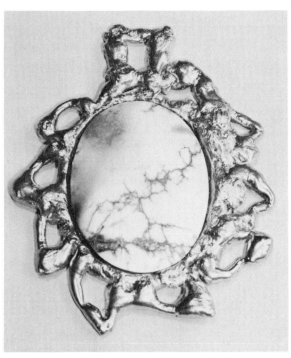

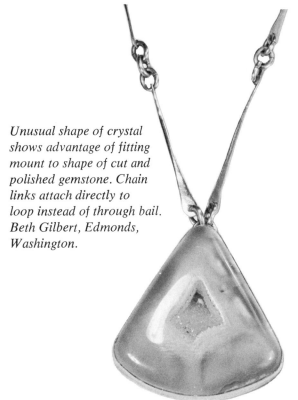

*Unusual shape of crystal shows advantage of fitting mount to shape of cut and polished gemstone. Chain links attach directly to loop instead of through bail. Beth Gilbert, Edmonds, Washington.*

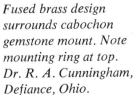

*Fused brass design surrounds cabochon gemstone mount. Note mounting ring at top. Dr. R. A. Cunningham, Defiance, Ohio.*

*Mounted gemstone fitted to textured sterling back with scalloped edges. Note fixed bail and combination loop and link chain. Anne Gries, Flushing, New York.*

*Bracelet links of dendritic agate mounted on sterling backs with fused designs. Note fabricated links and catch loop at right. William E. Garrison.*

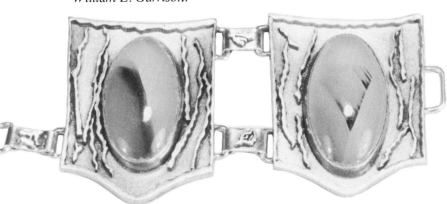

*Oval cabochon mounted in sterling using soldered-strip technique. Pierced designs sweat-soldered to antiqued sterling back.*
*William E. Garrison.*

*Multiple stone necklace connected with a dense chain of soldered jump rings. Note attachment loops at the side of the main pendant.*
*Beth Gilbert, Edmonds, Washington.*

*Free-form, forged brass edging soldered around cabochon mounting. Note the large attachment loop with decorated bail.*
*Oscar Yakopec, Gary, Indiana.*

# earrings
*Piercing Techniques*

CREATIVE, FREE-REIN DESIGN is the keynote for this chapter. You were introduced to metal sawing on outer edges in Chapter 3. In this chapter you will learn internal sawing, or piercing. The term "piercing" comes to us from the Middle East where the center parts of jewelry were once removed with small, sharp chisels. Today, we ordinarily drill a tiny hole in the metal, insert the jeweler's saw blade, and saw out the design. Very small files are used to remove the evidence of sawing.

Designs may be entirely free-form or geometrical and restrained. Try a free-form design first and, in effect, doodle in metal.

Crimp the four corners of two sheets of 22-gauge metal together (Fig. 6-1). By cutting through two layers of metal at the same time, you end up with two identical shapes for the earrings. Brass, copper, German silver, or aluminum sheets are readily available and inexpensive.

Drill two small holes (Fig. 6-2) through both sheets. One hole will be for assembly of the earring with a jump ring; the hole near the center will allow access for piercing the interior design. The distances of the holes from the edge of the metal will depend on the intended design. For true free-form shapes, the inside hole can be anywhere you wish to begin sawing. The hole for mounting the earring should be drilled to allow the final design to hang properly. About 1/16-inch metal minimum should remain between the edge of the hanging hole and the exterior edge of the cut sheet metal. First, center punch tiny dimples indicating the hole locations with a punch to prevent the drill bit from wandering (Fig. 6-3). Any size punch can be used, from a small brad to a 16-penny nail to a commercial punch ground to any of several angles. Second, chuck a 1/16-inch bit with only about 1/8 inch of the tip extending (Fig. 6-4). Small bits tend to break easily unless they are short.

Insert a No. 4-0 blade in the jeweler's saw and position it in the center hole, tightening the blade as shown in Fig. 6-5. Refer

*Geometric pattern pierced from sheet sterling rather than fabricated. Earrings are joined to ear-screws with soldered jump rings. Mrs. Taft Mitchell, Eugene, Oregon.*

to Chapter 3 for instructions on selecting the blade and inserting it in the saw. With the work supported on a bench pin, doodle around the area with long, gentle strokes (Fig. 6-6). Saw out an interior design that pleases you. After sawing the interior edge, remove the blade from the frame and begin sawing the outer edge from outside the blank or from a hole drilled close to the outer edge to be cut (Fig. 6-7). In piercing, always start at the center of a design and work toward the outside. By starting in the inner area, you retain the support and stiffness of the entire sheet with each succeeding step. If you start at the outside of the design, the piece of metal gets smaller and more flexible as you progress. Practice a number of doodling exercises while you gain experience and skill in using the saw.

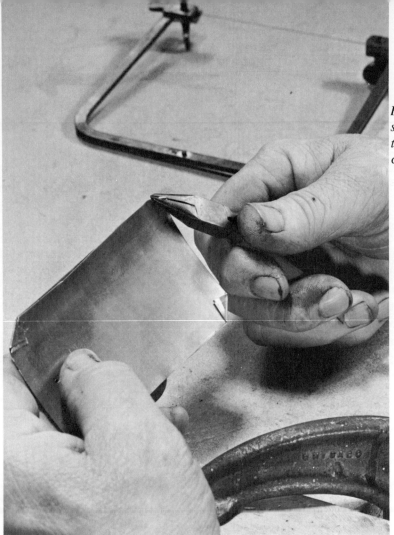

Fig. 6-1. - *Crimping the corners of two sheets of thin metal holds them together so that identical designs for earrings can be sawed.*

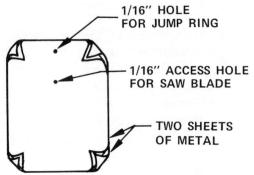

1/16" HOLE FOR JUMP RING

1/16" ACCESS HOLE FOR SAW BLADE

TWO SHEETS OF METAL

Fig. 6-2. - *Drill two 1/16 inch holes through the two sheets of metal. The upper hole will be used for assembling the earring and ear-screw or ear-wire with a jump ring. The hole near the center is the access hole for the saw blade when piercing the interior design.*

Fig. 6-4. - *Small drill bits break easily unless chucked deep into the jaws of the drill. If necessary, break off part of the shank end of the bit to make it shorter.*

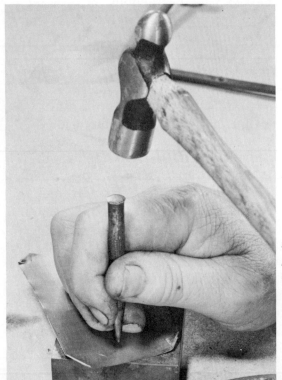

Fig. 6-3. - *Center-punch a tiny dimple in the metal to help control the position of the drill bit.*

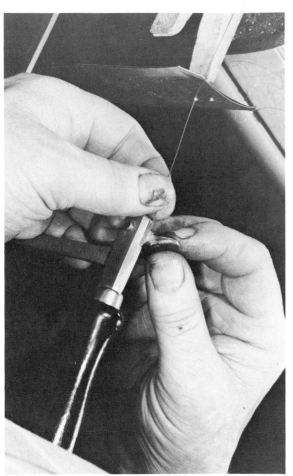

*Fig. 6-5. - To tighten the blade in the saw frame after it is inserted through the access hole, first hold the two sheets of metal in one hand. Lean against the handle to spring the frame and tighten the thumb screw.*

*Fig. 6-6. - Support the sheets on a bench pin while sawing around the center portion, doodling a design that pleases you. Be aware of the position of the jump ring hole and do not saw too closely to it.*

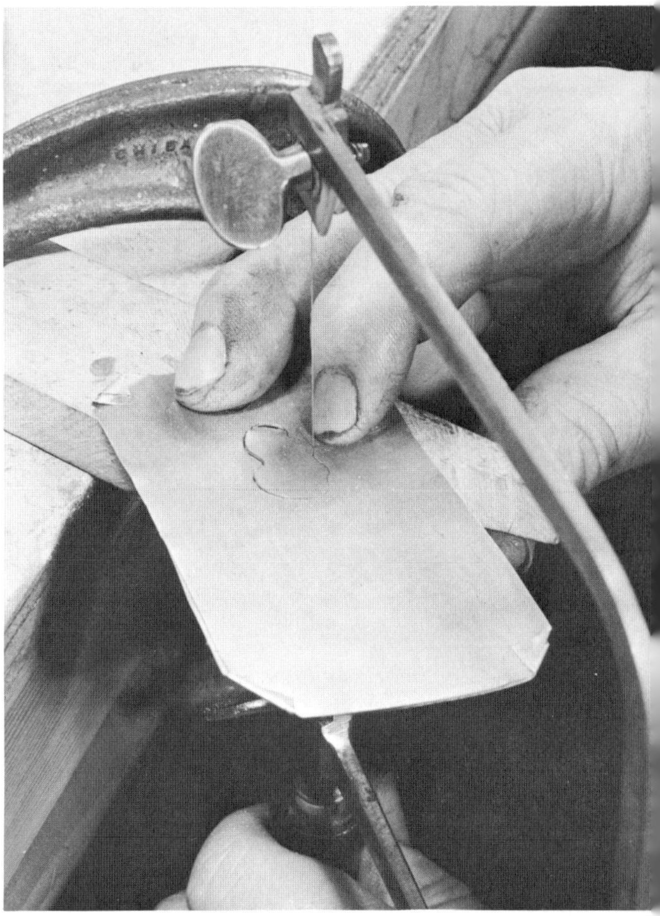

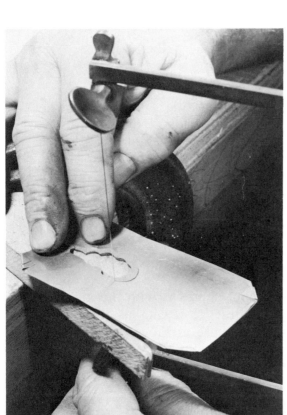

*Fig. 6-7. - Remove the blade, retighten it in the frame, and saw around the outer perimeter of the earrings.*

61

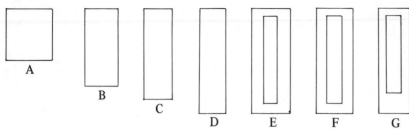

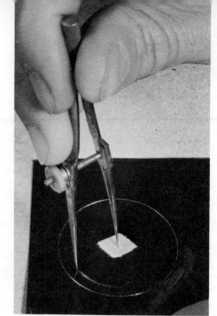

Fig. 6-8. - On paper sketch various size rectangles that would have equal areas of metal so that you stay within the weight limitations of 1/8 ounce Troy or 2 1/2 pennyweights. The size of the rectangle and related designs will depend on the metal and the thickness of the sheet. Repeat the layout sketches with different size triangles to keep the area of metal within weight limitations. Diamonds may be thick or thin as long as the basic area of metal remains approximately the same.

Fig. 6-9. - When scribing circles on metal, apply a chunk of adhesive or masking tape at the center of the circle to prevent the center point from slipping. Coat the metal with a felt-tip marker so the scribe marks can be seen easily.

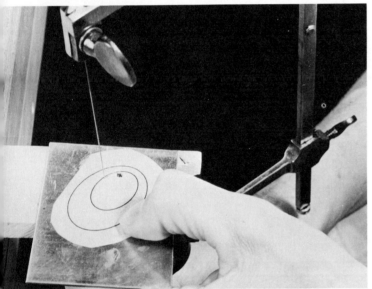

Fig. 6-10. - Ellipses are best drawn with the aid of templates. A design may be drawn on paper and cemented to a sheet of metal for sawing. Note the access hole for the saw blade on the inside of the inner ellipse.

## CALCULATING WEIGHT

About 1/8 ounce is close to the heavy limit for earrings. Some people will wear heavier earrings than others, and earrings worn for only a few hours at a party may be slightly heavier than earrings to be worn all day. Using the 1/8 ounce or 2 1/2 pennyweight limitation, determine the approximate size of earrings that might be cut from sterling sheet. Table 18C in Chapter 18 lists the weight of sheet metals according to the number of square inches for thicknesses (gauge) per troy ounce. For example, a 1-inch square of 22-gauge sterling weighs slightly under 1/8 ounce or 2 1/2 pennyweights.

With paper and pencil, lay out various geometrical shapes with equal areas to control weight. In Fig. 6-8 you can see how the shape of a rectangle may be varied while retaining about the same square area. The same principle is true for other shapes, such as diamonds and triangles. As outside dimensions get larger, you need to cut out more interior area to maintain relative weight.

Circular and elliptical shapes are best drawn with a compass on sheet metal (Fig. 6-9). But by far the simplest method of drawing ellipses is with the aid of a template. Practice sawing inside and outside a simple ellipse as shown in Fig. 6-10. It is

Fig. 6-11. - These three-circle dangling earrings were assembled with tiny jump rings. All the circles were cut from a single piece of metal to conserve material.

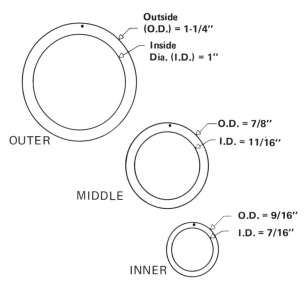

Fig. 6-12. - Dimensions of the three concentric circles used to make the earrings shown in Fig. 6-11. Each smaller ring is cut out from the center of the larger inner circle. Cut the smallest circle first and work outward.

important to remember in cutting all shapes that the outer diameter of a shape can be larger if a portion of the inner area is removed to reduce the overall weight.

## CRAFTING MULTIPLE DANGLERS

Multiple danglers can be hitched together with tiny jump rings that you make yourself (see Figs. 5-6 and 5-10 in Chapter 5). By using a simple circular design for multiple danglers, you can conserve material because each "cutout" leaves an inner circle that becomes the material for an even smaller circle. As with all other shapes, though, work from the inside to the outside. The finished earring is an eye-catching assembly (Fig. 6-11).

Begin the three-circle, dangler earring design by scribing the circles with a compass as shown in Fig. 6-9. Note the dimensions of each dangler as shown in Fig. 6-12. Locate and drill the holes as detailed in Fig. 6-13. Note that one set of holes is for assembling the three danglers with jump rings and the other set of holes is for access to pierce the inner circles. Center punch each of the holes to make a dent in

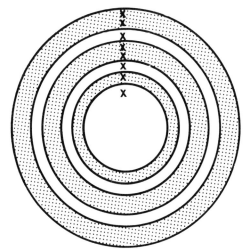

Fig. 6-13. - After scribing circles, but before piercing, drill No. 60 holes in the metal. Two sets of holes are needed: one set for jump rings to assemble the danglers and the second set for gaining access with the saw blade.

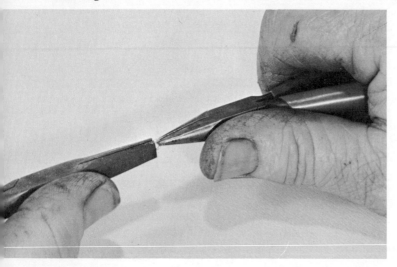

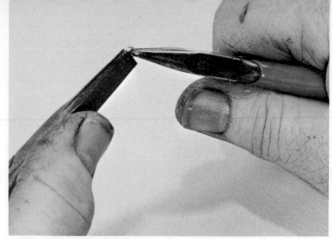

Fig. 6-14. - *When opening a jump ring, use two pliers and keep hands in alignment* (left). *For the opening action, rotate pliers around a common axis. If you hold your hands at an angle* (above), *you only complicate the action.*

the metal to mark the location and add a speck of light oil to the dent before drilling with a No. 60 drill.

Cut out all of the elements for the first earring, starting with the innermost circle. Using a No. 6-0 blade, saw out the scribed lines. Clean up any rough edges around the sawed perimeters of the elements with a file. Using the completed elements of the first earring as templates, mark and cut exact duplicates of the pieces for the second earring.

Fabricate at least ten jump rings for assembling the two earrings. Using 24-gauge wire, wind the rings on a 1/8-inch mandrel. Cut the loops apart with a No. 6-0 saw used for cutting fine wire. Refer to Figs. 5-7 and 5-8 for cutting techniques.

When opening, closing, or soldering tiny jump rings, the technique used to assure high quality craftsmanship becomes most important. To open a jump ring, hold the hands directly opposite each other and rotate the pliers around a common axis (Fig. 6-14). Closing the rings in preparation for soldering is even more critical than opening them. Jump rings should be closed with a slight built-in tension to hold the faces tightly together. To understand the technique (normally accomplished in one complex, continuous motion), the components are noted separately in Fig. 6-15. Practice the sequence of closing actions until you

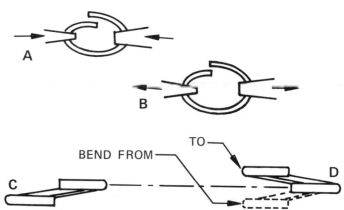

Fig. 6-15. - *Keeping your hands in alignment is even more critical when closing jump rings than when opening them. When closed, the two ends of the ring must be aligned with a slight built-in spring tension to hold the joint closed. In this illustration each of the actions is separated to show you what should occur in a continuous motion once you gain experience. First, with the pliers in alignment across from each other on the jump ring, push the ends together until they overlap (A). Second, pull the ends apart just enough to clear (B). Finally, rotate the pliers to bring the ends into alignment (D) from the cut position (C). Release one plier. If the ends stay in alignment and are closed with a spring tension, you have a perfect closure. Practice the motions detailed separately; then put them together until you can spring the coil in one continuous motion.*

*Fig. 6-16. - Misalignment, as shown here, usually occurs when springing a jump ring because both hands are not used together in the first step of the bending motion. Try using only one hand to make the bends while holding the ring with the other to see the results.*

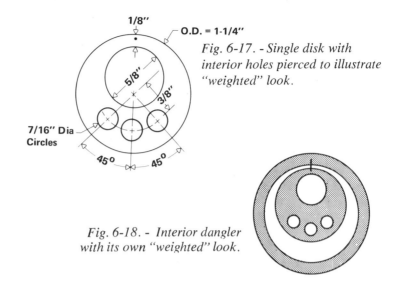

*Fig. 6-17. - Single disk with interior holes pierced to illustrate "weighted" look.*

*Fig. 6-18. - Interior dangler with its own "weighted" look.*

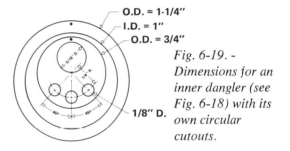

*Fig. 6-19. - Dimensions for an inner dangler (see Fig. 6-18) with its own circular cutouts.*

achieve consistent closures in one continuous movement. Both hands must take part in all motions. To understand this more clearly, use one hand (the left if you are right-handed) to simply hold one side of the jump ring stationary. Attempt to make all of the motions with your right hand. You will find that on the first couple of tries cut faces of the jump ring will likely end up out of alignment as shown in Fig. 6-16.

After closing the jump rings with a built-in tension, solder them as detailed in Fig. 5-10. Most problems in soldering tiny jump rings are caused by heating too slowly. Slow heating tends to burn off the little flux that sticks to such a joint, and by the time the metal reaches soldering temperature, the metal oxidizes because of the lack of flux and the solder fails to run.

**Assembling Multiple Danglers**

Assembling the interior circles of multiple dangler earrings calls into play the principle of "weighting." Each of the interior danglers should be hung closer together at the top than at the bottom. Such an arrangement creates the impression of "weight" at the bottom of the design. Two alternative designs illustrate this principle of weighting even more clearly. Note in Fig. 6-17 how the large interior hole is offset near the top of the large circle. The bottom of the large circle appears heavier, even

though three circles have been cut out of the thick section. An internal dangler with its own circles cut out (Figs. 6-18 and 6-19) has its own weighted look.

Begin assembling the three-dangler earrings by opening and closing a jump ring through the two smallest parts to be connected. Shift the danglers to the bottom of the jump ring away from the cut and solder the joint in the air. Refer to Fig. 5-11 in Chapter 5 for the proper procedure. Solder another jump ring to connect the two inner danglers to the outer circle. Build a chain of at least three jump rings to attach the earring to an ear-screw or ear-wire. Pickle the parts and polish or buff them to a high gloss before assembling the chain to the ear-screw or ear-wire. You may avoid soldering the jump rings by using oval jump rings that are cut at the side to attach interior danglers and the outer circle to ear-screws or ear-wires. Oval rings will not pull apart easily even when not soldered.

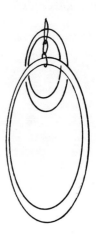

Fig. 6-20. - Multiple danglers
may be designed with the larger
element hanging below
the smaller element, again for a
weighted look. The larger
elements are assembled to the
jump ring at the top with a chain
of soldered round jump rings or
unsoldered oval jump rings.

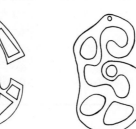

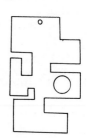

Fig. 6-21. - Note that in these
idea starters for a variety
of free-form shapes some of the
designs are somewhat symmetrical
while others are completely
asymmetrical.

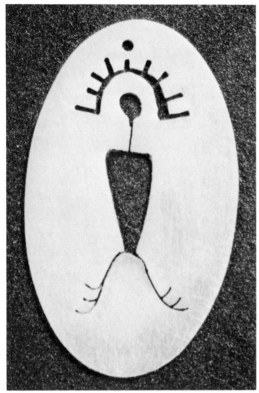

*Fig. 6-22. - This pierced design in oval brass features a petroglyph.*

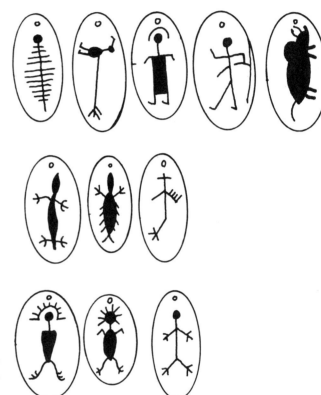

*Fig. 6-23. - Some alternative petroglyph designs that can be used for piercing.*

## ALTERNATIVE DESIGNS

Various geometric shapes can be cut out of single-piece earrings. Multiple danglers need not be circular, and they may be outside the piece attached to the ear-screw or ear-wire (Fig. 6-20). Mixed shapes may be combined with internal danglers. A variety of free-form designs to spark your creative instincts are shown in Fig. 6-21.

Piercing is not limited to geometrical designs. In fact, the range for pierced designs is limited only by the designer's imagination. Figure 6-22 shows an authentic Pacific Northwest Indian petroglyph tracing pierced inside a brass ellipse. These ancient tracings are found in several locations around the Pacific Northwest region. Additional designs from these tracings are detailed in Fig. 6-23. Other design possibilities include various art takeoffs from the Signs of the Zodiac, single initials or initials designed artistically in three's, and other abstract patterns created by your own imagination.

Leaf-shaped earrings pierced and
contoured. Beth Gilbert,
Edmonds, Washington.

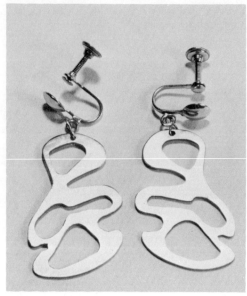

Abstract shape pierced from
sterling sheet. Note the
connection to the ear-screw with
a figure-8 link. Anne Gries,
Flushing, New York.

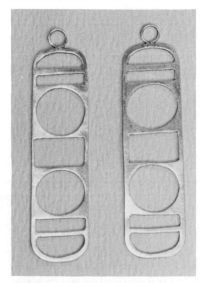

Combination of geometrical
shapes pierced from sterling sheet.
Carol Moch, West Hartford,
Connecticut.

Delicately curved and pierced
symmetrical design for earring,
contoured after piercing.
Catherine Kramer, West
Lafayette, Indiana.

AUTHENTIC, HANDCRAFTED CHAINS complement any jewelry item that hangs or swings, such as a pendant, medallion, key chain, bracelet, or choker. In fact, a beautifully handcrafted pendant doesn't look right hanging from a machine-made chain or one that looks as if it might have been made by machine. As a craftsman of personal jewelry, you should learn the skills needed to handcraft chains constructed with wire or short metal links joined with jump rings or other linkages.

Catches and clasps are considered interchangeable terms by some craftsmen. In this book, by arbitrary definition, the term catch will be used to mean any joining device with or without moving parts. Handcrafted catches, like chains, give your jewelry the look of authentic craftwork. Catches function to open and close a chain, necklace, or bracelet, and they should be constructed so that it is almost impossible for them to come loose accidentally. This requirement isn't as difficult as it sounds. There are a number of ways to design catches that are quite safe.

Conserve your bench time by designing and crafting chains that, while they complement the handcrafted look of your pendants or chokers and contribute to the authenticity of your handcrafted projects, can be finished in a minimum amount of time. For example, the shorter the links in your chain, the longer it will take to make. Long-link chains retain a handcrafted look and still keep chain crafting time down to a minimum. Although chains are an important accessory, they play only a supporting role to the major piece.

Interesting chains can be designed with links that do not require assembly with jump rings (Fig. 7-1). Flexible connections can be devised by joining the links directly to each other. The unique chain supporting the pendant in Fig. 7-2 is joined with a combination of integral end loops and an occasional jump ring.

## CRAFTING A LINK CHAIN

A simple, authentic link chain can be

# chains and catches
*Bending Techniques*

*Fused sterling pendant suspended from a unique bent wire chain that does not use solder or jump rings for connection. Beth Gilbert, Edmonds, Washington.*

fabricated by forging the ends of round wire in a metal to match the pendant or choker with which it is to be used. Then individual links are joined with one to three oval jump rings (Fig. 7-3). Begin making the link chain by cutting 1 1/2-inch pieces of 14-gauge wire. Links may be longer or shorter as you wish to complement a pendant, but 1 1/2-inch links afford flexibility and can be constructed in a reasonable amount of time. Forge the ends of the wire as shown in Fig. 7-4. Two variations of chain link ends can be forged (Fig. 7-5). Forge flats at each end of the links by holding the end forged first in a vertical

Fig. 7-1. - Chain links are joined with a balled end inserted through a drilled hole in the next link. Note the tiny prongs holding the crystal against the back in a free-form pendant design. Betty Tlush, Meadowbrook, Pennsylvania.

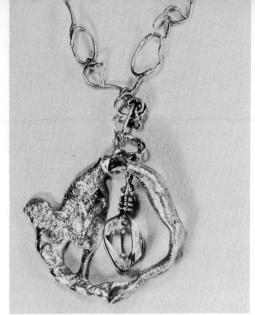

Fig. 7-2 - In this random design of bent wire links, some links are joined directly to the next link, others are joined with an irregularly shaped jump ring. The pendant is fused sterling with an agate bound in a wire swing hanging inside the opening. Betty Tlush, Meadowbrook, Pennsylvania.

Fig. 7-3. - An enlarged view of three-ring joint. Note the saw cut in the side of each oval jump ring. If jump rings are to be soldered, they must be closed so that the faces are in firm contact.

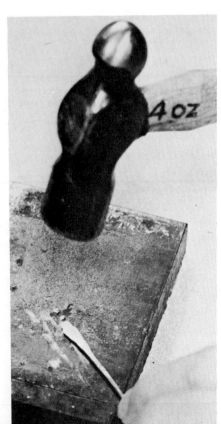

Fig. 7-4. - The ends of round wire can be forged flat to form chain links. A 4-ounce hammer provides more "heft" for flattening ends than does a 2-ounce hammer. The face of the 4-ounce hammer should be smooth to avoid defacing the link surfaces.

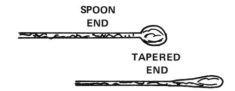

SPOON
END

TAPERED
END

Fig. 7-5. - A tapered and spoon end are alternative shapes for the ends of forged chain links.

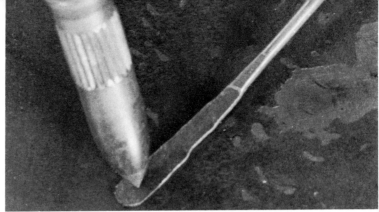

Fig. 7-7. - A center punch at the hole location defines the center point and dimples metal enough to keep twist drill from wandering over the surface of the metal. Apply a tiny bit of oil in the dimple with a toothpick to aid drilling.

3/32"

Fig. 7-6. - Locate the center point of the holes in chain links about 3/32 of an inch from the ends to increase flexibility and reduce tendency for the links to tangle.

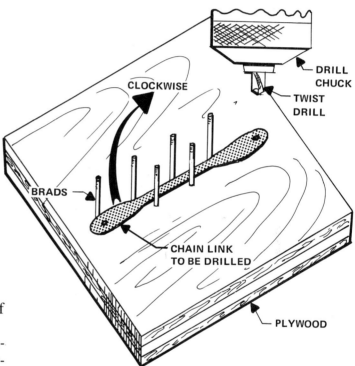

CLOCKWISE

DRILL CHUCK

TWIST DRILL

BRADS

CHAIN LINK TO BE DRILLED

PLYWOOD

Fig. 7-8. - A holding fixture made from brads driven into a plywood block prevents the chain link from turning as the ends are drilled. Rapid speed and light pressure will help to keep the twist drill from grabbing edges of the metal when the V-shaped point cuts through. Too much pressure on the bit may break the bit. Allowing the twist drill to extend only about 1/16 inch more than the thickness of the metal to be drilled protects the bit from breakage. Clean up any sharp edges remaining around the hole after drilling with a 1/4-inch twist drill. By hand, turn the point of the bit around both sides of each hole to remove any wire edge or metal slivers.

plane while forging the opposite end of the link horizontally on the steel block.

Drilling holes in the ends of the links requires special techniques. First, select carbon steel twist drills for making the holes, because they are less expensive and less brittle than high-speed twist drills designed for drilling steel. Holes in the ends of the chain links should be about 1/16 inch in diameter and should be located as shown in Fig. 7-6. To drill the holes, first center punch a dimple at the location of the hole (Fig. 7-7). A tiny drop of oil placed in the dimple left by the center punch eases the drilling. A holding fixture (Fig. 7-8) speeds the drilling of holes in the end of numerous links. Note how short the end of the twist drill extending beyond the end of the 3-jaw chuck is in Fig. 7-8.

71

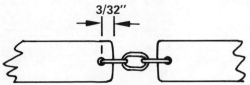

*Fig. 7-9. - Three jump rings are used to connect sheet metal links having a drilled hole in each end. By making connecting holes close to the ends, you improve the flexibility of the chain.*

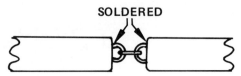

SOLDERED

*Fig. 7-10. - An alternative method for connecting sheet metal links calls for half-oval rings soldered to the ends of each section. A single oval jump ring connects each half ring.*

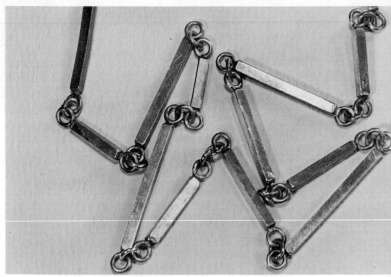

*Fig. 7-11. - A link chain formed with cut lengths of a sterling square bar. Round jump rings soldered to the ends of the links are joined with a third round jump ring, which has had its faces soldered after closing. William E. Garrison.*

To eliminate soldering the jump rings used to connect the links, oval jump rings can be used. A single jump ring can be used to join chain links, but such chains tend to tangle easily. A better joint is made when three oval jump rings are used (Fig. 7-3).

The overall length of the chain will vary according to personal taste. However, a large pendant or medallion ordinarily should hang lower on a longer chain than a small pendant.

You may vary the length of the links or cut them to a uniform length. Surfaces on one or both sides of the links may be decorated with stamped designs similar to those shown in Chapter 1. Edge treatments and piercing can also be adapted for decorating the sheet metal links.

Begin fabricating a sheet metal link chain by cutting enough metal pieces to assemble a chain that can be easily slipped over the head — at least 24 to 30 inches long. Links may be as narrow as 1/8 inch or as wide as 1/2 inch, or possibly 3/4 inch. When links

are wider than 1/2 inch, the chain may become tiringly heavy, depending on the weight of the metal selected. Cut the links from 14- or 16-gauge metal to match the pendant, medallion, or choker.

The easiest way to join the links is with three jump rings attached through holes drilled in the ends of the links (Fig. 7-9). Use wide oval jump rings to allow them to move easily in the holes drilled in the end of the links (Fig. 7-8). To assemble the chain, first open the oval jump rings (see Chapter 6). Insert the open jump rings through the end holes of the links and reclose them. Assemble the chain with a single oval jump ring that joins the jump rings at each end of the links. No catch is necessary if the chain is long enough to slip easily over the head.

An alternative method of assembling the links calls for soldering half rings to each end of the sheet metal links (Fig. 7-10). A single oval jump ring is used to join the half rings soldered to the ends of the links.

Links cut from square cross-section bar stock can be used to form another type of chain (Fig. 7-11). Round jump rings are soldered to each end of the bar, and a soldered round jump ring joins the ends of the links. The light twisted-wire chain shown in Fig. 7-12 has small wire loops at each end and is joined with a single oval jump ring. Bent-wire links are fabricated with round-nose pliers and may be joined without jump rings. Repetitive designs of bent-wire links may be bent quickly and easily with the aid of a wire-bending fixture (see Chapter 15).

## ATTACHING PIN CATCH

A pin catch may be soldered to the metal back of a mounted gemstone (Fig. 7-13) or may be soldered to fused designs in metal alone. Soldering these small findings to a large piece of metal poses a special problem of heat control. You must apply enough heat to make the solder run, but not so much that you melt the findings. While you can place the pin catch in almost any position on a back, consider how the pin will be worn. Gemstones generally look better from one angle rather than another. So, decide which end or side of the pin should be worn *up,* and locate the catch so the slot end will be *down* when the pin is attached and closed. The pin catch should be located above the horizontal centerline to allow the pin to hang gracefully.

A modified form of sweat soldering is used to attach commercial clasp pieces — a mount for the long pin and a safety clasp that accepts the end of the pin as shown in Fig. 7-13. Remove the long pin from its mounting before soldering it. Separately, turn the hinge pin and the clasp upside down on an asbestos heating block. Brighten the areas of the hinge pin and clasp that are to be soldered with silicon carbide paper and flux with heavy paste. Do not allow flux to run down the sides of the findings. Apply enough solder to cover the full area of the bases of both findings. Heat the solder until it runs over the two joining surfaces.

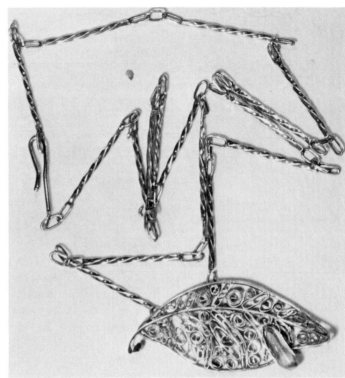

Fig. 7-12. - Twisted-wire links are joined with single oval jump rings. Note how the thin, twisted-wire links match the filigree design of the leaf with a single mounted gemstone. Leigh Garrison.

Fig. 7-13. - The two parts of a pin catch are soldered above the centerline on the back of a gemstone pin. The long pin is removed during sweat soldering. Use care not to allow the solder to run into the workable locking catch.

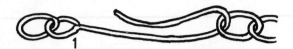

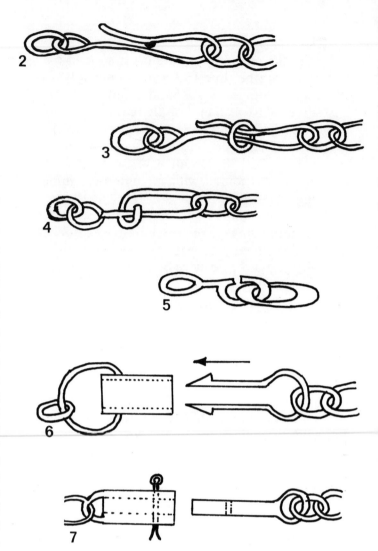

*Fig. 7-14. - Three principles are employed in making catches to prevent their coming loose accidentally: spring tension, gravity, and some sort of moving part, such as a slide or pin. Spring tension built into the hook keeps the catch shown in 1 together. In 2, a small knob or welded shot is used for increased safety in addition to spring tension. A sliding component in 3 makes the spring hook extra strong. A spring hook in 4 serves much the same purpose as a sliding ring. In 5 the end of the link can move through the slot only in one position that is different from its normal, in-place position. A sliding component in combination with spring tension in 6 adds complexity to the design of the catch, but also provides additional security. In 7 a more elaborate catch utilizes a locking pin. Some pins may be further secured with a small safety chain, or the pin may be retained with spring tension. Still other catches depend upon components designed in such a manner that accidental release is unlikely. In a sense, these resemble puzzle rings; that is, the components can be joined in only one way, and it is unlikely that they will accidentally become disengaged.*

With the mount or base face down on a heating block, brighten the spots where the hinge and clasp are to be soldered. Flux the two spots and place the hinge and clasp in position. Ordinarily you would expect to heat the assembly from the bottom to melt the solder already bonded to the ends of the hinge and clasp. However, if you have already soldered a bezel or other metal to the front surface of the piece, these joints might loosen if the assembly is heated from the bottom. Instead, keep the torch at medium heat and move it around the hinge or the clasp. The back must reach soldering temperature at the time the solder melts. Solder first one and then the other.

After cooling the assembly in water or in air, polish the back and clean the hinge and clasp. Finally, position the long pin in the joint and bend it closed with pliers.

**Designing and Constructing Clasps**

A clasp is used to join chains, necklaces, bracelets, and other pieces to facilitate wearing. In the accompanying photographs note the different kinds of clasps used to join pieces of jewelry. A number of design ideas for clasps are detailed in Fig. 7-14. Note also the details of clasps on jewelry pictured in other chapters.

Bent wire and bead choker with a long catch and short chain of soldered jump rings for length adjustment. David Graham, Seattle, Washington.

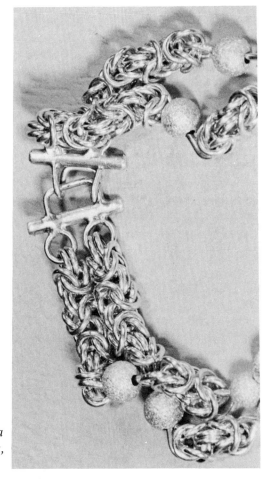

This full-width catch has a double hook. Beth Gilbert, Edmonds, Washington.

75

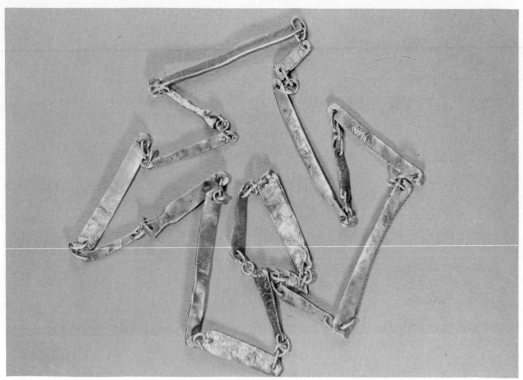

Random lengths of fused sterling
links connected with three oval
jump rings at each joint.
Leigh Garrison.

A bracelet clasp joins links of
jadite mounted in gold wire. Note
the ball at the end of the hook,
which prevents the catch from
coming loose.
William E. Garrison.

A fused gold thimble with a
useful catch-bail that permits
the thimble to be removed easily
for use in sewing. Jo Ann
Parsons, Seattle, Washington.

*Wire link chain with matching earrings decorated with plastic bits. Individual links were formed on a wire bending fixture and joined with oval jump rings. Dan Strahl, Seattle, Washington.*

*Bent wire choker with ceramic flags for decoration. Note the unusual combination of jig-bent wire elements in both the choker and earrings. Dan Strahl, Seattle, Washington.*

77

FORGING OR HAMMERING opens up a full range of design possibilities for shaping and texturing solid bracelets, chokers, belt buckles, earrings, pendants, buttons, and pins. A shaped bracelet also affords a mount for a gemstone (Fig. 8-1), added decorative fused elements, and space for pierced designs. Even earrings may be forged and domed (Fig. 8-2).

## FORGING TECHNIQUES

Before tackling a solid, forged bracelet, you should familiarize yourself with forging techniques and the specialized tools to be used. As a jewelry craftsman, you should understand the effect forging has on metals. Silver, gold, copper, brass, aluminum, nickel silver, and pewter are all malleable metals and are good for forging. Forging requires an enormous expenditure of time, even though the designs and textures appear quite simple.

To achieve the full richness of hand-forged work, you must move the metal enough to show the effects of forging — a change of thickness, length, width, or surface condition is required. In Fig. 8-3, for example, as metal is moved outward to widen one end, the metal becomes thinner.

Peening with a round-headed hammer, such as a ball-peen hammer, moves the metal out in all directions from the center of the ball (Fig. 8-4). As the metal moves out, it becomes thinner at the center. The overall effect is to cup the metal slightly.

A cross-peen hammer, in contrast to the ball-peen hammer, moves metal in two directions only (Fig. 8-5). The peen end of a cross-peen hammer resembles a blunted cold chisel (Fig. 8-6). The curve across the straight dimension of the cross-peen hammer may vary from broad to sharp (Fig. 8-7). On most cross-peen hammers, the straight dimension is 90° to the handle.

With the cross-peen hammer, you can extend the length of strips without changing the width (Fig. 8-8), or you can widen the strips without extending the length (Fig. 8-9). In either case, the cross-peen hammer

# bracelets, chokers, belt buckles

*Forging Techniques*

A forged and soldered sterling wire pendant hanging from a choker. Gordon Longley, Downers Grove, Illinois.

thins the metal being forged. Metal strips also may be thickened if the width of the strip is no more than two to three times the original thickness before forging (Fig. 8-10).

Edge-thickening increases the strength of bracelets and helps belt buckles and other pieces to hold their shape. Edge-thickening (Fig. 8-11) requires very careful handling to prevent buckling (Fig. 8-12). What happens to cause buckling is that forging the edge deforms the metal locally and

Fig. 8-1. - A sterling wire was forged and shaped before it was assembled and soldered into a full circle bracelet. Gwen Warren, Seattle, Washington.

Fig. 8-2. - The surface texture on sterling disks is highlighted by antiquing and polishing the surface with S-C block. Disks were formed to shallow dish shapes after surface forging. William E. Garrison.

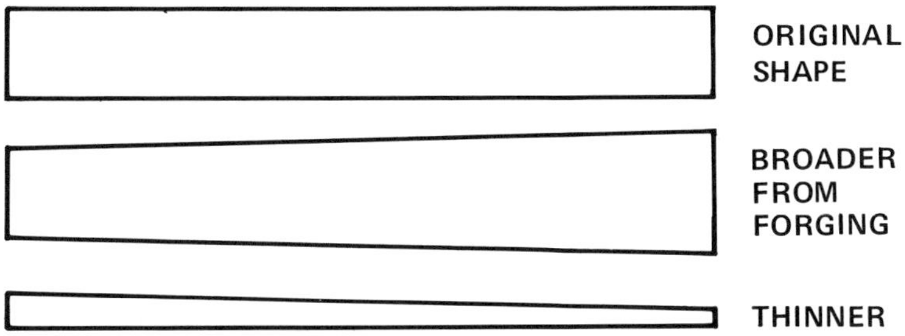

ORIGINAL SHAPE

BROADER FROM FORGING

THINNER

Fig. 8-3. - Before forging, the original shape of the blank is rectangular (top). As metal is moved to widen the right end, the thickness of the metal is decreased (bottom, side view).

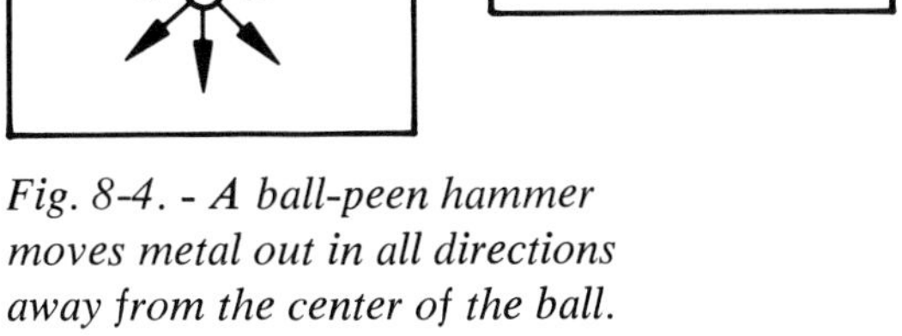

Fig. 8-4. - A ball-peen hammer moves metal out in all directions away from the center of the ball. This cupping action leaves the metal thin at the center.

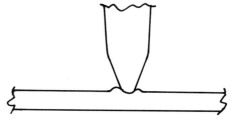

Fig. 8-5. - The cross-peen hammer is used to move metal in two directions only—away from the face of the hammer. With a cross-peen hammer the metal is thinned in a line rather than at a point as with a ball-peen hammer.

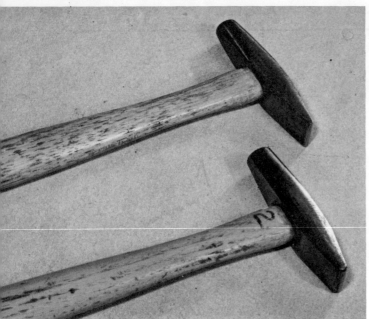

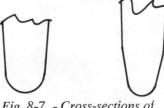

Fig. 8-6. - *Cross-peen hammers usually are built with the axis of the peen perpendicular to the handle.*

Fig. 8-7. - *Cross-sections of cross-peen hammers show varying radius of peen ends.*

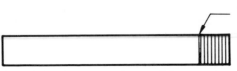

CROSS-PEEN AT RIGHT ANGLE TO LENGTH

Fig. 8-8. - *Cross peening enables you to extend a metal strip without widening it, since the metal moves in only two directions. The metal thins as the strip is lengthened.*

CROSS-PEEN PARALLEL WITH LENGTH WIDENS METAL

Fig. 8-9. - *Forging with a cross-peen hammer in the opposite direction widens the end of a metal strip without extending the length.*

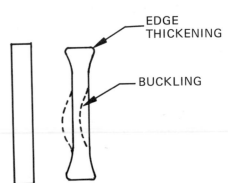

EDGE THICKENING

BUCKLING

Fig. 8-11. - *Thickening a strip at each edge increases the stiffness and springiness of the metal, which is particularly desirable for a bracelet. To thicken the edges each one must be hammered; the bottom edge in contact with the metal block will not be thickened by blows at the top.*

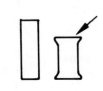

AFTER FORGING

Fig. 8-10. - *Forging may thicken a section of metal if the width of the strip is no more than three times the thickness before forging. In forging, hammer blows must be straight against the edge to prevent excessive rounding.*

BUCKLING

Fig. 8-12. - *Buckling at the center of a strip being edge thickened occurs when excessive hammering collapses the soft metal at the center. When metal at the edges being thickened no longer responds, it is work-hardened and further hammering will lead to buckling.*

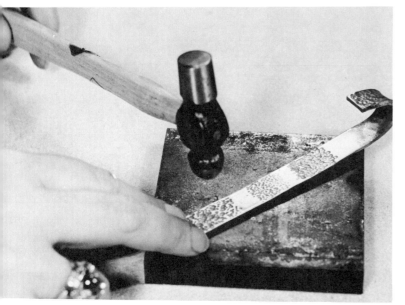

Fig. 8-13. - When texturing the surface of a formed bracelet by surface-forging, forging should be accomplished prior to shaping, except for local texturing. Varying textures can be achieved by even or uneven hammer strokes, combinations of ball peening, and striking the metal with the flat face edge of the 2-ounce hammer.

Fig. 8-14. - Stamped and shaped sterling bracelet with antiqued design. Catherine Kramer, West Lafayette, Indiana.

work-hardens the edge material. However, the metal away from the edge is not deformed and remains annealed. Continued hammering will cause the soft middle portion to bend or buckle. To continue edge-thickening without buckling the center, anneal the piece frequently to keep the edges soft and malleable.

Forging work-hardens metal, and some metals work-harden more rapidly and require more frequent annealing than others. See Table 16A for the difference in metals' tendencies to work-harden. Continuing to hammer on metal after it has work-hardened may cause buckling in the case of edge-thickening, or may cause local cracking. Jewelry materials may be annealed as often as necessary to keep them soft and malleable. You can tell when metals begin to harden by sound. The metal actually sounds harder while being hammered. Also, if you are holding a piece in your hands, you can begin to feel a sting as the metal begins to harden while being hammered.

## TEXTURING SURFACES

Various surface textures can be forged with ball-peen and flat-face hammers. Practice forging textures first on a 1/2-inch strip of brass. Using only the peen of the 2-ounce hammer, surface-forge one small section of the brass. Strike hammer blows over one part of the area so that the ball-shaped cavities are relatively the same size; that is, strike the surface with an even force from the hammer (Fig. 8-13). On a second small area, experiment with a variety of forces with the hammer to vary the depths of cupping on the surface. Add to the variety of surface textures by using the edge of the 2-ounce hammer's flat face.

## CRAFTING A FORGED BRACELET

Brass or copper strips 1/2 inch to 1 inch wide can be forged and bent into handsome bracelets by forging. To learn the skills required to make the bracelet, select a strip of metal 1/2 inch to 5/8 inch wide and about 7 to 7 1/2 inches long. Make sure the metal has been annealed and is thoroughly soft before starting. (Aluminum and pewter should not be annealed because they are soft metals to begin with.)

You may choose to surface-forge a texture on the surface of the bracelet or stamp a design of your own creation on it before forming it (Fig. 8-14). When you are more

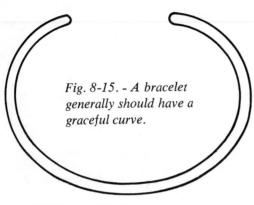

*Fig. 8-15. - A bracelet generally should have a graceful curve.*

GENERAL SHAPE OF BRACELET

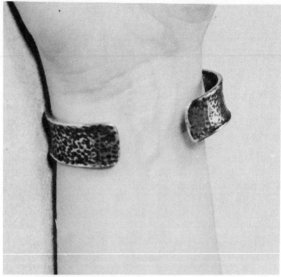

*Fig. 8-16. - To shape a bracelet that will fit most wrists, bend the ends first around an anvil horn, pipe, or other round object, then continue shaping the metal near the center.*

*Fig. 8-17. - Final edge thickening with the face of a 4-ounce hammer adds stiffness and smooths the edges of the bracelet. In its curved shape, the center portion of the metal is less likely to buckle than it is before bending.*

skilled, you might choose to fuse a design on the blank before bending it (see Chapter 11).

When the surface design is complete, turn the metal strip on edge on your metal block or anvil. With the *face* of the 2-ounce hammer, forge out any irregularities along the edge of the strip. At this point, edge-forging should make the edge only slightly thicker. Forge both edges of the blank; don't depend on the steel block to thicken or smooth the bottom while you are hammering on the top. Unit forces on the bottom edge of the blank are too little to cause edge-thickening while hammering on the top. Anneal the entire blank again to remove the work-hardening induced by surface texturing and edge-thickening.

Begin shaping the bracelet by bending each end. Start bending the strip at the ends — never in the middle. Use a soft-faced hammer to bend the ends around the horn of an anvil or some other curved object, such as pipe or a baseball bat. Attempting to bend the blank with a metal hammer will deface the design. The exact size and shape of the bracelet will vary somewhat — particularly if it is planned for a specific person. Generally, the bracelet should be shaped with a graceful curve as shown in Fig. 8-15. Or the bracelet may have the ends curved inward more sharply (Fig. 8-16). There will generally be enough "spring" in the metal to reshape it *slightly* by hand after final hammering.

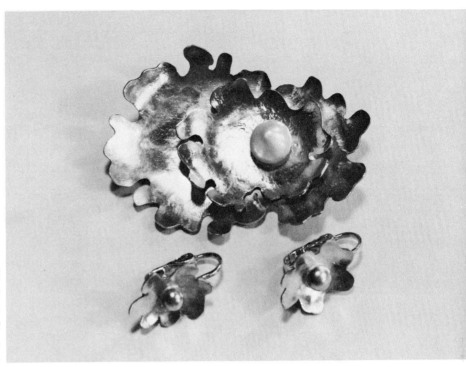

Fig. 8-18. - A matched set of pin and earrings forged in shaped sterling after the edge designs have been sawed. A pegged pearl is part of the design. Carol Moch, West Hartford, Connecticut.

Edge-thickening after shaping will work-harden the metal and give it more spring. Attempting to thicken the edges before shaping complicates the shaping because the bracelet will be even harder to bend into a graceful curve. Stand the shaped bracelet on the metal block or anvil. Begin hammering with straight downward blows with the handle parallel to the upper surface of the bracelet when the hammer face strikes the edge. Use considerable force with the 2-ounce hammer. Although a 4-ounce hammer wields more heft, the advantage of using a 2-ounce hammer is that you may use considerable force without collapsing the middle of the bracelet. Hammer both edges of the bracelet until you notice a definite thickening of the edge. (Fig. 8-17).

Pickle the bracelet to remove the oxidation resulting from annealing before any final finishing. Also, with a fine-cutting file, remove any burrs or sharp edges. Polish the piece lightly. The effect of the tool marks will be diminished if you polish and smooth the sharp, crisp edges and leave them rounded. Generally, the less metal removed during polishing and buffing, the better for final appearance.

Whether you decide to antique the bracelet or not depends on the metal used and the design. If the design includes deeply textured, stamped, or pierced designs, antiquing will highlight the design. If the design is relatively flat and even, antiquing will not last long enough to matter.

Shaping with the hammer resembles forging because it moves metal. Shaping or cupping changes the metal in three dimensions, as in the cupping of the back pieces holding the pearls in Fig. 8-18.

Off-hand shaping, in contrast to the precision of dapping, calls for practice and skill. Practice with scrap pieces first to develop a feel for shaping. A chunk of soft wood or a heavy canvas bag of sand is your work mandrel. Begin at the edge of the metal and tap the thin-gauge metal lightly. Heavy-gauge materials will require more force. Gradually work from the edges of the metal toward the center of a cupped shape. Always work with the hammer to bend metal up, because the soft mandrel will allow the metal to bend under the force of the hammer. Shaping will be a final step, after cutting and texturing but before polishing.

*bracelets, chokers, belt buckles*

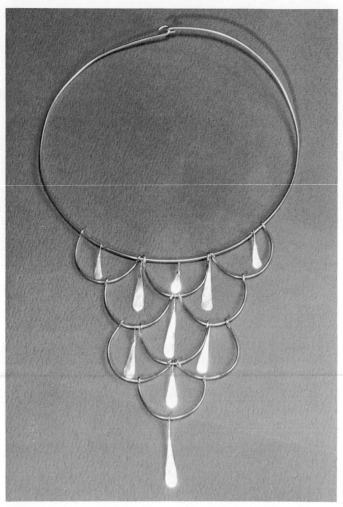

*Sterling choker with forged wire links hangs in half circles, which are soldered in position to assure symmetry. Gordon Longley, Downers Grove, Illinois.*

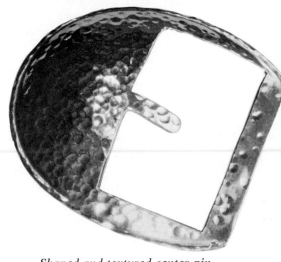

*Shaped and textured center-pin buckle. William E. Garrison.*

*Forged sterling bracelet with stamped design and bezeled peridot gemstones. Leigh Garrison.*

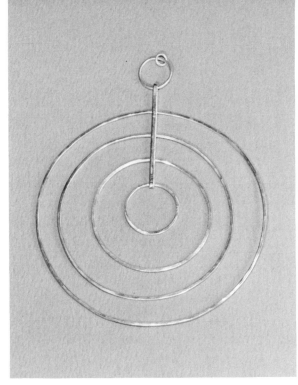

Sterling choker with forged
danglers spaced between drilled
balls. Simple, spring-loaded hook
catch joins choker at back.
Gordon Longley, Downers
Grove, Illinois.

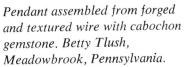

Pendant assembled from forged
and textured wire with cabochon
gemstone. Betty Tlush,
Meadowbrook, Pennsylvania.

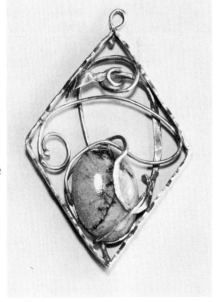

Buttons in sterling were forged
to dish shape after the surface
was textured. Beth Gilbert,
Edmonds, Washington.

85

MOUNTING LARGE CRYSTAL GEMSTONES in their natural shape without cutting and shaping the stone has challenged jewelry handcrafters for eons. Fusing a back from sterling sheet in a shape and size specifically designed for a large flat-backed gem not only solves the dilemma but produces a striking piece of finished jewelry in a minimum time (Figs. 9-1, 9-2, and 9-3).

Generally, to make the sterling mount you need a sheet of metal cut bigger than the outline of the stone. Then you cut strips of metal into but not beyond the outline of the stone (Fig. 9-5) and curve them upward. The torch is used to melt and fuse the metal into an irregular curved edge. Finally, projections of the edge are bent inward to secure the gemstone. A pin back or a bail may be fastened to the back to adapt the finished piece as a pin or pendant. This fusing technique is most effective in sterling, although gold may be used with a bit more difficulty because of its higher melting temperature. This technique is not adaptable for brass, copper, nickel silver, and other metals.

## FUSING THE MOUNT

Select a large, rough-surface crystalline gemstone to be mounted as a pendant. Set the stone on a sheet of 22- to 24-gauge sterling with 1/4 inch to 1/2 inch extending beyond the contour of the stone. Mark the sterling sheet with a felt pen (Fig. 9-4). Later, when you have gained experience, you may use a sheet as thin as 36 gauge for a lightweight, inexpensive mount.

Working quickly with the shears, cut around the edge *into* — but *not beyond* the marked perimeter of the stone (Fig. 9-5). Aim for random widths in irregular cuts. Compound-action shears with serrated jaws simplify this operation. Bend the cut strips until they stand nearly vertically from the flat base — not exactly vertical but nearly so. Using flat-jaw pliers, bend the cut strips around the stone to assure a custom fit (Fig. 9-6). Remove the stone before fusing the base.

# large gemstone pendants

*Fused Sterling Mount*

Emerald crystals in a fused gold setting. William E. Garrison.

Begin the fusing technique on the base by first turning it upside down on a heating pad that is big enough to rotate the work as you manipulate the torch. Work with a medium-to-low flame until the sterling begins to blacken from the heat. Add dry self-cleaning flux. Continue heating until the entire unit reaches a dull red. At this point, reduce the heat of the torch slightly and bring the blue cone of flame right down on the work (Fig. 9-7). Continue heating in spots until you see the silver begin to run as a liquid. Turn the heating pad to gain access to all edges. If necessary, touch edges of the cuts gently with the poker and scratch the surface to help the edges flow together, or fuse. Allow the work to cool.

Turn the work piece right side up on the heating pad and begin reheating the sterling. When the entire assembly approaches a dull red heat, reduce the heat of the torch

Fig. 9-1. - An amethyst crystal was
mounted without cutting or shaping
in a custom-crafted fused sterling
mount with a matching bail.
Note the varying lengths and shapes
of the individual handcrafted links
in the chain. William E. Garrison.

Fig. 9-2. - A fused sterling mount for a
polished gemstone is attached to a split
ring shank. Carol Moch, West Hartford,
Connecticut.

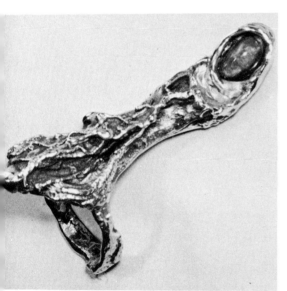

Fig. 9-3. - An extended gold ring was
fused and shaped with a torch.
William E. Garrison.

Fig. 9-4. - Begin fused setting for a
large gemstone or crystal by marking
the metal around the contour of the
stone with a felt marker. Allow
clearance for any projections beyond
the base if the edge that will hold the
stone will extend as high as the
projection.

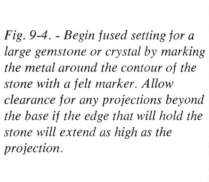

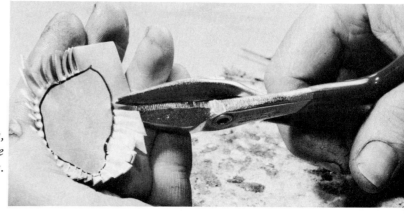

Fig. 9-5. - Using serrated-edge shears,
cut into the scribed line. Strips should be
of random width and irregular in shape.

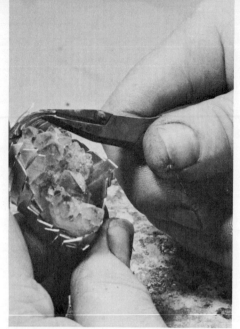

Fig. 9-6. - Using flat-jaw pliers, fit the cut strips of the setting around stone. Then bend out the strips only as far as necessary to remove the stone.

Fig. 9-7. - Turn the piece upside down on an asbestos heating pad. Using a medium-low torch flame begin fusing the bottom edge of the cut strips. Apply molten dry self-cleaning flux until it flows over the area being heated. Then, increase the heat until the piece reaches the right temperature—the metal will have a dull red color. Reduce torch heat and bring the tip of the blue cone into contact with the sterling. Slow the motion of the torch, but keep it moving over a small spot. The heated area should begin to melt, and it will look wet and shiny as fusion occurs. Keep working all the way around the perimeter of the base—not around the sides

and bring the tip of the blue cone right into the edge of the cut strips (Fig. 9-8). Slow the motion, but don't stop the torch completely, to concentrate heat in spots until the surface begins melting. Use your poker to reshape the bend of the slits or to tease the metal into fusing. Work all around the setting by turning the asbestos pad — not the piece, as it will be soft. Continue melting and fusing sides and edges of slits. The height of the setting should emerge irregular in a completely random design. Also, points of metal fused together but open along the sides should be left at strategic spots around the setting so that they can be bent to secure the stone.

After the initial fusing, you can patch and add more metal to change the shape. Suppose you end up with a serious gap along one edge of the mount. You can patch the opening by cutting a chunk of sterling sheet from the same gauge sheet as you used for the base and a bit larger than the gap. Reheat the base, and when it reaches a dull red heat, place the patch in the opening with tweezers. Stop the motion of the torch until the edges of the patch fuse and blend into the base. Then move the torch around the entire perimeter of the patch to bond it to the base piece and heal any wounds left during the insertion. If one or more points melt to a lower level than you want, build up the edge by fusing melted wire onto the area. You may need to cover the space being built up with molten self-cleaning dry flux (see Chapter 11 for application technique).

**ATTACHMENT OF FINDINGS**

At this point, depending on the size and intent of the project, attach whatever finding is required. If the stone is to be mounted as a ring, complete a band as detailed in Chapter 1. File a flat on the band and solder it to the back as noted in Chapter 4. Large

Fig. 9-8. - With the piece right-side-up on the heating pad, melt the sides in the same way as you melted the base to fuse the strips together at the top and along the sides. Allow strips to remain unfused where you expect to bend edges to restrain the gemstone. The height of the sides on the piece should end up irregular with a number of points not joined.

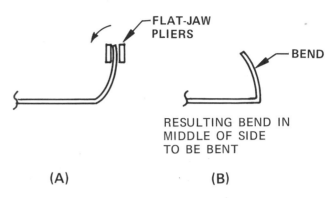

Fig. 9-9. - Note the position of the flat-jaw pliers on the side (A). The bend in the side should be made so that it crimps the top inward with the edge slightly canted from the base (B).

stones will normally be mounted as pins or pendants. Solder the two parts of the pin catch to the back as detailed in Chapter 7. A tube with a jump ring soldered at the center converts a pin to a pendant. For a pendant, solder a jump ring to the upper edge of the back for attachment to a chain with a bail (see Chapter 5).

Settings with edges fused will have irregular sides — both in height and contour. If you encounter a "holding problem" during the attachment of findings, try using a shallow tin level-full of powdered asbestos. Force the setting upside down into the loose asbestos until the top of the setting rests roughly horizontal and is stable. You may wish to set up a third-hand to hold a ring band, or other finding, in position on the back. Jump rings and pin clasps can be soldered onto the setting back if it remains stable and horizontal — as it will in the powdered asbestos.

## FINAL CLEAN-UP AND SETTING

For quick cleaning, heat the entire assembly once again to a cherry red and drop it hot into a pickle solution. Examine the edges of the fused sections and remove any sharp snags or edges with a file or pumice wheel in a flexible shaft. Antique the sterling, if you wish, following the directions in Chapter 17. Finally, polish exposed portions or highlights if base is antiqued — first with tripoli and then with rouge. Wash the assembly in 1:1 ammonia and water solution.

Place the gemstone in the mounting and decide where sections of the metal should be bent to hold the stone firmly in place. Avoid those sections which have become quite thick during fusion. During the fusion process you may have planned where bends should occur and left those edges open.

Remove the gemstone from the setting when making initial bends. Using chain-nose or flat-nose pliers, grasp edges about half-way down the side at a point to be bent inward. Bend each section inward rather sharply to move the metal toward the gemstone (Fig. 9-9). Replace the gemstone in the setting. If you have bent the edge too far 89

Fig. 9-10. - *Bend the sides of the piece with a flat-jaw or chain-nose pliers so they contact the stone.*

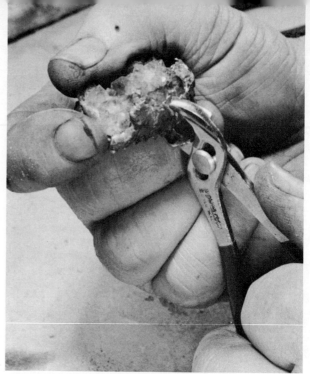

Fig. 9-11. - *Use a special prong-bending pliers to make the final bend of the sides. The hollow-ground jaws of prong-bending pliers neatly bend a tip curl on the sides. This tip curl bears on and secures the stone.*

inward, bend it back only enough to clear the stone. Bend tips inward onto the gemstone (Fig. 9-10).

With the gemstone in place, complete each bend with prong-bending pliers (Fig. 9-11). To avoid scarring the back of the setting with the lower jaw of the prong-bending pliers, place a small sheet of metal scrap between the bottom surface of the setting and the plier jaws (Fig. 9-12). Bend the sections that are to hold the stone until they bear on the surface with an edge curl. Examine the perimeter of the setting to see if any of the other edges of the setting protrude or are separated too far from the stone. You may need to bend in other areas slightly with prong-bending pliers (Fig. 9-13). You need not bend these other sections until they bear on the gemstone but only to bring them in to the contour of the stone.

## FUSING SMALL SETTINGS

Fused-back settings can be earring and tie tack size, as well as pendant or medallion size. Fusing the back for these small pieces is more difficult than for larger pieces because the back sheet is thinner to minimize weight, and heat control must be

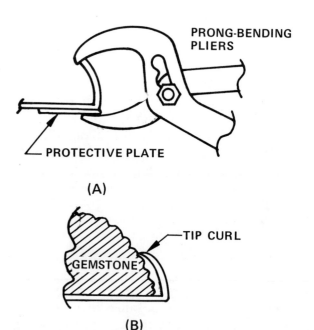

Fig. 9-12. - *During side bending, protect the underside of the piece from local deformation or scarring by using a protective plate (A). Prong-bending pliers apply pressure only to the topmost edge of the side to bend it into contact with the gemstone (B).*

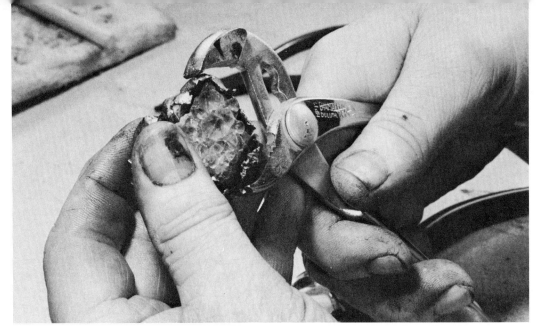

*Fig. 9-13. - Prong-bending pliers also are useful for bending edges into contour to fit a gemstone. Not all portions of the sides need bear on the gemstone, but sharp edges or projections should be bent into contour.*

more precise. Learn to use less heat when fusing small projects. Also, be alert to quickly melting metal and make it a habit to remove torch heat abruptly by jerking the torch to one side. Pulling back or up on the torch does not remove the heat from the object fast enough.

Follow the same general steps in constructing a setting for a small gemstone as you used for a large gemstone. Mark the back plate on 24-gauge sheet. Cut strips around the edge into the scribed mark. Because of its small size, strips must be cut more accurately for the base of a small gemstone. Check the fit of the stone during the cutting and bending.

Bend strips nearly vertical and begin fusion with the setting upside down on the heating pad. Adjust torch heat to low, but work with the blue cone right down on the work no matter how low the flame setting. Turn setting right side up and continue the fusion. Check fit of gemstone and make preliminary bends before attaching tie tack pin or jump ring for earring finding. You'll find the powdered asbestos essential for holding the setting during the attachment of findings.

Clean up and polish the setting before bending the sides to secure the stone. Use the small prong-bending pliers with a scrap piece under the back to prevent scarring as before.

### FUSING EXTRA-LARGE SETTINGS

For setting very large gemstones or crystals, use thin metal 28-30 gauge, for the back. Cut the back 1/2 inch to 3/4 inch or larger all around than the outline of the stone's edge. Instead of beginning fusion with the bent-up sides down against the asbestos and the back in the air, begin with the back against the heating pad. Begin immediately to melt down the nearly vertical strips. This action thickens the edges and helps to make the setting rigid. To fuse the lower part of the sides, lift up the setting with the poker and fuse the lower edge. Attempting to fuse the bottom portion of the cut strips with the back upside down will cause the thin metal to slump in the back. To help reduce the metal weight on extra-large settings, cut out a portion of the back after clean-up and attach the findings.

91

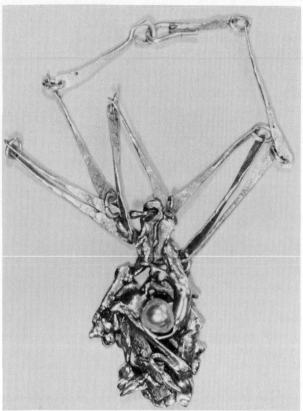

*A single pearl pendant in a random fused sterling mount. Note the chain links with a handcrafted clasp at the top. Leigh Garrison.*

*Symmetrical pearl nested in a fused mount and attached to a dual-wire ring shank. Carol Moch, West Hartford, Connecticut.*

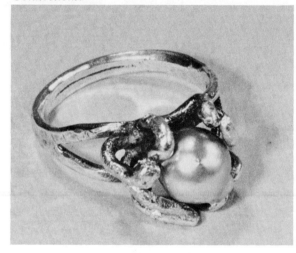

*Natural crystals mounted in fused sterling with soldered wire attachments for ear-wires. Anne Gries, Flushing, New York.*

# gemstones
*Prong Settings*

PRONG SETTINGS FOR GEMSTONES offer a versatile means for mounting natural, faceted, or cabochon gemstones in rings, pendants, earrings — nearly any kind of gemstone jewelry. Prong settings can be delicate and airy or strong and massive. When properly constructed, prong settings hold gemstones securely without sharp corners or edges to catch clothing. Prongs can be as safe as any mount except a full bezel (see Chapters 4 and 5).

The type of prong setting to be used depends on the gem to be mounted and the basic styling of the jewelry work. Tiny faceted stones are mounted with tiny prongs to keep the entire piece "in scale." Faceted stones also may require a special notch in the prong to seat the gemstone and hold it securely. Large cabochons, crystals, pearls, and other natural or cut stones may need prongs specifically designed for irregular shapes. Four methods of constructing prong settings are detailed in this chapter. While there are many different and specialized techniques for mounting gemstones with prongs, these four techniques, plus the method noted in Chapter 13 for use with wax models and casting, afford variety suitable for most of the gemstones jewelry handcrafters are interested in mounting.

## PRONG DESIGN

Prongs are usually used with other parts of a mount to secure a gemstone. As a definition, prongs are those projections on a mounting used for restraining a gemstone, bent into place *after* the gemstone is in place. Key elements in the design of prongs are:

1. Prongs contact the surface of the gemstone or pearl only at the tip, as shown in Fig. 10-1.

2. Prongs should be shaped and tapered to bend in an increasingly sharp curve near the tip. To meet this requirement, prongs must be tapered around all four sides (Fig. 10-2).

3. Prongs may be built up by fusion, or bits of shaped wire may be tapered and

*Sterling mount with decorative prongs bent to secure five-sided cabochon. Carol Moch, West Hartford, Connecticut.*

soldered or fused to a base or girdle. In either case, tapering permits the tip to be bent into a curl that restrains the gemstone without leaving snags.

## PRONGS CUT FROM
## INSIDE BACK SHEET

One simple, quick method for mounting large cabochon stones, either straight-sided or curved, for pins or pendants is to bend prongs out of a back sheet of metal larger than the gemstone (Fig. 10-3). Triangular prongs are pierced from the backing sheet of metal and bent up to accept the stone. Prongs are then bent to restrain the stone. A pin back may be soldered to the back sheet before the gemstone is finally mounted. Or, a jump ring may be soldered at the top corner for a bail and chain. Although the technique for mounting a large cabochon gemstone is detailed in sequence photos (Figs. 10-4 through 10-8), the same steps may be used for smaller gemstones to be mounted as rings, tie tacks, cuff links, earrings, and other pieces.

Begin the mount by selecting 14-gauge sheet metal for the back to complement the

93

*gemstones*

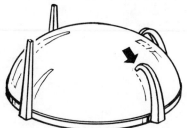

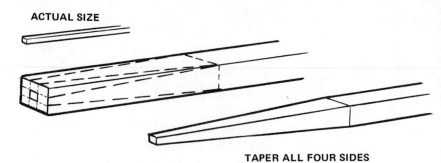

**ACTUAL SIZE**

**TAPER ALL FOUR SIDES**

*Fig. 10-1. - Prongs,
properly bent and placed,
secure all shapes and sizes
of cabochon and faceted
gemstones. Note the tip curl
on two of the prongs,
which touch the gemstone
at only one point.*

*Fig. 10-2. - Prongs for securing a gemstone must
be tapered around all four sides before being
soldered or fused to the base. Unless prongs
are tapered, they will not bend gracefully
with the desired tip curl.*

*Fig. 10-3. - This large cabochon gemstone
is attached to a brass back with four prongs
cut and bent from the interior of the back.*

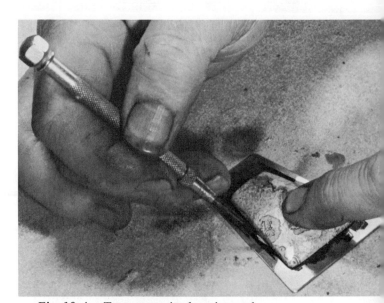

*Fig. 10-4. - To prepare for locating and
cutting the prongs, scribe around the edge
of the stone on the metal base. Before
scribing make sure the central area of the
base is coated with a felt marker pen.*

*Fig. 10-5. - If prongs are going to be
pierced from the base, mark their
positions and drill holes at the
end of each line where the prongs
will be bent. Insert the saw blade in
each hole and saw to the apex
of the marked triangle to assure
a sharp point on the prong.*

94

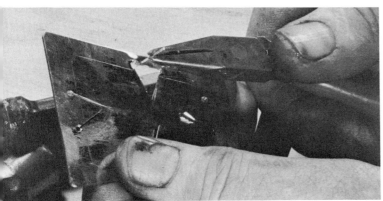

Fig. 10-6. - The apex of the prong is punched up before it is bent into a vertical position with a flat-jaw pliers. Position the gemstone to fit during bending.

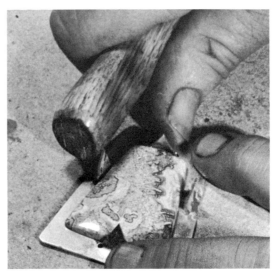

Fig. 10-7. - The first step in mounting the stone in the cleaned and polished base is pushing the prongs inward onto the stone; here it was done with the end of a hammer handle.

Fig. 10-8. - Use a prong-bending pliers to make the final, tip-curl bend.

shape and color of the gemstone. Mark around the edge of the gemstone, as shown in Fig. 10-4. Plan enough prongs to secure the gemstone, one for each side of the four-sided cabochon. Determine the number of prongs needed and locate them in a position to restrain the gemstone in all directions according to the shape of the stone.

Mark the position and size of the prongs to be pierced with a scribe. The size of the prongs should be in scale with the stone and back. Drill 1/16-inch diameter holes at each end of the prong-bend lines (Fig. 10-5) and saw two sides of the prong. Bend the prongs vertically and check the fit of the stone inside the prongs (Fig. 10-6).

Bend the prongs against the gemstone with a pusher (Fig. 10-7) and bend the tip curl with prong-bending pliers (Fig. 10-8). Smooth the edges of the prongs with a pumice wheel in a flex shaft or motor tool to eliminate any snags or rough edges. With the tip of the prong curled against the stone, there is little chance of the prong catching on clothing.

## PRONGS CUT FROM OUTSIDE BACK SHEET

Smaller cabochon or faceted stones to be featured in rings or other small pieces of jewelry may be mounted on a plate with the prongs bent up from outside the metal

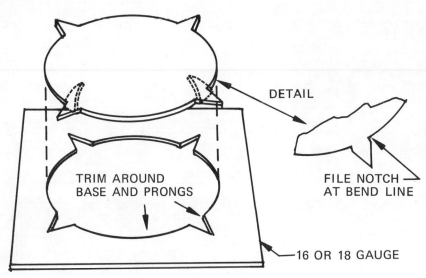

DETAIL

TRIM AROUND
BASE AND PRONGS

FILE NOTCH
AT BEND LINE

16 OR 18 GAUGE

*Fig. 10-9. - An alternative
method for using prongs
cut from the base sheet is to
trim the base even with the
perimeter of the stone and
cut the prongs from the
sheet stock outside of that
perimeter. The prongs
are then bent up around
the gemstone as shown in
Fig. 10-8.*

*Fig. 10-10. - Individual bracelet links of
matched gemstones rest in a nest of wire
prongs, two prongs for each side. The
prongs are soldered to a wire back.*

(Figs. 10-1 and 10-9). This method is the opposite of the method detailed in Figs. 10-4 through 10-8.

To mount a small stone, begin by scribing around the stone on a sheet of 16- or 18-gauge metal. Plan the location of the prongs according to the shape and size of the gemstone. Oval or round gemstones usually require four prongs. Straight-sided cabochons may require as few as three or as many as five prongs, depending on the shape of the stone.

Saw around the scribed perimeter of the gemstone, except where the prongs are to be located. At these points, jog out to cut the triangular-shaped pieces that are to be bent up as prongs. File and smooth the edges of the back to fit the base of the gemstone. At the base of each triangular prong, file a notch to define the bend line. Using flat-nose pliers and with the stone removed, bend prongs into a vertical position. Return the stone to the back and push the prongs down against the stone. Complete the bending of the prongs by using the prong-bending pliers to bend the tip curl on each prong (refer to Fig. 10-8).

The gemstone is now secured onto the metal backing sheet. If the stone is to be used as a ring, a ring shank should be formed and soldered to the back before final placement of the stone. Any other findings or attachments to the back plate should also be soldered or attached to the back before bending the prongs into contact with the stone. Clean up any rough edges.

Instead of simply bending triangular prongs up and into tip contact with a gemstone, an alternative to this technique is to solder tapered prongs onto the edge of a wire girdle (Fig. 10-10). Soldered prongs tend to look less bulky than those bent up from a base. When bending a prong soldered to a wire or sheet frame, the prong will not bend at the soldered joint. The prong should be shaped to bend gracefully from

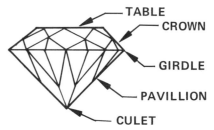

Fig. 10-11. - Faceted stone setting is built around a girdle band that leaves culet of stone open to the light. Prongs are attached to the girdle band to hold the stone securely.

Fig. 10-12. - Parts of a typical faceted stone mounted with a girdle band.

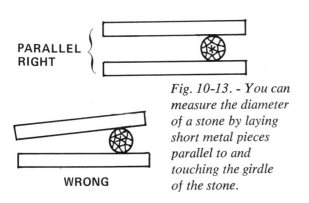

Fig. 10-13. - You can measure the diameter of a stone by laying short metal pieces parallel to and touching the girdle of the stone.

a true vertical position at some point up from the base. Soldered prongs are particularly adaptable to high-crown cabochon stones, either round or straight-sided.

## PRONGS FOR FACETED STONES

Faceted stones cut to display the light and fire resulting from their transparency, such as topaz or citrine, call for another type of mounting (Fig. 10-11). A girdle band (Fig. 10-12) slightly smaller than the girdle of the stone supports the gemstone around its full perimeter. Three or four prongs will then be fastened to the girdle band to secure the stone against the band (Fig. 10-11). Constructing the girdle for a round gemstone is easy, and is just slightly more difficult for an oval stone. However, constructing a girdle for a rectangular or square gemstone is difficult because the

slightest deviation from dimensions of the sides will be noticeable. Special or fancy cuts, such as the marquise, are about the same order of difficulty as ovals.

Practice the prong setting for a round faceted gemstone first. Important to the correct fitting of the girdle band to the gemstone is measuring the specific stone to be mounted. You'll find the easiest and fastest tool for measuring the diameter of the girdle is a sliding-jaw caliper. Simply slide the jaws of the caliper together until they touch the girdle and read the dimension on the scale. Or, as a substitute for the caliper, you may use a plastic circle template to determine the smallest circle through which the stone will drop. Turn the stone upside down (culet up). Press the circle template down gently until you find the largest one that will not allow the stone to pass through. If neither the caliper or template is available, place the stone upside down on white paper on a flat surface. Adjust two short pieces of straight-edged metal, one on each side, parallel and touching the stone's girdle (Fig. 10-13). Measure the distance between the parallel metal bars. If you constructed the girdle with the inside dimension equal to the measured diameter, the stone will drop through, so plan the gir-

97

dle band slightly smaller. How much smaller? That depends on the overall size of the gemstone and the angle of the culet. The inside diameter of the girdle band should be small enough to provide firm support for the stone — but no more.

Mark the inside diameter desired on a metal mandrel. For small stones, you may need to use a small tapered-shank tool, such as an awl, center punch, or small drift punch to mark the diameter. For larger stones, use the tapered ring mandrel. Wind 16-gauge sterling wire (or other material if desired) around the mandrel at a diameter smaller than the marked or desired diameter. The natural spring of the wire should allow the diameter to expand to the marked size. Wind on three rings and cut them apart as you did with jump rings. Use the center one for the girdle. Check the size of the girdle against the marked diameter with the cut faces of the stone in contact with the wire.

To adjust size file faces for the stone if necessary. Flux and solder the joint of the girdle in air. Clean off the remaining flux and file any excess solder from inside the joint before trying the girdle band on the actual stone. If the stone sits too high, the band is too small and may be enlarged by hammering. If the stone drops through, the girdle band is too large, and the excess needs to be cut away and the new joint soldered.

### Attaching Prongs

From three to as many as seven prongs may be attached to the girdle, depending on the shape and size of the stone being mounted. Three prongs are usually enough for a small, round stone (Fig. 10-11). Cut 5/16-inch lengths of 16-gauge sterling wire for the prongs. These prongs will be a little long, but the extra length will simplify bending. Two methods may be used for attaching the prongs:

1. If the prongs are attached around the outside of the girdle band (Fig. 10-14),

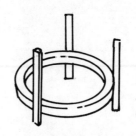

Fig. 10-14. - *Prongs soldered around the outside of the girdle band.*

PRONGS OUTSIDE GIRDLE BAND

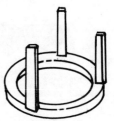

Fig. 10-15. - *Slightly larger diameter prongs soldered to the top of the girdle band afford a smoother and more finished look to a completed mounting.*

PRONGS ON TOP OF GIRDLE BAND

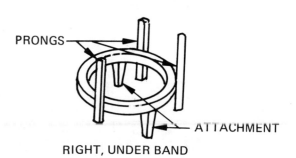

PRONGS

ATTACHMENT

RIGHT, UNDER BAND

Fig. 10-16. - *Attachment wires for mounting the girdle band and the stone assembly in a finding should be attached under the band—not on the outside of it.*

place the band on powdered asbestos. For ease in working, the asbestos should be placed in a flat tin tuna fish can, or similar container. The asbestos should be smoothed over by pressing a bottle or jar into the middle. Force the prongs down into the powdered asbestos until they are almost flush with the surface. In this position the girdle band is upside down with the prongs stuck down in the asbestos to hold the stone. Apply thick flux and two small bits of hard solder to each joint. Two small bits of solder are more effective than one large piece, because if either of the bits runs, you will get a joint that can be strengthened later. Use low heat to dry the flux, then turn up the flame to medium and heat until the solder runs. Use your poker to assure contact between the prong and the side of the girdle band; otherwise, the solder will not run.

2. A more finished-looking method for attaching the prongs is to solder them to the top of the girdle band (Fig. 10-15) rather than to the side, as in the preceding technique. Instead of holding the prongs in position upside down in asbestos, use a third-hand to hold one prong at a time while you solder it to the top of the girdle band. Do not position the prongs exactly over the band; otherwise, the stone will not fit. The prongs must extend just enough outside the band to allow the stone to slip down into full contact with the girdle band. This method calls for precise positioning of each prong.

Regardless of which method you choose, strengthen each joint with additional solder. Considerable force will be applied when you bend the prongs into contact with the stone, so this joint must be sturdy. Also, two round wires in point-contact form a "bad fit." Support the girdle and prongs on the powdered asbestos 1/8 inch or more above the surface to allow more heat around the joint. Apply flux and two bits of solder at each joint. Heat until the solder runs.

### Mounting Attachments

Although a great variety of attachments are possible, the simplest is to use two half-round pieces of sterling attached to the underside of the girdle band (Fig. 10-16). Soldering these attachments can be a bit tricky, as there is the possibility that the prongs may come unsoldered in the process. Protect the prongs and joints by covering them with yellow ochre or a mixture you can stir up yourself — lapidary polish or tempera powder mixed with enough water to make a heavy paste. Add a bit of alcohol as a wetting agent. Brush the paste onto the joints — and only the joints — before heating. Any of the "dirty" material around the girdle band will keep the solder from running to the attachments if the protective paste is not applied.

Fig. 10-17. - The third-hand holds the attachment wire in position for soldering. The girdle band with the prongs already soldered in place is upside down in the powdered asbestos. Solder one attachment wire to the base at a time.

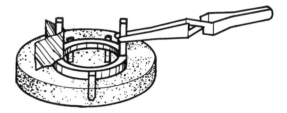

Fig. 10-18. - A heat shield protects first attachment wire while soldering the second (and others) in place. A piece of aluminum foil bent around the attachment wire reflects the heat.

Push the girdle band with attached prongs upside down into powdered asbestos. Position one half-round wire attachment and hold it with a third-hand (Fig. 10-17). Apply flux, bits of solder, and heat until solder runs. Repeat this procedure for the second (or more) wires. If succeeding attachments must be soldered close to the first or other attachments, protect the previous joints with a heat shield (Fig. 10-18).

If the attachments are to be fastened to a larger mount, as shown in Fig. 10-11, there is no problem of fitting the attachments around the culet. If you plan to use the girdle-mount for a ring, solder the ends of two or three wires forming the ring shank to each side of the girdle. Use the powdered asbestos to hold the girdle with

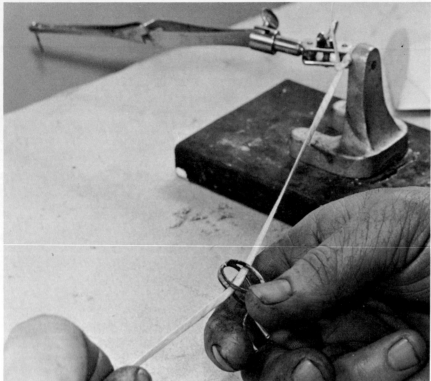

*Fig. 10-19. - Strumming is a technique for cleaning the many inaccessible nooks, crannies, and corners that result when prongs and attachment wires are assembled on a girdle-band mount. Tie a flat cotton cord securely at one end. Then load the cord with tripoli by rubbing the waxy cake back and forth on the cord. Thread the loose end of the cord through the girdle-band mount, reaching places ordinarily inaccessible with other polishing tools. Pull the cord tight with one hand and move the setting back and forth, exerting side pressure as necessary to clean corners and odd places. Use a second string similarly loaded with red rouge for a final polish. Strumming takes little time and often makes the difference between amateur and professional quality.*

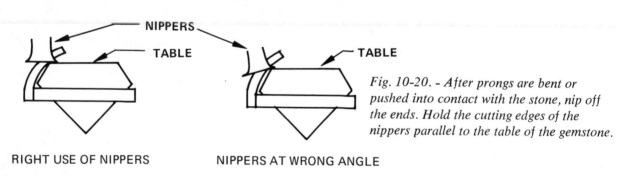

RIGHT USE OF NIPPERS          NIPPERS AT WRONG ANGLE

*Fig. 10-20. - After prongs are bent or pushed into contact with the stone, nip off the ends. Hold the cutting edges of the nippers parallel to the table of the gemstone.*

attached prongs upside down when soldering attachments.

### Cleaning the Mount

After completing all soldering but before setting the stone, clean the assembly in a pickle and follow with tripoli and rouge in succession. This type of assembly challenges most craftsmen because of the many places difficult to reach, the "dirty" material added for heat control, and bits of asbestos sticking to the metal. One technique for cleaning a difficult assembly, such as a pronged mount, is "strumming" (Fig. 10-19).

### Setting the Stone

Place the gemstone in the case formed by the girdle band and prongs. Using flat-nosed or chain-nose pliers, bend each prong part way in toward the stone. If you attempt to bend one prong all the way at once, chances are you will end up with a stone sitting crooked or off center in the setting. You will find it hard enough to align the stone perfectly as you bend each prong a little at a time. After several partial bends, you are ready to cut off the excess prong length (Fig. 10-20). The last bends must be made by pushing on the prongs with your thumb, because the pliers will get in your way. Cut off the prongs only after they are touching the gemstone.

Shape the prongs after cutting with the nippers (Fig. 10-21). While prongs could be cut and shaped first, the extra length available before cutting simplifies bending.

Final bending of the prongs to secure the gemstone firmly in place is most easily accomplished with prong-bending pliers (Fig. 10-22). After final bending, remove any rough spots and polish the piece.

## Mounting Oval Gemstones

Mounting an oval or unusual rounded gemstone follows the same steps detailed for a round stone, except for finding the size of the stone and using a special mandrel. Measure the minor and major axis of an oval stone and construct an ellipse on a piece of scrap metal coated with a felt pen. An ellipse template simplifies this operation. Saw out the ellipse or other shape slightly smaller than the perimeter of the gemstone. Wind annealed sterling (or other metal) wire around the template, mark the cutoff point, and solder the joint of the wire to fit the template. Check the size of this girdle band on the gemstone. Change the size if necessary, as you did with a round girdle band. Once you have constructed a girdle band that fits the gemstone, proceed with soldering prongs and attaching wires as you did with the round girdle band. For an oval gemstone, an even number of prongs is required.

## Mounting Rectangular Gemstones

Rectangular or square gemstones are the most difficult to mount because of the need for absolute precision in measuring and constructing the girdle band or box. Either of two techniques may be used with rectangular or square gemstones.

The first technique follows generally the method for mounting round or oval gemstones. A girdle band is fitted to the stone and prongs and attachments are soldered to the band. For a rectangular or square stone, the girdle band may be constructed with square wire or sheet stock.

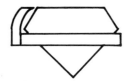

PRONG BEFORE BEING SHAPED

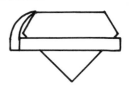

PRONG AFTER SHAPING

*Fig. 10-21. - Prongs are shaped after bending to permit an extra length of prong to ease the bending procedure. By tapering the prong toward the tip, you remove that bulky look. The easiest way to shape prongs is with a pumice wheel in a flex shaft. The pumice wheel rotating at high speed will remove metal, but will not damage the gemstone. A file may be used, but if it touches some gemstones it may leave a mark.*

PRONG BEFORE BENDING, PLIERS PROPERLY PLACED . . .

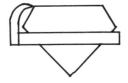

PRONG AFTER FINAL BEND . . . BEND SOMEWHAT EXAGGERATED IN SIZE.

*Fig. 10-22. - Final bend of prongs with prong-bending pliers adds a tip curl that secures the stone against the roughest of treatment. The lower jaw of the pliers should be engaged at the girdle band—not at some lower point.*

101

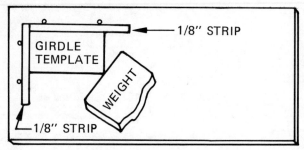

*Fig. 10-23. - Brads placed in an asbestos block to form a square corner hold the pieces to be used for part of a rectangular or square girdle band. Note the template in place to hold the wire or sheet square while soldering butt joints. Solder one corner joint first.*

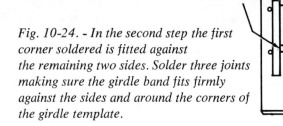

*Fig. 10-24. - In the second step the first corner soldered is fitted against the remaining two sides. Solder three joints making sure the girdle band fits firmly against the sides and around the corners of the girdle template.*

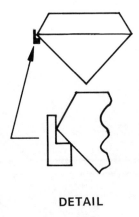

DETAIL

*Fig. 10-25. - A cross-section of a commercial bezel wire shows how the girdle of a gemstone rests on the shoulder. The bezel is later crimped around the perimeter of the gemstone. Or, prongs may be soldered to the top or sides of the bezel wire.*

Begin by measuring the stone and building a template slightly smaller than the dimensions of the stone's girdle. Drive brads into an asbestos block to form a square corner for holding the pieces to be soldered, similar to the soldering fixture used in Chapter 4. Dirty the edges of the template to keep solder from bonding to the edge by heating it in an oxidizing flame or applying yellow ochre. Solder the first corner as shown in Fig. 10-23. Trim the ends of the first two sides flush with the edges of the template.

Assemble the remaining two sides against the corner pins in the soldering fixture and place the soldered corner in position to form the four-sided girdle band (Fig. 10-24). Solder the three remaining joints. Check the fit of the constructed girdle before continuing. Minor adjustments can be made by unsoldering one or more of the joints, but attempting to adjust the fit can be a time-consuming and often frustrating task. Sometimes you may save yourself time and effort by starting fresh, possibly with a revised template if the fit is too far off.

Prongs may be fitted at the center of each face or at the corners. Proceed with attaching prongs and other attachment points as detailed for the round stones.

## COMMERCIAL BEZEL MOUNT

A fourth way to mount stones in any shape is to use one of the commercial bezel wires, a few of which are shown in Chapter 16. Instead of using wire to form a girdle band, the bezel wire is soldered to a shape that fits the stone. The girdle of the gemstone should fit against the inner face of the bezel above the shoulder (Fig. 10-25). Instead of adding prongs to the girdle band, the thin bezel edge may be bezeled around the full perimeter to secure the stone in the mount (see Chapters 4 and 5).

Working with one of the commercial bezel wires calls for minor changes in technique from that outlined in the preceding pages. First, because the commercial bezel wire is formed by rolling, it will be work-hardened, and no amount of annealing will remove all of its stiffness. Therefore, you may need to use the soldering fixture and weight to hold ends of the wire together for soldering.

Second, when forming rectangular or square mounts, you will need to miter the corners of the girdle rather than construct butt-joints as detailed in Figs. 10-23 and 10-24. Otherwise, the shoulders and bezel strips will not form perfect corners. Miters may be filed on the joints, and this operation increases the precision required for mounting rectangular gemstones.

## ADDITIONAL DESIGNS

Decorative or protective additions for a gemstone mount may be built into the basic setting or added later. Fragile stones may need protection from bumps or surface contact, and a high-wall mount nestles the stone deep in a protective shell of metal. There is, of course, no limit to the variety and extent of decorative elements that may be added to a mount. Size may limit some additions to a ring or tie tack, but size is no problem with a pendant or medallion.

*Deep flaring rim surrounds fragile opal. William E. Garrison.*

*Australian opal mounted in an inverted girdle band with prongs securing gemstone from square underplate. William E. Garrison.*

103

*Gemstones may be mounted in a variety of different ways; the two pendants on the left feature gemstones mounted with prongs cut from inside the back area. Gladys McKinnis, Battle Ground, Washington.*

*Square Australian fire opal
mounted in a square girdle band
with square wire ring shank.
William E. Garrison.*

*Carved jade with two prongs at
each end of oval is surrounded by
decorative wire rim.
William E. Garrison.*

*Extra petals in sterling surround
high-crown cabochon secured
with prongs from girdle band.
Carol Moch, West Hartford,
Connecticut.*

*Carved cameo secured in wide
girdle band with fences at
both ends and overlapping, ring-
shank wire prongs.
William E. Garrison.*

# rings, pendants, tie tacks
## *Fusion Techniques*

FUSION IS A METHOD OF JOINING METALS without the use of solder. What happens during fusion is not completely clear. However, in the presence of heat and an atmosphere controlled by flux, an interchange of molecules takes place well *below* the melting point of the metals. Permanent bonds occur between metals with no visible surface flow or distortion of the metals. Sterling silver that has been fused becomes permanently hardened to some extent, and this hardening cannot be removed by annealir

You should understand the clear distinction between fusion and welding. In fusion, metal components are joined without the addition of metal as noted above. One of the earliest types of fusion was the bonding of wrought iron by hammering pieces together while they were red hot. Welding calls for the addition of metal. Where the additional metal is the same as the components being joined, the process is termed "fusion welding." Ordinarily, welding implies the joining of components by the addition of an alloy different from the components being joined. Both fusion and fusion welding are jewelry techniques. The most common is fusion, the technique detailed in this chapter.

With the fusion technique, decorative elements may be added to rings, bracelets, tie tacks, pendants, and other pieces. The fusion technique can be adapted for decorating any piece of handcrafted jewelry. Sterling may be fused to sterling (Fig. 11-3). Or gold wire may be fused to sterling (Fig. 11-9). Various metals may be fused to one another, just as in sweat soldering, but without the use of solder.

To understand fusion, you must understand what happens to metals during the process and the special conditions that must exist before fusion can occur. When heat is rapidly applied to the surface of metals, the heated surface of the metal reaches its melting temperature before the central part. This melting point is called "fusion temperature." During fusion, the

*Sterling ring with fused wire design. Anne Gries, Flushing, New York.*

molten surface of one metal interacts with the molten surface of the contacting metal while the inner portions of both remain relatively solid. Ordinarily, the surfaces of the metals oxidize rapidly under these near-melting temperatures. However, when surface oxidation is controlled through the use of flux, the molten surfaces will flow together — or fuse. You must learn to control two elements during fusion — heat and flux action.

Before tackling a fusion-decorated sterling ring, try two small practice stacks of sterling on sterling (Fig. 11-1). Apply a thick flux paste to one of the stacks. Here you should dip down to the bottom of your flux bottle and bring up the solids. Water added to dry borax flux aids only in spreading the flux over the work. So, the less water the better during fusion. Later in this chapter you will be introduced to a method for applying a dry self-cleaning flux to aid the fusion of gold on sterling. Remember, apply the thick flux to one stack of sterling only.

Warm both stacks with the torch at low heat until the flux is dry. Turn the torch up to medium or hot and move in quite close to continue heating. If you work in a dim light, you will be able to see the silver change to a dull red and finally a bright red as it heats. Try to keep both stacks at the same temperature. Continue heating until the surface of the fluxed sterling takes on a "wet" look. This is the fusion temperature. Play with the flame to keep the surface of the metal "wet" without allowing the chunks of silver to slump or change shape (Fig. 11-2). You will note that the surfaces of the two stacked pieces that were fluxed have "run together" or fused. The two pieces that were not fluxed remain separated. The small upper piece of the unfluxed stack may actually ball up, indicating complete melting with no surface interaction. Oxidation of the metal surfaces blocks any fusion of the surface metal, just as oxidation prevents solder from bonding to metals.

Back off with the torch and allow the fluxed stack to cool enough for it to lose its "wet" look. Then apply heat once again to bring the stack back to fusion temperature. You will find that once the two pieces have been fused, you can repeat this cooling-reheating cycle several times without really changing the sterling.

When using the propane torch working with sterling is easy, because sterling melts at about 1658° F. — well within propane's 2000° F. flame temperature. Therefore, you may work directly on an asbestos heating block when fusing sterling. When working with brass, which has a higher melting point than sterling, you are taxing the heating capacity of a propane torch. Many craftsmen use oxygen-acetylene when working with brass to gain more heat. However,

Fig. 11-1. - Stack two tiny chunks of sterling on two larger base pieces in preparation for testing and becoming familiar with heat effects during fusion. Coat one of the stacks with thick flux paste; leave the other stack bare.

Fig. 11-2. - Note differences in effect of heat on fluxed and unfluxed stacks of sterling. Fluxed stack reaches a "wet" stage and top piece fuses to base. Oxidation on unfluxed stack prevents fusion regardless of how much heat may be applied.

for small pieces of brass, you may work on a charcoal block. The charcoal absorbs and builds heat to make the propane torch more effective.

## CRAFTING A FUSION-DECORATED BAND RING

Each of the sterling band rings in Fig. 11-3 was decorated with sterling fused to 107

*Fig. 11-3. - Early student practice rings with fused sterling designs.*

*Fig. 11-4. - Sterling band ring with raised geometric design fused to the surface. The base is antiqued to contrast with the polished surfaces of the decorative bits fused to outer surface.*

*Fig. 11-5. - Cut bits of sterling may be arranged randomly for a creative geometric design.*

the surface. The geometrical shapes of the pieces fused to the band in Fig. 11-4 show another example of how sharp edges were achieved using the fusion technique. In fusing shapes to a metal band ring, generally you should follow the directions for constructing a plain band ring from Chapter 1, but with several variations. For example, once you have determined the length of the band according to the ring size (consult Table 18E), leave about 1/16 inch extra metal. A 3/8-inch width allows room for adding decorative elements. Men's rings generally will be wider than rings designed for women.

Use 18-gauge sterling for the band and 22-gauge sterling for the decorative bits. With shears or your jeweler's saw, cut the thin sterling sheet into strips 1/8 inch to 1/16 inch wide and up to 1 inch long. Arrange the cut bits into a casual design as shown in Fig. 11-5. Or, use your own creativity to come up with a design of your

own. Rather than geometrical shapes, consider using curved slivers of sterling arranged randomly.

Apply thick flux to the surface several times to assure complete coverage. Warm the heavy flux gently with the torch adjusted to a low heat to dry the flux without disturbing the strip overlays. Bubbling of flux may lift up pieces, but they will usually sink back into place as the flux melts to a fluid. A poker may be used to reposition the pieces. When the flux is dry, adjust the flame to medium and bring it in closer — moving it at all times. Aim to bring the surface of the base and the overlays up to fusion temperature at exactly the same time.

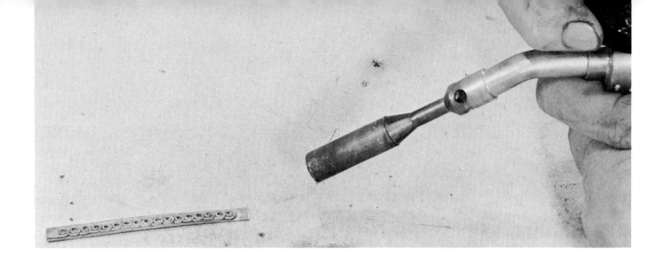

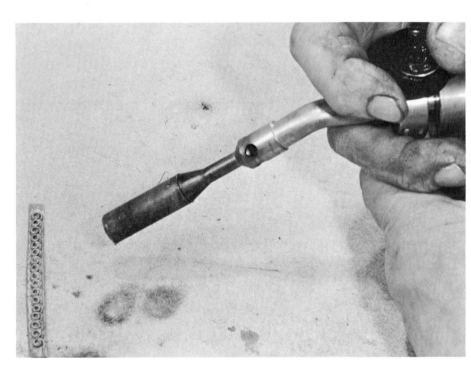

Fig. 11-6. - Locate the band on a heating block in a position that allows you to aim the torch down the full length of the strip (top) *rather than from side to side* (left). *By moving the torch lengthwise, the band is bathed continuously in heat.*

Work with the torch aimed down the length of the band — not across the band (Fig. 11-6). If you apply too much heat too quickly, the thin strips or small cut overlays on top will melt and ball up before the base reaches fusion temperature.

The metal will be molten when the surface exhibits a "wet" look (Fig. 11-7). The full length of the band may not reach or be kept at fusion temperature at the same time. Sterling may reach fusion temperature with the surface appearing "wet" while the heat from the torch is directed at a small section. And as soon as the torch moves to another section, the surface immediately cools to a solid once again.

If you wish to add new cut pieces as overlays, the fusion process permits you to do this — even after the pieces have cooled. Simply replace the assembly on the heating block, apply new flux, and reheat the work to fusion temperature. Add new pieces that have been heavily fluxed, and cool the fused assembly in air or by dunking it in clear water.

Because of the heavily decorated surface, you will need to use a different system for soldering the butt-joint in the ring. File the ends of the band at an angle as detailed in Fig. 11-8, with the exact length measured on what will become the inside of the ring. When the band is rounded on a ring

*Fig. 11-7. - Decorative bits and the base metal should reach fusion temperature at exactly the same time. You can judge when the metal reaches fusion temperature by noting the "wet" look to the piece—actually liquid metal moving quickly under the force of the flame.*

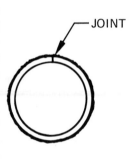

FILE ENDS AT ANGLE TO FIT FLUSH WHEN ROUNDED.

FACES IN FIRM CONTACT

JOINT

*Fig. 11-8. - Rather than bend the decorated band with squared ends into alignment, file the ends at an angle and round the ring to bring joint faces into firm contact. If necessary, file the ends further so they fit together cleanly. Measure the length of the band to match the ring size around the inside.*

mandrel, the joint should be in contact across the full face. Sharp bending to align faces, as noted in Chapter 1, not only affects the design but may cause the band to break. Fusion sometimes leads to crystallization of sterling, which will increase breakage hazards.

Solder the ring on the heating block. When rounding the ring after soldering the joint, use a soft-face hammer to prevent defacing the decorative overlays. If the ring becomes work-hardened during shaping, anneal it and continue the shaping. If the ring should be slightly small, a metal hammer will be necessary to stretch the ring to enlarge it more than 1/4 size.

To clean and polish the ring, first remove any rough spots around the edges with a fine cutting file. Pickle the ring to remove oxidation. If you wish to antique it, follow directions for heating it in a bath of liver of sulfur and water (see Chapter 17). Smooth any surfaces you wish to leave bright with the silicon carbide board followed successively with buffing using tripoli and rouge.

**FUSING 18K-GOLD TO STERLING**

Fusing overlays to a base of the same material, sterling to sterling in the case of the band ring (Fig. 11-4), is easier than fusing one metal to another. In this project, you learn to fuse decorative overlays of 18K-gold wire to a sterling base (Fig. 11-9).

It seems that 18K gold is better than 14K for overlays, because 18K conducts heat better than 14K. The melting point of these metals is not as important as their heat conductivity.

Cut the sterling band about 1/16 inch longer than the length indicated in Table 18E for the ring size you choose. Wind 18K wire on a mandrel — 1/4-inch diameter to fit on a 3/8-inch wide band base. Cut the circles in half to form the design shown in Fig. 11-10. Make sure the pattern matches at the joint. With the pattern in Fig. 11-10, allow quarter circles at the ends, so that when the band is rounded and joined, the pattern of half circles will be the same all over.

1/4 CIRCLE → ~~~~~~~~~~~~~ ← 1/4 CIRCLE

Fig. 11-9. - Sterling band with half circles of 18K gold wire fused to the surface. The sterling is antiqued to contrast with the polished gold decoration.

Fig. 11-10. Suggested design layout for half circles of 18K gold wire to be fused to a sterling band. Arrange quarter circles at the ends so the design will be continuous when joint is soldered.

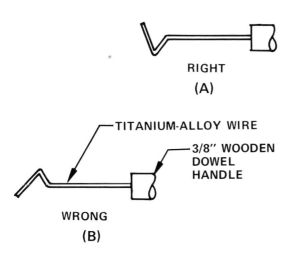

RIGHT
(A)

TITANIUM-ALLOY WIRE
3/8" WOODEN DOWEL HANDLE

WRONG
(B)

Fig. 11-11. - The flux applicator is a titanium alloy wire with a wood handle. The end of the applicator is bent to a V shape. When using the applicator, the bottom of the V should be down to hold blob of flux (A). If the V is upside down, molten flux will run off the end (B). Solid flux is charged on the applicator by first heating the applicator and dipping the hot end into a container of dry flux. Magic Flux, used in this exercise, contains a cleaning agent in addition to borax. Dry flux is more concentrated than flux mixed in water, because only the dry materials are useful in preventing oxidation of metal surfaces during heating.

You may continue to use wet borax flux applied thick and heavy over all of the design. Or you may prefer to learn a new technique using a self-cleaning dry flux. *Magic Flux* is one proprietary flux that removes oxidation when applied hot. Therefore, you may begin heating the base with the 18K-gold design in place — without fluxing. Align the strip so that you can move the torch up and down the same axis as the torch motion (see Fig. 11-6). This action continues to bathe the full length of the band in heat. Keep the torch well away (twice the length of the blue cone) from the surface of the band to prevent the force of the flame from blowing the tiny 18K half-circles out of position. As you heat the sterling base, watch the color turn

a light golden-brown, then a darker brown, and finally a blue-black. At this point you can add dry flux as follows:

Heat a flux applicator — titanium wire bent with a V at the end (Fig. 11-11). Dip the applicator in the flux and if the flux drips off, you have charged the applicator with excessive flux. Allow the excess to drip off into the flux container to be reused. Touch the flux-charged applicator to the ring base at a point away from the gold half-circles, because molten flux is sticky and will pick up or move the light decorative pieces if it is applied too closely. If the sterling is at the right temperature (surface black), the flux will flow over the surface. The dry flux flows toward heat. Continue charging the flux applicator and con-

111

veying the flux to the band until the full surface is covered. While heating the applicator and flux, keep the flame moving and directed down the length of the band to keep the sterling base hot.

As flux flows over the band, it will first become transparent and colorless. You can easily see where flux has flowed because the black will instantly disappear as the cleaning action removes oxidation. As the flux and band approach fusion temperature, the flux will begin to show green spots and then turn to a light golden brown. If the band was overheated during flux application (above 1200° F.), oxidation from the metal will dissolve in the flux and show some dark-red opaque spots.

When flux turns a golden brown, the band is approaching fusion temperature. Slow the motion of the torch and concentrate heat on the "near" end of the band until the flux pulls in from the edges. (Note — flux will pull in only at the spot where heat is concentrated, so the pulling-in action of the flux will not happen over the entire band at the same time.) Fusion should be occurring while the flux is pulling in from edges. Gradually move the torch (while keeping it moving in a circle) the full length of the band until all of the decorative pieces are fused to the base. You can test the fusion bond between decorative overlays and the base by touching the poker to each piece to make certain it has fused. When using the poker, avoid direct flame on it. The poker can become red hot and, if touched to decorative half-circles, may cause them to melt.

If any piece is not solidly bonded, reheat the band to fuse the overlay, applying additional flux and concentrating heat around the area where fusion did not occur. Continue heating until flux pulls in from the edges rather violently and black areas appear temporarily at the edge of the band where flux has pulled away.

While the band is hot, drop it in plain water or a pickle bath to clean away the flux. File the ends and bend the band into a round shape for soldering the butt joint as shown in Fig. 11-8.

You also may wish to use the dry flux system for soldering the butt joint of the ring. Hold the rounded ring with the joint faces in contact with a third-hand or self-locking tweezers held in a hand vise. Grasp the ring at the top with the joint flat against a heating block. Charge the flux applicator with a small amount of dry flux and heat it enough to turn the flux sticky. Touch the sticky end to a bit of solder. Heat the joint area of the ring before bringing the flux-solder blob into contact with the joint. While the flux applicator is holding the flux-solder blob at the joint, direct the heat away from the applicator itself. *Magic Flux* flows toward moderate heat, but it may run up the applicator if the tip is red hot. After positioning the flux-solder blob, continue heating until the flux flows into and around the joint. This action releases the solder bit. Continue heating the joint, keeping the flame always moving, until the solder runs.

Begin cleaning the band by dropping it into a pickle bath while the ring is still hot. Antique the sterling as noted in Chapter 17.

Use a soft-face hammer only for final rounding of the ring on a ring mandrel. The tiny half-circles of 18K gold will be defaced if hit with a metal hammer. Finally, clean and polish the inside of the ring, first with 400-grit wet-dry paper (see Chapter 1) followed by tripoli and rouge. Use tripoli on the edges of the band but only *very lightly* on the face. Polish the face with rouge to bring out the luster of the gold without disturbing the antique finish on the silver base.

Fused erratic pattern on domed sterling earrings. Note series of unsoldered oval jump rings attaching domes to ear-wire.
Carol Moch, West Hartford, Connecticut.

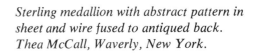

Sterling medallion with abstract pattern in sheet and wire fused to antiqued back.
Thea McCall, Waverly, New York.

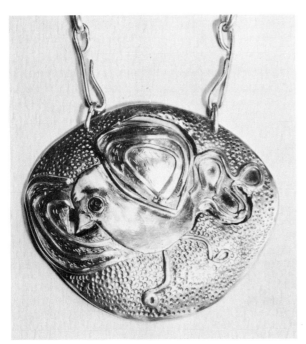

Sterling pendant with fused design on forge-textured base. Note double connection to fabricated wire-link chain. Anne Gries, Flushing, New York.

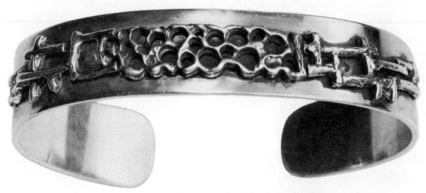

*Abstract design of fused wire on sterling bracelet. Thea McCall, Waverly, New York.*

*Sterling pendant with design fused to back and flame surface textured. Carol Moch, West Hartford, Connecticut.*

*Sterling earrings with design fused to surface with back flame textured before antiquing. Anne Gries, Flushing, New York.*

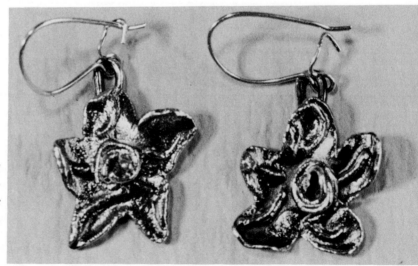

Bright sterling pendant with half domes of sterling fused to the base. Matching half domes connected to manufactured chain. Thea McCall, Waverly, New York.

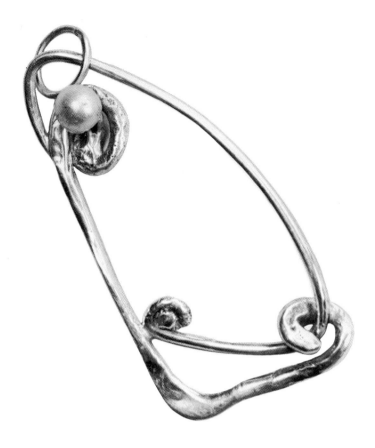

Fused and forged sterling pendant with pegged pearl. Betty Tlush, Meadowbrook, Pennsylvania.

Tie tack with fused sterling and turquoise cabochon stone. Carol Moch, West Hartford, Connecticut.

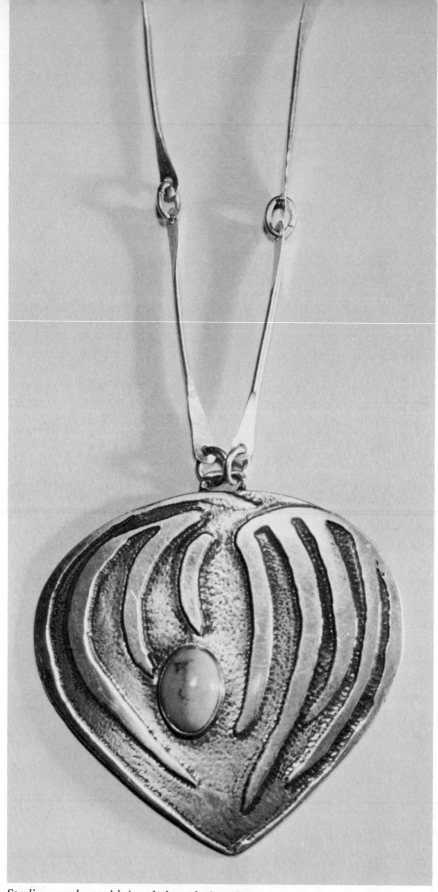

*Sterling pendant with fused sheet design plus
a small off-center cabochon gemstone.
Note connection with jump rings
to forged-wire link chain. Thea McCall,
Waverly, New York.*

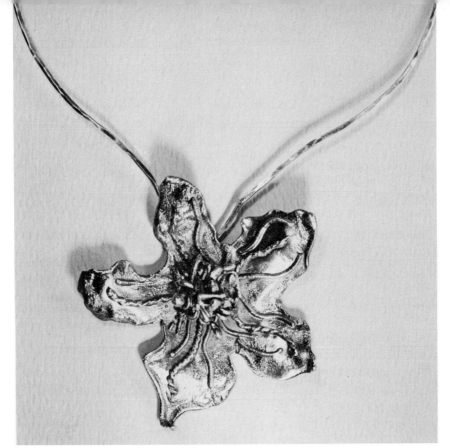

Massive pendant with fused wire decorative
pattern and flame-textured back. Leaf was
forged to an irregular shape after fusion.
Note the single choker wire attached to
a hidden mounting ring. Anne Gries,
Flushing, New York.

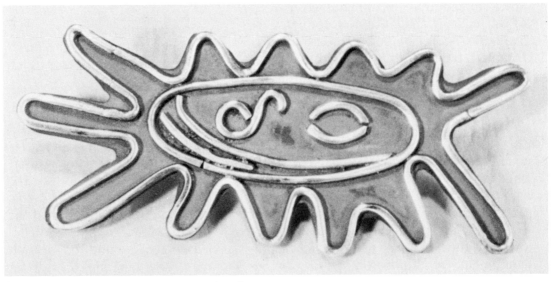

Pin with bright sterling wire design fused to
antiqued sterling back. Carol Moch,
West Hartford, Connecticut.

# free-form originals

*Lost Wax Casting*

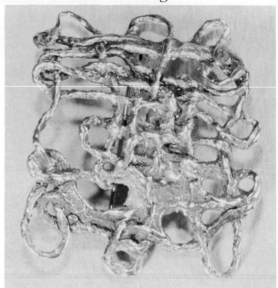

*Abstract pin design crafted in wax and cast in sterling. Leigh Garrison.*

METALCRAFTING CALLS FOR A VARIETY OF SKILLS in crafting wire and sheet metal. Casting introduces a completely different technique from those already discussed. The term, lost-wax casting, refers to a process that begins by investing a wax model in mold material (investment). The wax model and mold are then heated to melt out the wax, leaving a cavity the exact shape of the model. Molten metal is then poured or forced into the mold cavity. When cooled and the investment removed, the casting should be the exact shape of the model, possibly with an allowance for some shrinkage.

Various techniques are available for shaping the wax model which, in turn, controls the shape of the final metal casting. Wax may be carved or shaped while cold. Models may be built up by adding hot, molten wax to a basic shape. This chapter details the lost wax process; Chapter 13 details techniques for modifying an existing wax model.

Free-form design for rings, pendants, or other jewelry cast in a lost-wax mold can literally free you from many of the shaping and joining limitations of metals. A number of wax carving and build-up techniques are available — enough, in fact, to fill another complete book. Therefore, in this chapter you will learn how to form the wax model for a ring, cast it, and complete it — ready for wearing.

Special equipment and tools are necessary for this free-form, hot-wax model technique (see Chapter 19 for supply sources). Those with artistic talent may form figures, such as *Modern Woman* (Fig. 12-1), but you need no special talent to free-form your own delightful rings. You need not own or know how to use special casting equipment for this lesson. Until you become very proficient and wish to invest in professional equipment, you will do better to send your models to one of the custom casters noted in Chapter 19, than to attempt the casting yourself. Casting re-

quires completely different skills than free-forming a wax model and finishing the casting into a beautiful piece of jewelry.

## FREE-FORMING A RING WAX MODEL

You will need a stepped, lightweight ring mandrel to make a ring wax model. Wind on at least two laps of plastic tape around the ring mandrel 1/2 size larger than the finished ring size you desire (Fig. 12-2). Seal the loose end of the tape with a dab of hot wax. Apply a silicone or other release agent around the full outer surface of the plastic tape and the adjacent metal surface of the mandrel to assure that the free-formed wax model will be released easily from the tape.

The well of the camel wax application tip should be loaded with fast wax that has

*Fig. 12-1. - Tiny wax figures can be created with a camel—a special fountain pen tip for wax application and build-up. Note the size of the figure in relation to a dime.*

*Fig. 12-2. - Plastic tape (without adhesive) is wound on stepped ring mandrel 1/2 size larger than the desired ring size. Plastic tape allows wax model on mandrel to be slipped off easily when completed. A tiny drop of wax should be used to seal the edge of the plastic tape after two winds of tape have been completed.*

been carved off corners and edges of a wax block after the well has been heated. The wax melts easily after being placed in the heated application tip. Fast wax is not a soft wax, and its melting point is considerably higher than that of most common waxes. The high melting point allows the wax to retain its shape even in hot weather, and yet it will not break easily except after chilling. Fast wax is intended only for build-up through the fountain-pen action

of the camel tip and is not formulated for cold carving. When using fast wax, adjust the heating control to a high temperature, one that will keep the fast wax fluid but not so thin that the wax drips from the end of the pen. Fast wax at the correct temperature will flow from the tip of the pen when in contact with the plastic tape or another part of the wax model. Adjust the heat control of the pen so that it functions in a true "fountain pen" action.

119

Fig. 12-3. - A camel wax pen applies a thin
bead of wax to the plastic as the
mandrel is turned. Fast wax is heated in the
well from an electrical resistance coil in
the pen's handle. The wax should be
hot enough to flow freely when the tip
touches the plastic or wax already deposited,
but not hot enough to drip from the end.

Fig. 12-5. - Chrysocalla crystal
mounted in a gold casting made from
a free-form wax model. William E.
Garrison.

## Wax Application

Begin the wax application by touching
the tip of the camel to the center of the
plastic winding (Fig. 12-3). Turn the mandrel with one hand while you free-form a
design with the pen. Instead of simply
turning straight or slightly curved lines
around the mandrel, deliberately develop
an asymmetrical band having curves and
angles (see Figs. 12-4 and 12-5).

Continue to apply a number of layers of
wax to build up the thickness and width of
the model by turning the mandrel and allowing the wax to flow from the tip. You
may wish to develop a parallel, or roughly
parallel, circle around the mandrel in a
later design. But for this first model stick to
a single band that may include various
thick-and-thin sections. Imagine the final
design by "seeing" the wax building up on
the mandrel as metal. Be sure to deposit
enough wax at any corners or angles to
avoid weak spots in the final casting.

Build up a design for the top of the ring
(Fig. 12-6). Spread out a series of loops or
other designs of your own choosing for the
portion of the ring that will be on top. The
four-petal design (Fig. 12-7) is only one
suggestion. Part of the excitement of the
free-form technique is the range of design
possibilities open to you.

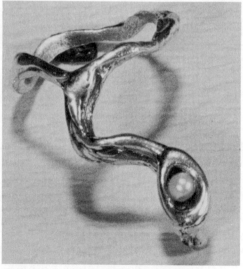

Fig. 12-4. - Sterling free-form ring
with finger extension that mounts a
small pearl. William E. Garrison.

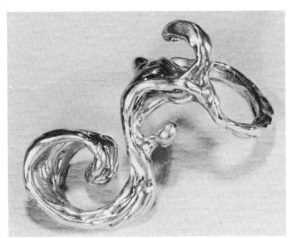

*Fig. 12-6. - Abstract finger form crafted in wax and cast in sterling. William E. Garrison.*

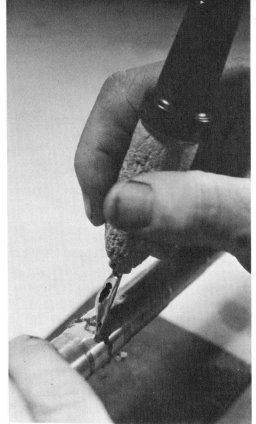

*Fig. 12-7. - Free-form design with four loops takes shape on the mandrel as the camel deftly deposits wax from the point. The top design for a ring is created along with the shank in a completely unstructured pattern. Free-forming with wax opens a whole new field for jewelry handcrafters.*

When the free-form design is finished, remove the wax model with plastic tape attached from the mandrel (Fig. 12-8). When you strip the plastic tape from the inside of the wax model, the tape surface should be mirror smooth. Using the sides or tip of the hot camel, smooth and touch up any surfaces of the model that appear rough or where wax may have spilled onto the plastic tape.

### Custom Caster

Your wax model is now ready to be sent to a custom caster. See Chapter 19 for casters who do business by mail. Or you may walk your fingers through the yellow pages of your local telephone directory to find a custom lost-wax caster. Look under Castings — Investment or Jewelry Manufacturers.

The professional custom caster who receives your wax model will add any sprues necessary to assure a full flow of metal to every part of the casting. Since the caster is responsible for the casting, he will determine the number and placement of the sprues as part of the casting operation. Adding sprues is not part of the model making.

When your casting returns, it will have been cut loose from the button and will be

*Fig. 12-8. - The wax model is self-supporting after it has been slipped off the mandrel and the plastic tape has been removed from the inside. The edges of the wax model should be smoothed and cleaned in preparation for the casting.*

121

clean but not polished (Fig. 12-9). If you do your own casting, remove investment and prepare to clean and polish the ring.

### Sprue Removal and Cleaning

First pickle the casting, preferably by heating the pickle with the casting in it to 180-190° F. An even better way to pickle the casting or other jewelry is to heat the metal to a dull red and drop it hot into hot pickle solution. Prolonged soaking in a pickle bath may not remove some of the discoloration and other dirt that comes off quickly with the help of heat. Scrub the casting with a soft brush to remove any investment still embedded. A soft-bristle toothbrush is ideal for this job. If the brush does not remove all traces of investment, use a sharp-pointed instrument, such as a scribe or salvaged dental tool, to remove embedded investment. Scrub again to remove all traces of investment.

Next, remove the sprue with a jeweler's saw, using a 2-0 blade (Fig. 12-10). Cut the sprue as close to the ring band as possible. Remove any sprue material not sawed away with a file and finish the surface with fine silicon carbide wet-dry paper. Use a half-round ring file to remove excess metal from the inside surface of the ring. The half-round ring file will have a sharper radius for the rounded portion, allowing you to clean up the band with minimum interference at the edges.

Cleanup of the ring is a simple task if you have access to power equipment, such as a rotary file or abrasive point in a flex shaft handpiece or a hand-size motor tool. Use 400- to 600-grit wet-dry, silicon carbide paper *wet* for final abrasive finishing. When wet, the abrasive cuts faster, smoother, and tends to clog the grits less easily.

Shape the ring on the ring mandrel, tapping it during rounding only with a soft-face rawhide or buckskin hammer. Most plastic hammers will be too hard for this task. Check the ring for roundness and size from both directions. If the ring is slightly under the size desired, you may stretch it slightly by hammering on the tapered ring mandrel, again using a soft-faced hammer. Switch the ring frequently to prevent building in a taper from the mandrel. If the ring is too large, cut the band opposite the top or at a joint where metal may be removed without being obvious. Solder the joint, as described in Chapter 1, and finish.

Buffing and polishing a free-form ring by hand is, at best, tedious and, at least, unsatisfactory. Some kind of power equipment is essential for this task. An electric motor salvaged from some appliance or other source can be fitted with a double-ended spindle to mount buffing wheels. Or use one of the small buffing wheels mounted in a flex shaft or motor tool. Buff first with tripoli on a muslin buffing wheel. Continue buffing until the surface is clean and smooth. Clean with a 1:1 ammonia-water mixture; a soft-bristle toothbrush helps to clean out crevices.

Rather than clean the casting by hand, you might try tumbling as an alternative. Jewelry manufacturers have tumble-finished jewelry for years, using a mild abrasive in the tumbling charge. However, a charge made by cutting common brass wire into quite small bits burnishes whatever it contacts without abrasion. Round brass wire approximately 16-gauge, cut into random lengths of 1/16 inch to 1/4 inch yields good results when combined with additional material. Two of these materials are *Metal Magic* and *Magic Tumbling Compound*. Total charge in the tumbler should weigh somewhat less than the tumbler's capacity. Cast jewelry may require as long as twelve hours of tumbling time to clean the piece. Tumble cleaning does not polish metal but cleans it thoroughly and removes surface discolorations, highlights areas that have been antiqued, and produces a pleasing matte finish. A high polish may be added with the polishing disk. Tumble

Fig. 12-9. - Rough casting of ring created from wax model shown in Fig. 12-8. Note that the sprue, added to assure free flow of metal to base portion of the ring, is still intact. Investment material from mold also remains in pockets of the ring. This must be removed as part of the cleaning process.

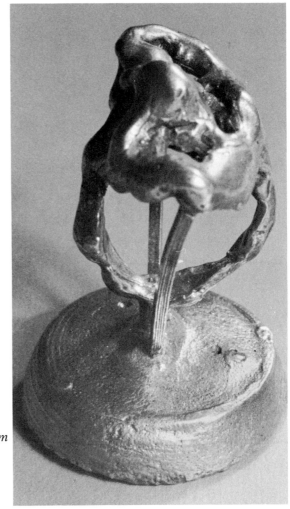

Fig. 12-10. - The sprue should be cut from the remainder of the cast ring with a jeweler's saw. Extra material should be filed from both outside and inside the ring before clean-up and polishing.

Fig. 12-11. - This polished free-form ring was cast in gold.

cleaning takes most of the drudgery out of jewelry making; you will find it effective even if only one or two pieces are in the tumbler.

If your ring is sterling, you may wish to antique it as detailed in Chapter 17.

Final polishing calls for red jeweler's rouge. You will want to polish only a few highlights, allowing depressions and some flat surfaces to remain antiqued. Finally, wash thoroughly in an ammonia-water wash and dry with a soft cloth (Fig. 12-11).

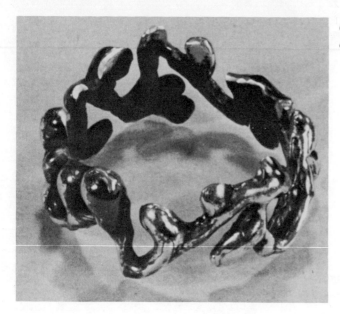

*Gold free-form ring crafted in wax, cast, and antiqued. William E. Garrison.*

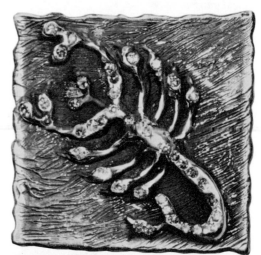

*Scorpion pin crafted originally in wax and cast in gold with small diamonds. William E. Garrison.*

*Faceted smoky quartz mounted in an ornamented gold free-form casting. William E. Garrison.*

124

*Synthetic emerald in free-form cast sterling mounting. Leigh Garrison.*

*Synthetic sapphire mounted in a free-form gold casting. Leigh Garrison.*

*Gold mounting for pearl with cast-in-place prong. William E. Garrison.*

*Free-form design crafted in wax and cast in sterling. William E. Garrison.*

125

## Chapter Thirteen

# redesign of models

*Lost Wax Casting*

CHAPTER 12 INTRODUCED YOU TO a free-form technique for building ring models in wax on a ring mandrel. In this chapter you begin with a wax model that has been molded into a ring shape (Fig. 13-1). Through various techniques, you can modify the wax model to suit your own design ideas. You may want an all-metal ring, or you may want to add a seat and prongs for a cabochon stone.

One word about wax models — through another step not really practical for most craftsmen, but common among craftsmen who design and sell their jewelry, a master for a ring, spoon handle, pendant, or other piece of jewelry may be constructed in metal or other material. A rubber mold is formed around the metal master and allowed to cure. The rubber mold is parted and the metal master is removed, leaving a cavity. Hot wax is then cast in the rubber mold. Since the mold is rubber, it may be peeled away from the delicate design of the wax. Wax models may be produced in quantity from these rubber molds, which are available at supply sources.

Wax models prior to modification and the rings cast from modified models are shown in Figs. 13-2, 13-3 and 13-4. In Fig. 13-5, two different modifications of the same basic model are shown with one cast ring.

Tools needed for modifying wax models are an alcohol lamp or electrically controlled unit and various welding and carving tools (see Chapter 15). In Chapter 12, you were introduced to an electrically heated camel for the application of hot wax. The camel may also be used for hot carving. However, to get started and experiment, simple hand tools resembling those used by a dentist are all that are needed to modify the wax models.

## SHAPING A MODEL WITHOUT A GEMSTONE

Decreasing the width of a wax model calls for taking wax off both sides or removing it from the center. Slitting the wax model and removing a section from the center

*Geometric ring modified in wax and cast in sterling. W. H. Laffoon, Seattle, Washington.*

narrows the model quickly (Fig. 13-6). But, if you wish to preserve the central design of the piece, simply remove wax from both sides of a ring wax model with a hot cutting tip.

Very little wax is ordinarily required to repair and weld those areas of the wax model where cutting occurred. Heat a welding tool in the alcohol lamp, dip it into a block of welding wax, and transfer the hot wax quickly to the model. Repair the cut areas with the addition of wax and by smoothing, to remove any evidence of the cut. In all wax carving or shaping, develop the knack of seeing the wax model as finished metal. Every detail, every little crack or ridge will be reproduced exactly as the wax is shaped during casting. While you can burnish, file, and smooth the final metal, shaping the wax model is infinitely easier and faster.

Opening up, thinning, and reshaping the wax model allows you to develop your own

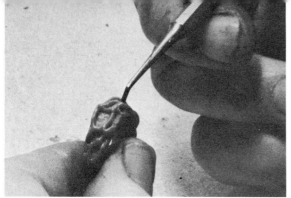

Fig. 13-1. - A wax model for casting a
ring, either with or without a gemstone,
can be modified to reflect your own
ideas. Hand tools similar to those used
by a dentist aid in shaping the wax.
Carving cold wax or adding and welding
with hot wax affords a variety
of design options.

Fig. 13-2. - A wax model and resulting cast
sterling ring. William E. Garrison.

Fig. 13-3. - Solid sterling band cast from
decorated wax model. William E. Garrison.

Fig. 13-4. - Wax model before modification
and sterling ring cast from modified
model. William E. Garrison.

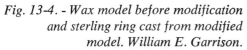

Fig. 13-5. - Original wax model at left with
slightly modified cast sterling ring in the
center. A greater modification of the
wax model is shown at right. William E.
Garrison.

127

*Fig. 13-6. - A wax model can be narrowed easily by first slitting the center of the pattern with a hot cutting tip (left). With the center removed and ends tapered, the wax pattern is pushed together (right). Welding with hot wax and smoothing with various tips repair the slit.*

*Fig. 13-7. - Opening up a design (left) calls for increasing the size of the holes in the model (right). Remove the wax between existing holes, or lighten the wax on the ribs and connections that make up the design.*

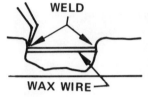

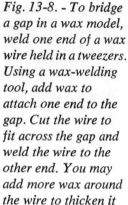

*Fig. 13-8. - To bridge a gap in a wax model, weld one end of a wax wire held in a tweezers. Using a wax-welding tool, add wax to attach one end to the gap. Cut the wire to fit across the gap and weld the wire to the other end. You may add more wax around the wire to thicken it or to build a shape compatible with the rest of the wax model.*

creative designs without having to start from scratch. With a hot carving tip, you cut away portions of existing holes, open up new spaces or holes, pull out ridges to expand the width, and build up portions as you desire (Fig. 13-7).

New wax may be added to an existing wax model by one of two techniques — welding in new pieces, wax wire or sheet, or building on wax bit by bit. The technique of adding wax wire is detailed in Fig. 13-8. The technique of building on bit by bit is detailed in Fig. 13-9.

## MODIFYING A MODEL FOR A GEMSTONE

Cast jewelry need not be all metal. You can modify a wax model to fit a gemstone. When the metal is cast, you mount the gemstone in the prepared opening. Here's how —

Select a wax model that is wide enough to accommodate the gemstone you wish to mount. The gemstone should not be fragile or one that requires special protection. Before touching the wax, set the stone in the planned position and examine its relationship to the model. Imagine how the stone will look in place and make certain it is where you want it. Mark around the gemstone location with a sharp stylus and remove the stone. With a cutting and welding tip, remove wax to the approximate size of the stone to be set (Fig. 13-10).

Try the stone in the opening after applying a release agent to the gemstone so that it won't stick to the wax model. After the gemstone has been positioned, the hole should be enlarged to be slightly larger than the gemstone (Fig. 13-11). Place the gemstone in the mold and turn it upside down on the bench and fit the wax model over it to allow you to work on the back side of the gemstone (Fig. 13-12). Add enough wax around the perimeter of the gemstone to form a seat (Fig. 13-13).

With the ring right side up again on a stepped mandrel (see Chapter 12) or held

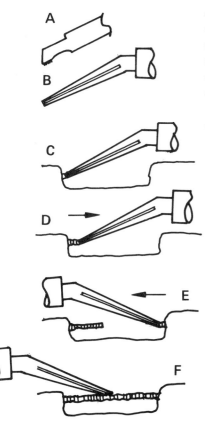

Fig. 13-9. - A second, and more difficult technique for bridging a gap, other than the wax-wire technique, is worth learning because it also can be used for building wax sculptures. A long barracuda tip (A) in an electrically heated element works best, although a welding tip (B) heated in an alcohol lamp can be used. Adjust the heat until wax is barely above melting point and just hangs from the tip. Touch the tip to one side of the gap (C). Blow furiously while you pull the tip gently away (D). As the wax begins to harden, keep pulling the tip away very slowly. An electric bench fan saves a lot of blowing. Repeat this procedure as necessary to build a bridge half way across the gap. Begin bridging from the opposite side of the gap (E). Build out the wax bridge until it meets the first half (F).

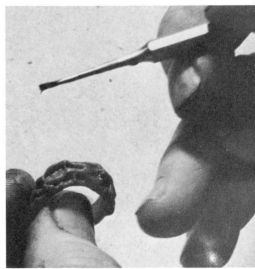

Fig. 13-10. - A hot carving tip quickly removes the central part of wax model for fitting the gemstone. Cut out wax all the way through to the bottom. Later you can add wax to build a seat for the gemstone.

Fig. 13-11. - Try the gemstone in the hole. Continue to enlarge the hole until the opening is slightly larger than the gemstone.

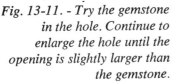

Fig. 13-12. - In fitting the gemstone into the opening of the modified wax model, the stone should fit loosely in the opening to allow for shrinkage.

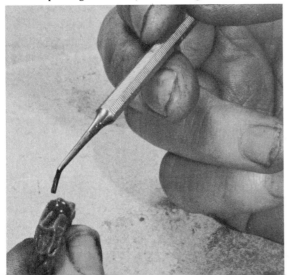

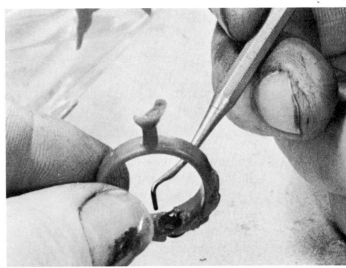

Fig. 13- 13 - With the wax model upside down and the gemstone in place, add wax around the base of the stone to form a seat. To provide for the gemstone's removal later, apply a release agent to the top and bottom (see Chapter 12). With a warm welding tool, pick up wax from the block and transfer it to the bottom of the stone.

129

Fig. 13-14. - Smooth and repair the opening around the top of the gemstone, adding wax as necessary. However, make sure you do not build in an overhang around the edge that will prevent the gemstone from slipping out easily.

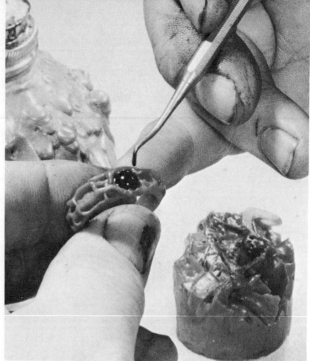

Fig. 13-15. - Build up metal for prongs directly on the surface of the gemstone. The release agent will prevent the wax from bonding to the surface. Transfer bits of warm wax with a welding tool or use the tip of the camel.

Fig. 13-16. - When building prongs, start 1 or 2 millimeters back from the edge of the stone to allow for metal shrinkage during casting.

in one hand, build up small prongs with wax to retain the stone. Wax may be added bit by bit (as in Fig. 13-9), or for perfectly even, smooth prongs, weld round or rectangular wax wire to the base model around the stone as shown in Fig. 13-8.

When building prongs bit by bit to achieve a more "natural" look, apply a release agent to the stone in position and apply wax directly onto the stone (Fig. 13-14). Remember, you must bend the prongs of built-up wax away from the stone to remove the stone from the model. Therefore, you should use a flexible wax for this prong-building work. With a welding tip heated in the alcohol lamp, pick up wax from a block and transfer it directly onto the gemstone (Fig. 13-15). But don't start building

a prong flush against the base of the stone — or the shrinkies will get you! You must allow a millimeter or so of space between the inside surface of the prong and the gemstone (Fig. 13-16). If you add prongs of wax wire, hold the upper end of the wire in a third-hand while you weld the lower end to the model (Fig. 13-17).

Remove the gemstone from its position on the wax model when you have finished building prongs. With a sharp-pointed tool, gently pry all of the prongs loose from the surface of the stone (Fig. 13-18). If you have used a release agent, the wax prongs should lift easily. When all prongs have been loosened, slip a pointed tool under the gemstone and ease it out of the wax model.

Prongs should remain vertical for casting. However, since the prongs were formed directly on the stone, the wax will tend to return to its curved position. Straighten the prongs with heat, if necessary (Fig. 13-19). Unless the prongs are cast vertically, you can expect trouble on two counts — in the casting and later when you insert

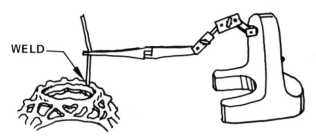

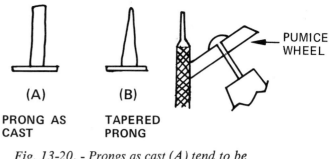

WELD

Fig. 13-17. - An alternative method for building prongs is to weld a wax wire to the base, 1 to 2 millimeters away from the gemstone — not right up against it! Don't attempt to weld short lengths of wax wire. Instead, grasp a long wire in a third-hand and join the base of the wire to the wax model with welding wax. As soon as the wax joint is firm, cut off the wire slightly longer than will be used for the prong.

(A)

PRONG AS CAST

(B)

TAPERED PRONG

PUMICE WHEEL

Fig. 13-20. - Prongs as cast (A) tend to be bulky and crude with a squared tip. Each prong should be tapered to permit the tip to be bent into a gradually tighter curve. Small files enable you to taper prongs by hand, but a quicker and much more satisfactory technique is to use a small grinding wheel. Even fine abrasives tend to "eat up" the small prongs before you realize it. An ideal abrasive for shaping and tapering prongs is a pumice wheel operating at high speed. To enable you to begin tapering from the base, shape the pumice wheel on a file to work with a sharp edge. Remember — taper the prongs on all sides.

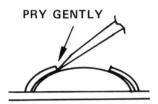

PRY GENTLY

Fig. 13-18. - Pry the ends of the built-up prongs gently away from the gemstone and bend the prongs vertically to remove the stone.

Fig. 13-19. - Prongs formed against the gemstone tend to remain curved. To straighten prongs to permit casting them vertically, apply a heated smoothing tool in an up-and-down motion to the inside surface of each prong.

the stone. If the prongs are curved, you must first bend them back to insert the stone. Then you must bend them into position to restrain the stone. Cast metal does not bend readily, so plan to bend the prongs only once — when you are setting them against the stone.

When the wax model is ready for casting, package it carefully and send it to one of the custom casters noted in Chapter 19 or to a local shop. When the casting comes back, clean it of investment and polish it according to the directions detailed in Chapter 12.

**SETTING THE GEMSTONE**

All cleaning and polishing of the ring casting must be completed before setting the stone. Turn your attention first to the prongs. Slim and taper the prongs as detailed in Fig. 13-20. The taper on the prongs can mean the difference between a graceful curve that increases toward the tip or a chunky-looking prong that bends mainly at the base. Therefore, do not skip this step of tapering the prongs.

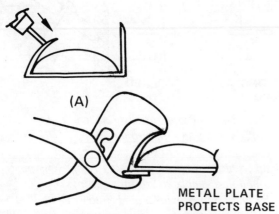

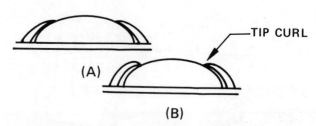

TIP CURL

Fig. 13-21. - *The first step in setting prongs is to force them against the stone. A pusher will move the tapered prongs against the stone (A). An alternative method is to use a prong-bending pliers. A piece of metal under the base may be necessary to protect the surface from the action of the lower jaw.*

METAL PLATE PROTECTS BASE

Fig. 13-22. - *No matter how much simple bending you may do, metal springback will prevent the tips of the prongs from bearing on the gemstone to hold it securely in place. Final bending is accomplished in two steps. The tips are first pushed to bend in a slight curve and to bring only the tip into contact with the stone (A). Finally, the fine tip of the prong is bent into a sharp curl to bear against the gemstone (B).*

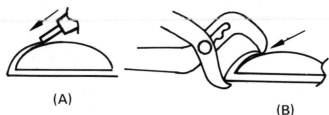

Fig. 13-23. - *The tip curl on prongs may be bent with a pusher (A) or with the prong-bending pliers adjusted so that it bends only the tip of the prong (B).*

Set the gemstone in place on the mount and check the fit around the seat. A slight hump or two may prevent the gemstone from seating firmly all around its perimeter. Remove any projections with a scraper, file, or rotary file. With the stone firmly in place, force all prongs down against the stone, using a "pusher" or prong-bending pliers as shown in Fig. 13-21.

Finally, a tip curl should be bent on each prong to lock the gemstone into place (Fig. 13-22). Unless the prong has been properly tapered, you will be unable to form this tip curl with a pusher (Fig. 13-23). If you cannot form the tip curl on the prong with the pusher, use the prong-bending pliers as shown in Fig. 13-23B. The mechanical advantage from the prong-bending pliers affords both the force and control needed to bend the tip tightly against the gemstone without slipping or possibly scratching the stone.

Clean up any rough spots on the prongs or setting with a pumice wheel rotating at high speed.

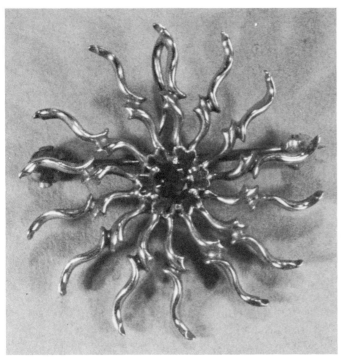

*Cast gold pin.*

*Ring band cast in gold from modified wax model. William E. Garrison.*

*Opals mounted in a modified wax model and cast in sterling. Leigh Garrison.*

133

# jewelry from found objects

TALK ABOUT UNIQUE, PERSONAL JEWELRY! There's nothing that allows you more opportunity for creativity — for letting your imagination run free — than developing jewelry from "found" objects.

What is a "found" object? It's something you find — something you can adapt for a piece of personal jewelry with little or no change. Found objects have an endless range — from bits of stone you find on a beach to shells, driftwood, and tumbled glass. Where you find these objects is less important than letting your imagination "see" the object as a finished piece. Some of the places that have an abundance of found objects are:

1. Antique shops — Here you may find old buttons and obsolete or foreign coins that might be used with only a good cleaning either as a piece of jewelry or as an element in constructing some new piece. Look too for bits of porcelain, particularly those with fine hand-painted designs. Put on your magic glasses that allow you to convert what you see into what might be. Look at everything with these questions — "Could this object be used in jewelry? What kind of jewelry would show off a found object's distinctive characteristics best?"

2. Industrial surplus or scrap dealers — All kinds of metal, plastics, various types of wood, glass, and ceramics crowd the usual surplus shop in unkempt abandon. Possibilities are so unlimited that you should really take a look for yourself. Look up scrap and surplus dealers in the classified section of your telephone directory. Then visit the shops or outlets — again with your magic glasses on. Some of the examples in this chapter should get your imagination going in high gear.

3. Look also in attics, your own basement, import shops, used-goods and bargain stores, rummage sales — any place where out-of-the-ordinary objects collect or are displayed.

134

Found objects can be used in two dis-

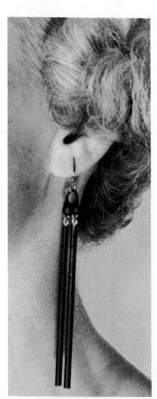

*Fig. 14-1. - Long, dangling earrings were made from solid plastic rods that were sprayed black and connected with brass oval jump rings to a small symmetrical hanger picked up in a salvage shop. A large jump ring connects the assembly to an ear-screw. William E. Garrison.*

Fig. 14-2. - Polished
brass dog tag suspended
from a manufactured
chain becomes a small
pendant. Rose Boyles,
Seattle, Washington.

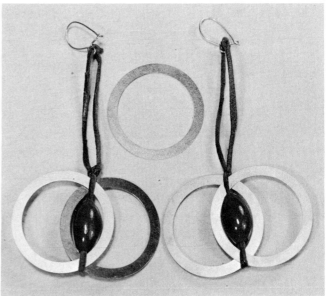

Fig. 14-3. - Swinging
earrings are assembled from
two stainless steel washers
connected with a thin
leather thong through a
painted wood bead. One of
the original stainless steel
washers is shown above.
Rose Boyles, Seattle,
Washington.

tinctly different ways. A found object may
be made into a piece of jewelry or incor-
porated into the design of a piece with little
or no change in its shape or form. For
example, the earrings shown in Fig. 14-3
were made from two small stainless steel
washers. Only a minimum of effort was
required to develop this one-of-a-kind pair
of earrings. Many found objects need only
some kind of finding or chain to convert
them to a piece of fun-type jewelry.

Other found objects require some kind

of molding or shaping to convert them to
wearable jewelry. The lapidary enjoys a
distinct advantage in working with porcelain or ceramic objects. He can grind or
shape a large piece of porcelain into smaller pieces usable in jewelry.

The jewelry items displayed as examples
of found objects in this chapter offer only a
limited sampling of possibilities. Some
may appear wild or extreme — or they may
be considered highly imaginative. It all
depends on what you like.

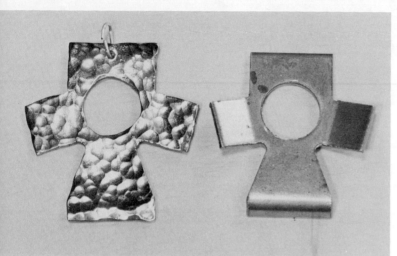

Fig. 14-4. - Forged and polished pendant with an unusual shape was converted from a steel punch-out — a scrap piece of metal punched out of a larger piece on a punch press. Punch-outs are sold by the pound or barrel at surplus outlets. Rose Boyles, Seattle, Washington.

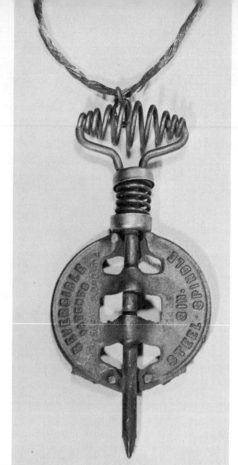

Fig. 14-6. - This king-size medallion was formerly a smoke-pipe damper. It has a spring handle that was used to reduce the chance of being burned while adjusting its position. Stranded copper wire is used as a choker. Rose Boyles, Seattle, Washington.

Fig. 14-5. - Imaginative earrings assembled from snap ring washers picked up in a surplus outlet because they were rusted. A quick polish and plating with chromium, plus the addition of a column of beads strung on an eye-pin converts these scrap pieces into eye-catching danglers. Original snap ring shown above. Rose Boyles, Seattle, Washington.

Fig. 14-7. - Twin key fobs from a hotel with the usual "Drop in Any Mailbox" on one side were easily converted into earrings. Rose Boyles, Seattle, Washington.

136

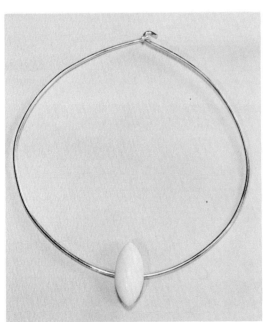

*Fig. 14-8. - Choker of plain wire features ceramic "egg" as a single, eye-catching element. Rose Boyles, Seattle, Washington.*

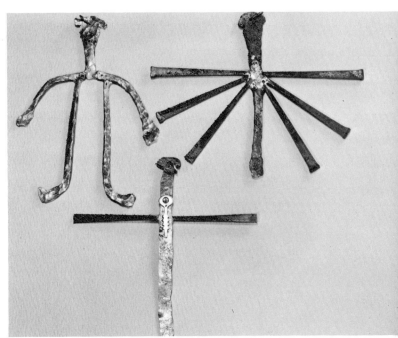

*Fig. 14-9. - Jewelry art was made from copper nails picked up at a scrap outlet. This trio shows how nails may be shaped into a rough figure* (top left), *forged with a surface design* (bottom), *and simply joined in a unique array* (top right). *Rose Boyles, Seattle, Washington.*

*Fig. 14-10. - Sparkling and colorful imported glass beads are displayed on ring bands of bright copper. The glass beads were cemented to the handwrought copper bands. Dr. R. A. Cunningham, Defiance, Ohio.*

137

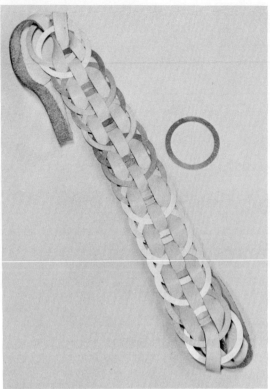

*Fig. 14-11. - In this bracelet two completely different materials — stainless steel washers and soft glove leather — are combined in a unique design. Rose Boyles, Seattle, Washington.*

*Fig. 14-12. - Two scraps, one a punch-out and the other a round washer with symmetrical holes, combine to form a forged, polished earring. The copper centers are polished and sweat-soldered to a six-point star. Rose Boyles, Seattle, Washington.*

*Fig. 14-13. - A copper circle with punched holes is forged to texture the surface before it is soldered inside a steel, internal gear punch-out. These earrings could be too heavy for some people. Rose Boyles, Seattle, Washington.*

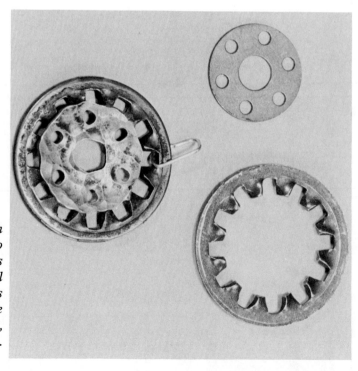

Fig. 14-14. - This simple yet striking pendant is fabricated from a steel punch-out and has a copper circle soldered in the center. A long, flexible spring supports the pendant at choker length. The choker is connected by a close-fitting plastic sleeve. Rose Boyles, Seattle, Washington.

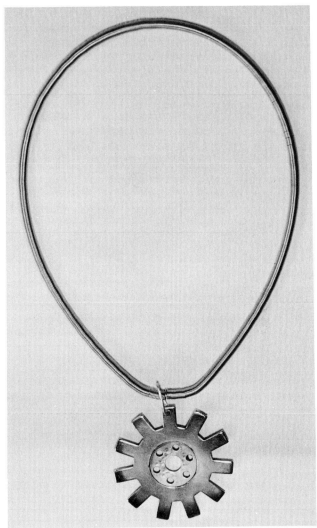

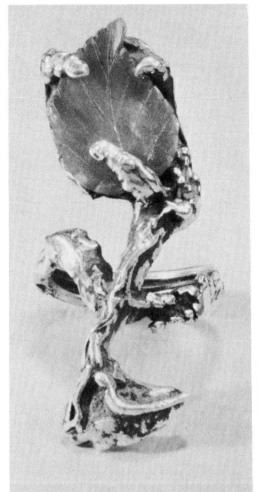

Fig. 14-15. - Oriental, carved jade leaf is mounted in a fused sterling ornamented ring. Kit Gifford, Queen Charlotte Island, Canada.

139

*Fig. 14-16. - Tiny pine cones "found" in the woods, invested in mold material, and burned out like wax form a model for gold earrings. Jo Ann Parsons, Seattle, Washington.*

*Fig. 14-17. - Carved jade fish found in a curio shop is used to highlight a fused sterling pin. Kit Gifford, Queen Charlotte Island, Canada.*

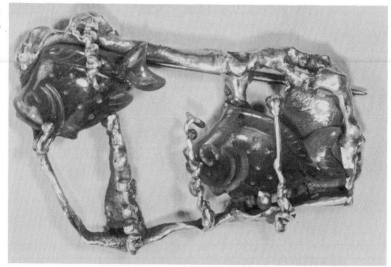

*Fig. 14-18. - Scrolled pendant or pin in hammered, antiqued brass. Japanese ceramic scene was found in a scrap heap. Note the mounting prongs soldered to the outside of the forged mount. William E. Garrison.*

*Fig. 14-19. - This large ring in antiqued brass incorporates another found ceramic Japanese object. Note that the looped prongs for holding the ceramic face also protect the edges of the piece from bumps. William E. Garrison.*

*Fig. 14-20. - Large antique gold-plated buttons with greenish stones from the front of a garment were combined into a triangular pendant on a wire frame. The smaller sleeve buttons were fitted with a wire for attaching to ear-wires. William E. Garrison.*

141

# tools

TOOLS ARE KEY ELEMENTS in jewelry crafting. This chapter describes the essential characteristics of basic hand tools and introduces optional tools and powered equipment that aid specific tasks or speed up work. Additional tools for specific tasks become more useful as you develop your skills and master metalcrafting techniques using basic hand tools.

## BASIC HAND TOOLS

All of the tools illustrated and described in this section are used in jewelry making.

**Pliers** — These "fingers of metal" are among the most used tools for crafting jewelry. Three basic types, available in a variety of sizes, are needed:

1. Chain-nose pliers are an all-purpose type for grasping, holding, and some special bending. The inside faces are flat without serrations, and the back of the jaws are rounded.

2. Flat-jaw pliers are tapered slightly but have flat, straight jaws.

3. Round-nose pliers have tapered circular jaws. These pliers are used mainly for bending wire and thin metal into loops, such as eye-pins or "figure-8" links. The tapered jaws permit bending a range of loop diameters.

**Hammers** — The two ball-peen hammers described below (4 ounce and 2 ounce) are used for two specific purposes.

The 4-ounce hammer is an all-purpose hammer used mainly for striking stamps, center punches, etc. Although the 4-ounce hammer comes with a polished face, it is likely to become scarred through use with a variety of scratches and gouges. The 4-ounce hammer is seldom used for hammering or forging jewelry metals, because marks on the hammer face will mar metal surfaces. Sometimes the random texturing from a scarred hammer becomes a design element. The peen end of the 4-ounce hammer, however, is often used for shaping metals when added heft is useful.

The 2-ounce hammer is used mainly for forging jewelry metals, such as ring shanks.

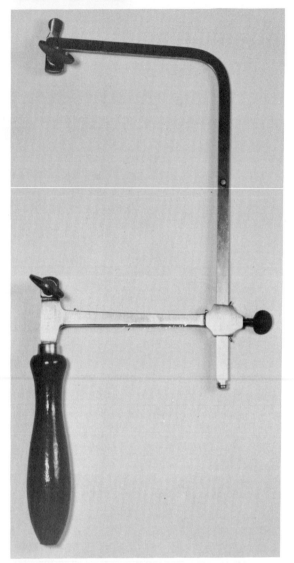

*Fig. 15-1. - Jeweler's saw frame.*

The flat face of the hammer comes with a smoothly polished finish and should be kept smooth. The 2-ounce hammer should not be used for driving nails, striking punches, or hitting hard steel. Otherwise, the face of the 2-ounce hammer will become scarred.

**Shears** — Short handles on the metal-cutting shears prevent their being used for cutting metal thicker than 14-gauge or for

## TABLE 15A — Jeweler's Saw Blades

| Size No. | Thickness (Inches) | Blade Width (Inches) | Teeth Per Inch |
|---|---|---|---|
| 8-0 | .006 | .013 | –– |
| 7-0 | .007 | .013 | –– |
| 6-0 | .007 | .014 | 76 |
| 5-0 | .008 | .015 | 73 |
| 4-0 | .008 | .017 | 70 |
| 3-0 | .010 | .019 | 66 |
| 2-0 | .010 | .020 | 64 |
| 0 | .011 | .023 | 60 |
| 1 | .012 | .025 | 56 |
| 2 | .014 | .027 | 48 |
| 3 | .014 | .029 | 44 |
| 4 | .015 | .031 | 40 |
| 5 | .016 | .034 | 36 |
| 6 | .019 | .041 | 32 |
| 8 | .020 | .058 | 24 |

cutting hard steel. The curved jaws of the shears permit metal to be cut with the plane of the shears perpendicular to the plane of the metal.

**End nippers** — Although end nippers resemble pliers in appearance, the nippers are for cutting only. End nippers are mainly used for snipping wire.

**Jeweler's saw** — The frame of the jeweler's saw is a holding device for very thin, fine-toothed blades (Fig. 15-1). The frame can be adjusted to accommodate blades of various lengths. Thumbscrews control the top and bottom jaws for chucking the blades. Tension on the blades is critical for effective cutting. Blade tension is controlled by the amount of spring forced into the frame as blades are mounted in the chucks. Blades are mounted in the frame in such a way that they will cut on the downward or pull stroke.

**Saw blades** — Jeweler's saw blades are fine-toothed, thin blades with straight ends for cutting various jewelry metals. Saw blades range from Size 8-0 to 8, as noted in Table 15A. Most sawing is accomplished with 2-0 blades on 18-gauge metal and thicker with 4-0 blades being used on metal 20-gauge and thinner.

**File** — One all-purpose, 6-inch half-round file is used for most filing. The half-round cross section permits flat or curved surface filing. The slim taper of the file allows it to be used for the inside of ring shanks. See Optional Hand Tools for a description of other files.

**Hand drill** — Commonly referred to as the "egg-beater" type, the hand drill includes a 3-jaw chuck for holding twist drills and mandrels for winding jump rings.

**Twist drills** — Metal cutting, straight-shank twist drills are used mainly for drilling holes in metal (Fig. 15-2). One 1/16-inch diameter and one No. 55 twist drill are useful for drilling holes in chain links, sheet metal earrings, and the like. Table 15B lists the sizes of twist drills according to three groups — fractions of an inch, such as 1/16 inch, numbered sequence, and letter sequence. A fourth column indicates the proper size twist drill to use for clearance with specific wire sizes. The letter and number sequences permit a greater variety of drill diameters than would be practical with only fractional sizes in small diameters.

**Tweezers** — Two types of tweezers are commonly used in crafting jewelry — direct action and self-locking. Both types can be

143

## TABLE 15B — Twist Drill Sizes and Wire Clearance

| Size Fraction | Decimal | Letter | Size Decimal | No. | Size Decimal | No. | Size Decimal | Wire Clearance Wire Gage | Wire Clearance Drill Size |
|---|---|---|---|---|---|---|---|---|---|
| 1/16 | .0156 | A | .234 | 80 | .0135 | 40 | .098 | 24 | 76 |
| | | | | 79 | .0145 | 39 | .0995 | | |
| 1/32 | .0312 | B | .238 | 78 | .016 | 38 | .1015 | 22 | 72 |
| | | | | 77 | .018 | 37 | .104 | | |
| 3/64 | .0468 | C | .242 | 76 | .020 | 36 | .1065 | 20 | 67 |
| | | | | 75 | .021 | 35 | .110 | | |
| 1/16 | .0625 | D | .246 | 74 | .0225 | 34 | .111 | 18 | 60 |
| | | | | 73 | .024 | 33 | .113 | | |
| 5/64 | .0781 | E | .250 | 72 | .025 | 32 | .116 | 16 | 55 |
| | | | | 71 | .026 | 31 | .120 | | |
| 3/32 | .0937 | F | .257 | 70 | .028 | 30 | .1285 | 14 | 52 |
| | | | | 69 | .0292 | 29 | .136 | | |
| 7/64 | .1093 | G | .261 | 68 | .031 | 28 | .1405 | 12 | 46 |
| | | | | 67 | .032 | 27 | .144 | | |
| 1/8 | .1250 | H | .266 | 66 | .033 | 26 | .147 | 10 | 38 |
| | | | | 65 | .035 | 25 | .1495 | | |
| 9/64 | .1406 | I | .272 | 64 | .036 | 24 | .152 | 8 | 30 |
| | | | | 63 | .037 | 23 | .154 | | |
| 5/32 | .1562 | J | .277 | 62 | .038 | 22 | .157 | | |
| | | | | 61 | .039 | 21 | .159 | | |
| 11/64 | .1718 | K | .281 | 60 | .040 | 20 | .161 | | |
| | | | | 59 | .041 | 19 | .166 | | |
| 3/16 | .1875 | L | .290 | 58 | .042 | 18 | .1695 | | |
| | | | | 57 | .043 | 17 | .173 | | |
| 13/64 | .2031 | M | .295 | 56 | .0465 | 16 | .177 | | |
| | | | | 55 | .052 | 15 | .180 | | |
| 7/32 | .2187 | | | 54 | .055 | 14 | .182 | | |
| | | | | 53 | .0595 | 13 | .185 | | |
| 15/64 | .2343 | | | 52 | .0635 | 12 | .189 | | |
| | | | | 51 | .067 | 11 | .191 | | |
| 1/4 | .250 | | | 50 | .070 | 10 | .1935 | | |
| | | | | 49 | .073 | 9 | .196 | | |
| | | | | 48 | .076 | 8 | .199 | | |
| | | | | 47 | .0785 | 7 | .201 | | |
| | | | | 46 | .081 | 6 | .204 | | |
| | | | | 45 | .082 | 5 | .2055 | | |
| | | | | 44 | .086 | 4 | .209 | | |
| | | | | 43 | .089 | 3 | .213 | | |
| | | | | 42 | .0935 | 2 | .221 | | |
| | | | | 41 | .096 | 1 | .228 | | |

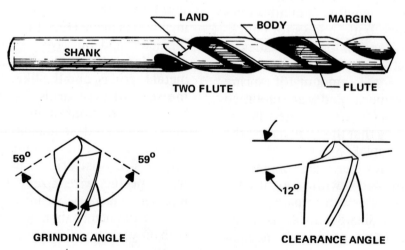

Fig. 15-2. - *Twist drills with cutting angles and cutting-lip clearance.*

used to hold parts in the heat of the torch without damaging the ends of the tweezers. With the direct action tweezers, pressure must be maintained on the tips to hold the object. The self-locking tweezers are spring loaded so that an object can be held without continuous finger pressure.

**Hand vise** — One of the handiest and most versatile tools on the bench is the hand vise, a device with jaws controlled by a large wing nut. A handle permits work to be shifted around for easier filing, shaping, or minor hammering. The hand vise also can be used in combination with self-locking tweezers for holding work as a substitute for a "third-hand."

**Steel block** — Although nearly any kind of steel will do, a simple chunk of steel bar provides a flat surface as a backup for stamping and forging. Sharp and small-radius edges on the block act as a form for bending wire or sheet metal. The steel block can be used instead of the traditional anvil for most forging.

**Ring mandrel** — Heavy and tapered, the mandrel with its circular cross section is essential for forming band rings, ring shanks, and small-diameter wire loops. The ring mandrel is marked to indicate approximate ring size, but these marks should be calibrated against the ring sizer.

**Center punch** — Before any hole is drilled in metal it must be center punched. Otherwise, the twist drill wanders over the surface.

**Bezeling rocker** — This small rocker (Fig. 15-3) simplifies the crimping of bezels around stones. The curved end and the large handle help to concentrate considerable force during the rocking motion. Burnishers can be used for this function, but the bezeling tool applies considerably more force.

**Design stamps** — The two most-used metal stamps are one ground with a straight end and one ground with a curved end. Stamps may be ground from hardened concrete nails and can be used separately or in combination for an infinite variety of designs.

*Fig. 15-3. - Rocker end bezeling tool.*

**Ring sizers** — Ring sizes normally range from 0 through 13½ by "half sizes." Table 18E notes the ring size, inside diameter, and the length of a straight blank necessary to form a circular band for each size. Ring sizers, either plastic or metal, are used to find the ring size that fits a finger comfortably.

**Scribe** — This sharp-pointed metal tool scratches lines on metal that are used as guides for sawing or shearing.

145

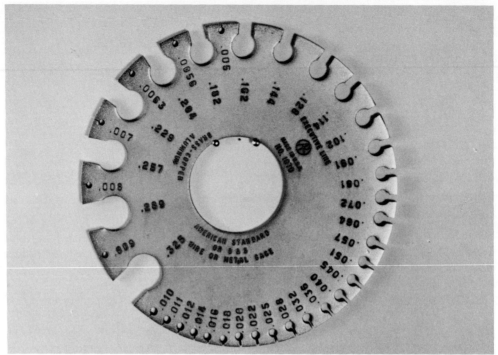

Fig. 15-4. - American Wire Gauge, also known as the Browne & Sharpe wire gauge.

**Steel rule** — The steel rule is used for measuring lengths of wire and metal. A common rule is marked in 64ths of an inch and is 6 inches long.

**Polishing buffs** — Hand polishing buffs are used with tripoli, a next-to-last polishing compound and jeweler's rouge, a final polishing compound. Hand buffs are simply pieces of felt glued to a wood handle. Buffs should be kept separate for use with each compound. While hand buffs can be used, powered buffs will do a better job in considerably less time.

**Felt marker** — A black marking pen with a wide felt tip can be used for two purposes — to coat sheet metal surfaces for marking with a scribe and to darken the cuts left by stamps to highlight a design. The cap should be replaced immediately after each use to keep the felt tip from drying out.

**Flux brush** — The 5-0 artist's brush has an extremely small tip to permit application of only a minimum amount of flux. When wet, the flux brush also simplifies the positioning of tiny bits of cut solder.

**Flattening sheet** — The small rectangle of tough springy metal is used to flatten wire loops after bending and soldering. The flattening sheet is used with the steel block.

## OPTIONAL HAND TOOLS

Tools discussed in this section are useful in crafting jewelry. However, they are not essential, because the same tasks can be accomplished with other tools.

**Parallel-jaw pliers** — In addition to various sizes of the three primary pliers previously noted, parallel-jaw pliers with rectangular or pointed tips simplify tasks that require considerable gripping power. The action of the parallel jaws provides more mechanical advantage for gripping metal or bending pieces together. Other special purpose pliers are available for ring bending, ear-clip adjusting, and bow closing among others.

**Anvil** — A small jeweler's anvil is useful for two purposes — as a base for flat surface hammering and as a horn for bending curves in wire or sheet metal. The usual anvil is

*Fig. 15-5. - Bench vise with soft wood jaws holding ring shank for bezeling with the bent-tip bezeling tool.*

too small to rest by itself on a bench without restraint. One simple way to hold the anvil is to soft-solder it to a chunk of metal.

**Wire gauge** — The Browne & Sharpe wire gauge (Fig. 15-4), also known as the American Wire Gauge, is the standard for measuring wire diameter and sheet metal thickness. See Chapter 18 for tables on wire and sheet metal gauge dimensions. This precision gauge measures wire and metal at the slots cut into the perimeter of the gauge. Each numbered slot identifies the gauge thickness of wire and metal.

**Ring clamp** — This holding device clamps the shank of a ring between jaws at one end by wedging the opposite end. The ring clamp is useful for holding ring mounts during bezeling. A hand vise with soft liners for the jaws can be substituted for the ring clamp.

**Bench vise** — A sturdy machinist's bench vise (Fig. 15-5) solves many holding problems in the crafting of jewelry. The bench vise has a flat forging surface.

**Files** — There is almost no limit to the variety of files available for special tasks in metalcrafting. For classification, files can be divided into three broad categories — smoothing and cutting, needle, and riffle.

Smoothing and cutting files, the kind normally employed for general use, may be rectangular, square, half-round, round, or one of many special shapes. Files also vary in their coarseness of cut. In the American system, files range from coarse to fine as — bastard, second cut, and smooth. In the Swiss system for grading coarseness, No. 0 represents coarse, and numbers range from 0, 1, 2, 3, 4, 5, to 6 — the finest. The file size denotes the length of the actual cutting surface. Therefore, a 6-inch file would have 6 inches of cutting surface regardless of its cross-section shape.

Needle files used in the crafting of jewelry are available in a profusion of shapes, cuts, and sizes. A set of twelve needle files with different shapes will satisfy most requirements for advanced jewelry metalcrafters.

Riffle files are even more specialized than needle files. Rifflers, as they are often called, are files with curved, tapered, or angular tips with only a very small cutting surface or edge. Rifflers are used mainly to reach difficult areas where end or small motion filing is required.

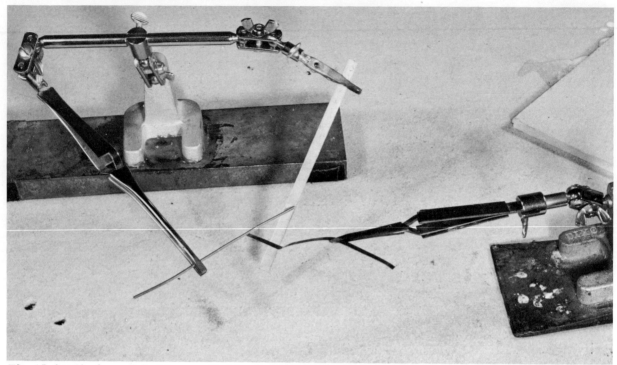

*Fig. 15-6. - Single- and double-arm third-hands for holding work being soldered.*

**Soft-face mallet** — Hammering with a steel hammer may alter design elements on the surface of a piece during shaping. Using one of the soft-face mallets instead of a steel hammer prevents such surface damage. Wood, rawhide, or plastic are of variable softness and can be used for shaping metal without inflicting local damage.

**Bench shear** — Cutting blanks for multiple production can be tiring and time consuming. The lever-operated bench shear is a handy accessory for such tasks.

**Special hammers** — In addition to the flat face and peen of the usual hammers, specific shapes of hammers are available for metalwork. A chasing hammer includes a wide round face for shaping metal directly or for use with chasing tools. Shaping metal with a chasing hammer is little used today because of the time required. Cross-peen hammers have a cylindrical shape rather than the spherical shape of the usual peen end. The cross-peen head is useful for stretching or thinning metal during forging. The planishing hammer has a highly polished surface, and it is used for forging a smooth surface on formed sheet metal. Raising hammers include peen ends that are only slightly rounded and are longer in one direction than the other. Raising is another technique that is little used today — it involves the forming of rounded shapes from flat metal.

**Gravers** — These sharp-ended tools are used by engravers for removing surface metal from selected areas. Engraving is an art by itself and is beyond the scope of basic metalcrafting.

**Third-hand** — This mechanical restraining and holding device is aptly named (Fig. 15-6). Essentially the third-hand includes a heavy support base. A swiveled arm grasps one or two pairs of self-locking tweezers that hold work pieces in a convenient spot. Thus, both hands are free to work on the piece. Self-locking tweezers clamped in the hand vise can be substituted for the third-hand.

**Binocular magnifiers** — Hood mounted to leave hands free, the binocular magnifiers

(Fig. 15-7) can be focused for magnification to aid in working with small details. Magnification is fixed for one set of glasses, but the units may be purchased from 1½ to 4 orders of magnification and with varying focus distances. Similar magnifiers that can be clipped onto regular glass frames are available.

## POWER TOOLS AND ACCESSORIES

Most jewelry craft workers can do almost everything essential with one simple powered unit. An electric motor with a double-ended shaft and a speed of 3500 rpm is ideal for most work. But a single shaft motor with a normal 1750 rpm speed will do the same job though a bit slower. A tapered spindle is attached to each shaft on the motor with the spindle on the left having left-hand threads. Accessories designed for these spindles are readily available. Such accessories include buffs of various sizes and weights, which are ideal for buffing and polishing. One set of buffs should be used for tripoli and another set for rouge. Wire brushes of various diameters available in both steel and brass are also easily mounted on the same spindle. Abrasive wheels with grit bonded in rubber can also be used, and the end of the spindle will hold a cone for buffing the inside of rings for fast cleanup.

The next logical extension beyond this simple powered unit is the installation of a flexible shaft. With an adapter, the flexible shaft can be run off the same motor that is used for the tapered spindle. This unit is not very efficient because the speed is too low, but it is economical, and it does work.

**Powered flexible shaft** — Probably the most popular piece of powered equipment is a small, high-speed motor with a flexible shaft attached (Fig. 15-8). A foot-controlled rheostat for varying the speed is a useful addition. A variety of specialized hand pieces can be used on the same shaft to hold tools. A prime advantage of the powered flexible shaft is that the rotating tool can be manipulated while holding the work piece steady. The powered flexible shaft is only a

*Fig. 15-7. - Headband-type focusing magnifiers.*

device for rotating a small tool at high speed. The usefulness and versatility of the powered flexible shaft depend on the tools available. These are usually divided into three main classes — grinders, polishing heads, and drills.

Grinders may be the metal burr type or the abrasive wheel type. Both types come in an almost unlimited variety of shapes. They are mounted on straight shanks for attachment in the collet chuck of the drill's hand piece.

Polishing heads include smooth abrasive wheels, wheels for holding cylinders or disks of abrasive paper or cloth, and soft, buffing wheels for use with polishing compounds.

Drills or tapered piercing bits drill holes in metal.

**Bench grinder-polisher** — High speed is essential for good power-polishing results, but grinding may require slower speeds. The motor-powered grinder-polisher should, therefore, be equipped with a rheostat that permits varying motor speed. The grinder-polisher should include two usable shaft ends. One end is for mounting muslin buffs for polishing; the opposite end is designed for mounting grinding wheels.

149

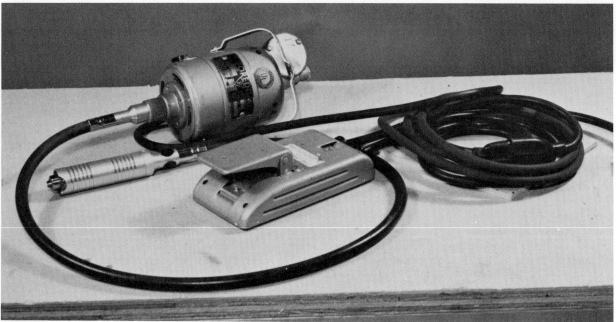

*Fig. 15-8. - Powered flexible shaft with foot-operated rheostat for speed control.*

**Disk polisher** — This tool is mainly a disk sander that can be adapted for silicon carbide, metal-cutting abrasive papers. The abrasive sheet cemented on the disk surface rapidly smooths and rough polishes certain kinds of metalwork.

**Electric soldering machine** — Electric soldering is beyond the scope of this book. But for your information the electric soldering machine uses a carbon pile for extremely rapid heat buildup and is useful for some types of production and specialized repair work.

**Drill press** — A drill press greatly simplifies the task of drilling holes in jewelry metals. The work can be held steady, and the speed of the twist drill reduces the chances of catching a corner and breaking the bit. For jewelry work, the drill press need be no larger than 1/4 inch. Some means for varying spindle speeds should be available. The chuck should close to zero rather than the 5/64-inch minimum closure of many 1/4-inch chucks.

**Electric pickle-pot** — A luxury item for most shops, the electrically heated pot keeps pickling solutions, such as *Sparex No. 2,*

heated at all times. This convenience saves time when many pieces are being chemically cleaned of oxidation, particularly if a piece must be cleaned after several successive steps.

## FABRICATED TOOLS

Certain tools, fixtures, or equipment greatly facilitate the crafting of jewelry. Many of these special items are not available or are excessively expensive. A simple and practical workbench, for example, is easily built at home with simple hand tools. Workbenches are available commercially, but their cost is prohibitive compared to the simple bench top that serves adequately. A number of other special tools are useful and may be built at home or in the shop.

**Workbench** — Figure 15-9 details the construction of the bench with its panel construction. Unbolting eight locations separates the panels for easy storage. The top unbolts from the supporting stand with four bolts. The top size, 18 by 36 inches, offers plenty of working space without occupying excessive floor space. The block

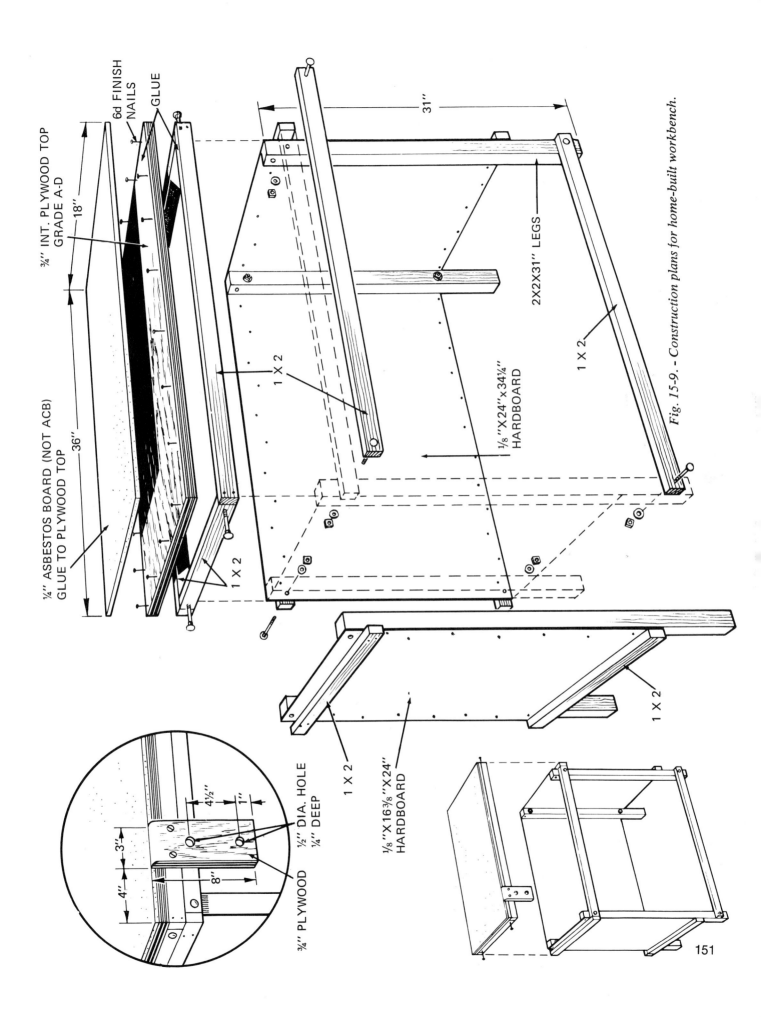

¾" INT. PLYWOOD TOP
GRADE A-D

6d FINISH
NAILS

GLUE

18"

36"

¼" ASBESTOS BOARD (NOT ACB)
GLUE TO PLYWOOD TOP

1 X 2

1 X 2

31"

2X2X31" LEGS

1 X 2

⅛"X24"x34¼"
HARDBOARD

1 X 2

1 X 2

⅛"X16⅜"X24"
HARDBOARD

4½"

1"

3"

4"

8"

½" DIA. HOLE
¼" DEEP

¾" PLYWOOD

*Fig. 15-9. - Construction plans for home-built workbench.*

151

*Fig. 15-10. - The top of this workbench with an asbestos board surface is portable and can be used in any convenient location, such as on top of a kitchen table.*

with a hole, mounted at the front left corner of the bench, supports the end of the ring mandrel. This block rides against the edge of the table when in use, or it can be removed by unscrewing wing nuts from machine screws through the frame. This board may also control the end of a mandrel when winding jump rings. The bench pin can be removed by unscrewing two wing nuts from two machine screws. With 1/4-inch asbestos board (AB) over the full top surface, you can use the torch on any part of it. However, for most work, a smaller, expendable AB block is normally placed on top of the bench for heating. The workbench can be built in two parts — a top surface and a supporting stand. The top surface with its frame of 1 by 2 lumber can be used alone at a temporary location (Fig. 15-10).

**Bench pin** — This thin hardwood board

with a V-slot sawed in the end is used mainly for sawing. The V-slot supports thin metal as it is being cut during the downward, or pull, stroke of the jeweler's saw.

**Silicon carbide board** — This abrasive grinding and polishing board is simply a thin plywood sheet with silicon carbide paper cemented to both sides. The board measures about 2 3/4 by 9 inches. The silicon carbide paper on one side is close-coat 240 grit. The opposite side is 400-grit paper. The silicon carbide paper is waterproof and is intended to be used wet. Therefore, the SC paper should be bonded to the board with waterproof contact cement. These boards do wear out and lose their cutting and polishing effectiveness. SC boards must, therefore, be replaced periodically.

**Heating block** — Expendable blocks of

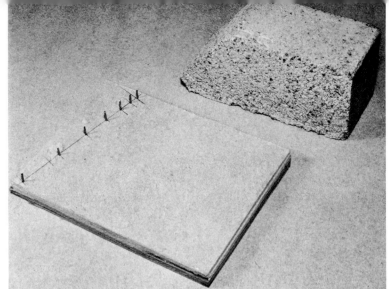

Fig. 15-11. - Soldering fixture,
firebrick weight in background.

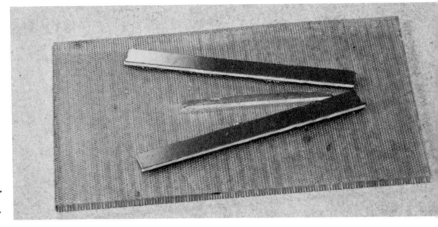

Fig. 15-12. - Holding fixture for
bezeling pins and pendants.

asbestos board protect the bench top where flux or molten metal could disfigure the surface. Heating blocks can be made simply by cementing two pieces of 1/4-inch or 1/8-inch thick asbestos board together with common white household glue. Or you can simply cut squares or rectangles from 1/2-inch asbestos board.

**Soldering fixture** — Small stainless steel pins driven through an asbestos heating block into an underlying piece of plywood make up the soldering fixture (Fig. 15-11). The pins are for holding the thin bezel-strip of metal as it is soldered to a back sheet for mounting gemstones. Stainless steel pins are used because solder does not stick to them. Varying distances separate the pins. The soldering fixture is required in Chapter 3, which introduces the technique of soldering a bezel-strip to a back sheet. The weight for holding the work piece against the pins for soldering is a chunk of firebrick or serpentine.

**Holding fixture for bezeling** — Pin and brooch backs, tie tacks, and other mounts without a ring shank are difficult to hold steady while the thin bezel is crimped around the perimeter of the gemstone. Therefore, a special holding fixture for bezeling is useful (Fig. 15-12). The bezeling fixture is fabricated from plastic because wood deteriorates rapidly with use. The slot down the center of the fixture is for clearance so that pin clasps will not interfere with the bezeling.

**Circular anvil** — When the size of a loop earring exceeds the diameter of the ring mandrel, some other device is needed to aid in hammering the loop into a circle after soldering. Probably the easiest and best large-diameter anvil can be assembled from a junk ball bearing wedged onto a stick of wood (see Chapter 2). The outer surface of the ball bearing case should be unrusted. These cases can usually be picked up for a few cents from a junk auto shop or used auto

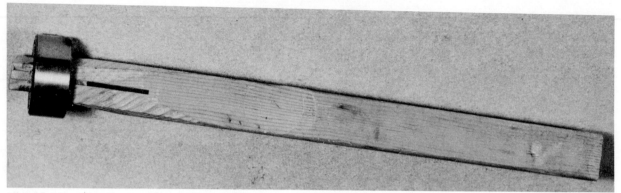

*Fig. 15-13. - Circular anvil made from junk ball-bearing case.*

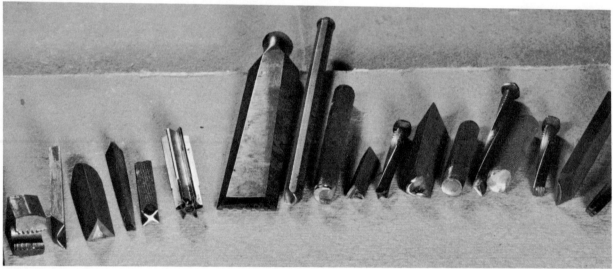

*Fig. 15-14. - Steel stamps ground from a variety of scrap tool steel.*

parts dealer. Mount the bearing on a piece of wood shaped to fit through the inner diameter of the bearing. With the end slotted, a wedge driven into the slot after assembly will hold the bearing to the end of the stick (Fig. 15-13). Clamp the stick to the workbench with a stout C-clamp.

**Steel stamps** — Steel stamps can be ground from miscellaneous chunks and pieces of tool steel (Fig. 15-14). Nearly any discarded piece of tool steel can be converted into a special stamp to build a varied repertoire of designs.

**Bezeling tool** — The rocker-type bezeling tool (see page 145) requires considerable strength if it is to be used properly. A modified screwdriver with a bent-over tip may be used with the 4-ounce hammer to achieve the same results as the rocker-type bezeling tool. The bent tip of the screwdriver is placed against the bezel edge. A tap with the hammer crimps the metal against the stone. This action is repeated around the perimeter of the stone. The bent-tip bezeling tool is introduced in Chapter 5.

**Poker** — The pointed poker is an aid in soldering. It is fabricated by brazing a looped-end wire onto a special alloy tip or inserting a 4-inch length of titanium alloy wire into a wood handle. The tip of the poker retains its strength in the heat of the propane torch and does not stick to solder.

**Bending jigs** — Wire can be formed into an unlimited variety of designs for earrings, pins, and pendants. However, when two articles of exactly the same design are needed, as for two earrings in a matched pair, bending two wires exactly alike can be difficult. Bending jigs can be fabricated by driving nails into a wood block to define a pattern (Fig. 15-15). For some jigs a piece of plastic or wood can be cut to a shaped contour for defining large-radius curves or complex shapes. Bending jigs also simplify large quantity production of bent-wire designs.

**Prong-bending pliers** — Prongs are defined as projections from a mounting that are used to restrain a gemstone and are bent into place *after* the stone is in place. Some stones, such as the pearl, will be damaged if the stone is used as a fulcrum for applying force to bend the prong. Therefore, special prong-bending pliers are needed to apply force to the tip of the prongs without touching the stone. Wide-jaw pliers are ground with a curve on the inside of the upper jaw (Fig. 15-16). In use, the moving jaw forces the tapered tip of the prong into a curve that contacts the stone only at the point of restraint.

## HEATING TOOLS AND ACCESSORIES

Crafting metal jewelry with or without the addition of gemstones requires heat for soldering and annealing. Techniques in this book require no hot bending or hot shaping of metal. Therefore, the propane torch that generates about 2000° F., provides enough heat to bring metals to soldering temperature and to melt very hard silver solder. The tools and equipment necessary for these tasks are described in this section.

**Propane torch** — The most practical all-purpose heating equipment is a torch tip attached to a propane fuel cylinder, which is widely available. The torch tip should burn with a reducing flame so that the flame produces a minimum of oxidation on the metals during heating. An oxidizing

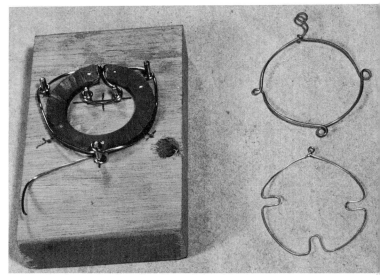

*Fig. 15-15. - Wire-bending jig at left with two sample bent wires.*

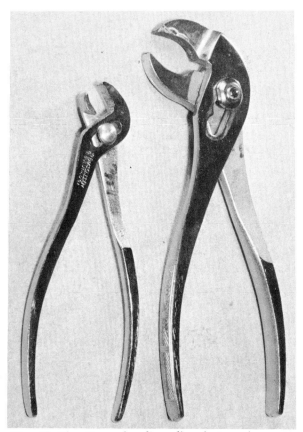

*Fig. 15-16. - Prong-bending pliers in two sizes.*

155

flame in contrast to a reducing flame creates considerable problems in soldering.

**Fuel tank and tube torch** — A torch connected to a remote fuel cylinder will reduce weight and cost, when beginning production metalcrafting. A torch tip can be connected to a fuel cylinder with a flexible, pressure-tight hose. The fine control valve at the torch tip controls the heat of the flame. The valve at the tank is turned off when work stops for the day. For long periods of handling, the weight of the fuel cylinder, even when cradled on or under the arm, becomes uncomfortable. The lightweight torch tip at the end of the light tubing reduces overall weight to a fraction of the tip plus cylinder weight. For large-scale use, the tubing may be connected to a large refillable propane fuel tank. Tubing and tank can be purchased or rented from propane fuel suppliers.

**Oxygen-acetylene outfit** — When metalcrafting requirements exceed the temperature attainable with the propane torch assembly (about 2000°F.), the next step up is to an oxygen-acetylene system. For example, if hot steel is to be brazed or shaped, temperatures higher than those attainable with a simple propane torch are required, and you will need an oxygen-acetylene outfit. Techniques involving an oxygen-acetylene outfit are beyond the scope of this book.

**Charcoal heating block** — Normally an asbestos board block is used when soldering, annealing, or fusing jewelry materials. However, the AB blocks reflect the heat. For certain kinds of work, such as fusing metals or in free-form sculpturing, a charcoal block is needed to absorb and collect heat to aid in building temperatures to a high point. Three types of charcoal or carbon blocks can be used — charcoal, sintered carbon, and wood.

Charcoal blocks, chemically treated to prevent flaming, are inexpensive and readily available. However, these blocks will glow under a flame and will gradually burn away, although at a much slower rate than ordinary charcoal used for heating. Although

*Fig. 15-17. - Charred surface of a hardwood tree trunk is used as a charcoal block.*

these blocks can be used in metalcrafting jewelry, they are not too practical, because they are used up rapidly.

Sintered carbon blocks are not true charcoal. Carbon is compressed and prepared in a furnace so that it can be used specifically for metalcrafting. Sintered carbon blocks last through many uses, but they tend to dust off and are dirty.

Wood blocks cut from green limbs or kept damp by sprinkling water on them are inexpensive and quite practical (Fig. 15-17). The burned fissures and cavities can be used to shape free-form sculptured jewelry. A chunk of green tree trunk or a large limb is best. A chunk of 4 by 4 or 6 by 6 lumber cut across the end grain is a satisfactory substitute if tree chunks are not available for wood blocks. If the wood is dry, sprinkle the end with water before each use.

**Heating frame** — Typical heating frames consist of an iron ring supported off the bench on three steel legs. A heavy iron mesh across the top of the frame supports work to be heated from underneath, mainly pieces to be sweat soldered. The heating frame also supports the beaker of pickling solution to be heated with the propane torch. A satisfactory, low-cost substitute for the usual heating frame can be made from a

156

No. 10-size food can, such as the can used for holding three pounds of coffee. After cutting out one end of the can, a number of nail holes are punched in the center of the top. The punched holes should be close together, but not so close that the metal between them will burn away after a few uses. Also, the metal between the holes needs to be strong enough to support the beaker of pickling solution. On one side of the can, use the metal shears to cut away a portion of the metal to provide access for the torch tip so that heat can be applied to the underside of the punched-hole top.

## WAX WORKING TOOLS

Building or modifying wax models for casting jewelry requires special tools that fall roughly into two broad categories — those used for melting or cooling the wax, and metal tools used for shaping the wax.

### Heat Sources

**Alcohol lamp** — The traditional source of heat for metal tools is the alcohol lamp fueled through a wick. Tools used with the lamp are called "lamp" tools. Many wax carvers prefer the alcohol lamp to an electrical heating unit because it provides a variable source of heat that does not overheat the tools when properly used. Production jewelers use a gas burning lamp instead.

**Electrical heat units** — Controlled electrical heat offers many advantages over the alcohol lamp in heating metal tools. First, electric heat can be controlled precisely. Second, electric heat can be applied continuously through a heating element in an insulated handle. Third, and this is the most important characteristic of all, the unit permits continuous heating of tools and using of wax instead of the bit-by-bit procedure when using the alcohol lamp. Electrical heat is supplied by a resistance that can be controlled simply by turning a dial (Fig. 15-18). The working tools are screwed or slipped into the end of the heating element that also serves as a handle. A two-element heating unit permits two

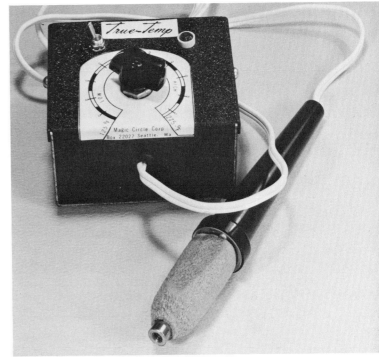

*Fig. 15-18. - A variable heat control with a handle that accepts a variety of wax carving and build-up tools.*

kinds of tips to be kept hot for use in working with wax.

### Wax Carving Tools

**Lamp tools** — Hand tools for working with wax resemble those used by dentists. A variety of end shapes is available (Fig. 15-19). These tools are designed to be used with an alcohol lamp for welding, cutting, carving, and patching. Transferring wax bit by bit tends to extend the time necessary for developing the wax model.

**Wax-well tools** — Carving and embossing tools developed expressly for wax carving include a slot, or a "well," for storing wax. Tools that continue to deliver wax decrease the time for building wax models. These tools (Fig. 15-20) come in a variety of shapes and sizes.

**Electrically heated tips** — Two types of tips that fit into electrically heated handles

157

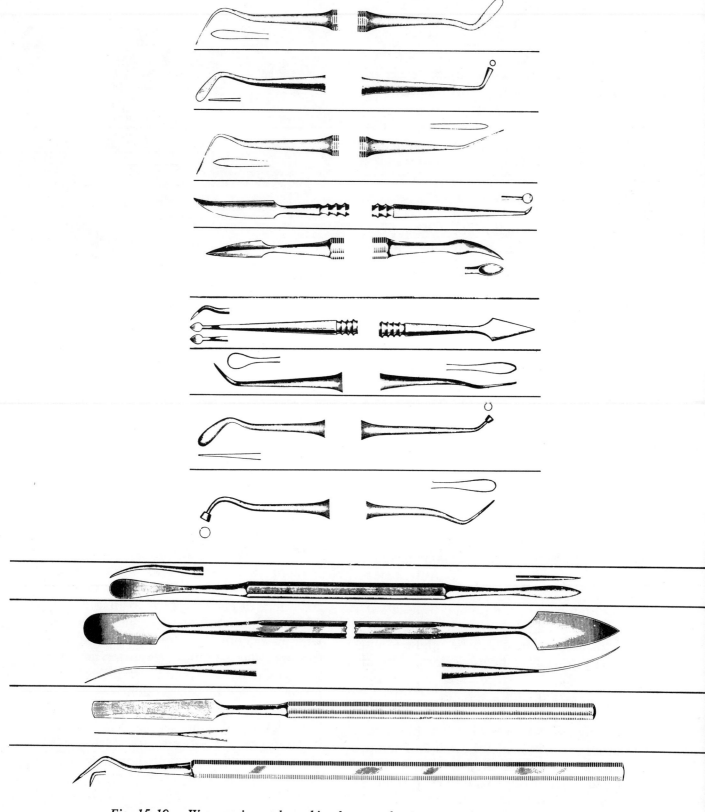

*Fig. 15-19. - Wax carving and patching lamp tools. Courtesy, Romanoff Rubber Co., Inc., New York, New York.*

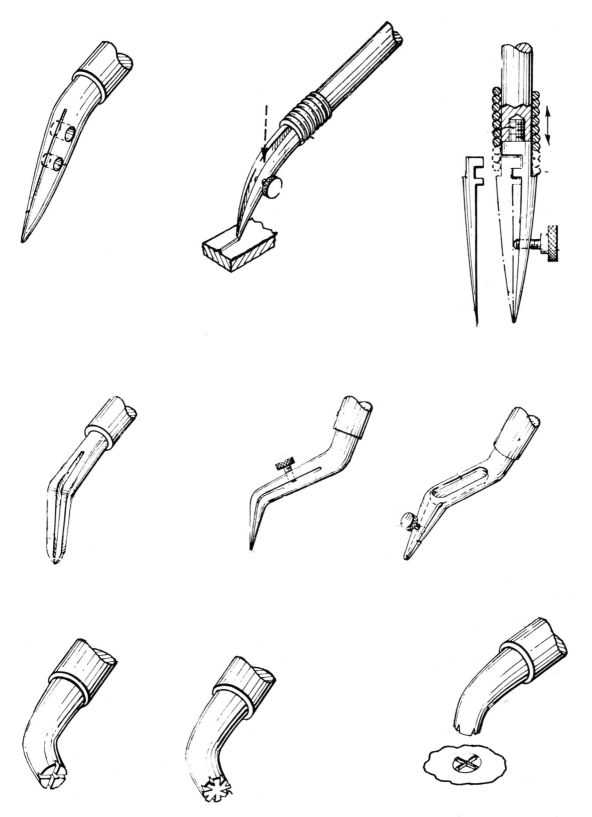

*Fig. 15-20. - Lamp tools with built-in wells for wax. Patents Pending, Magic Circle Corporation, Seattle, Washington.*

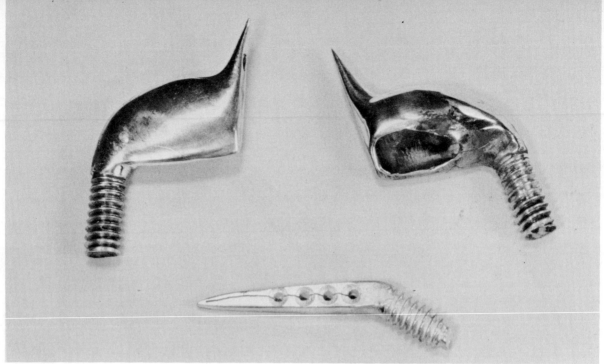

Fig. 15-21. - Two views of camel wax
carving tool (top). Note well for heating
wax. Barracuda tip (bottom) includes four
small wells for wax. These tips screw into
handles heated by controlled
electrical current.

simplify the various functions of carving,
building, and smoothing wax. The camel
(Fig. 15-21) is a tool expressly designed for
free-form building (see Chapter 12). The
camel fits into the end of an electrically
heated handle. A well continuously supplies melted wax through a tip that functions much like a fountain pen. When
heated to the right temperature, the wax
will not drip or flow unless the tip is in
contact with a surface that pulls it from the
well through the hole to the tip. A "barracuda" tip (Fig. 15-21) is designed expressly
for adding on wax, either in modifying a
model or in sculpturing. The barracuda
tip feeds wax to the tip through a slot cut
through the metal. Both the camel and the
barracuda tips fit into the same electrically
heated handle.

**Accessories**

**Bench cooling fan** — A small 5- or 6-inch
diameter electrically driven fan reduces the
amount of blowing necessary to cool wax
during placement either with lamp tools or
with electrically heated tips. The fan should
operate quietly and blow only a relatively
small volume of air. One of the fans sal-

vaged from a television chassis or slide or
movie projector works quite effectively.
A foot-controlled switch permits turning
the fan on or off without interfering with
the wax work.

**Wax pot** — Melted wax maintained
automatically at the desired temperature
with an electrically controlled heating unit
saves time by keeping the wax just above
the melting point. A simple wax pot may
also be constructed for use with an alcohol
lamp. The heat of the wax pot can be
controlled by varying the height of the flame
and/or the flame's distance from the pot.

**Thermometer** — A water-immersible
thermometer with a temperature range of
80 to 120° F. is handy for testing the
temperature of water used for warming the
wax to be bent.

**Stepped ring mandrel** — This lightweight
ring mandrel is turned in flat steps rather
than tapered and mounted from one end
on a rack. The stepped ring mandrel is
used as a base for forming ring shanks in
wax (see Chapter 12). Stepped ring mandrels are available in full sizes or in full and
half-size models.

# materials

CRAFTSWORKERS DEVELOP A TRUE LOVE affair with their materials. Regardless of whether the basic material is slick and goopy clay being shaped with slurry-coated fingers or 18-karat gold being fashioned with the tiniest of burins or rifflers, the craftsman knows and understands his materials intimately. By developing a working rapport with his materials, the jewelry craftsman can manipulate them skillfully and creatively.

Many of the finest jewelry makers work with only one material, because they feel they cannot develop the necessary rapport with more than one material. A jewelry worker, for example, may execute all designs in sterling silver. The worker knows and understands what he can do with sterling — and what he can't do. Attempts to work with any of the other common materials would be like trying to speak in a foreign language with all the idiomatic flair of his native tongue.

Other jewelry workers learn to create with more than one material. They revel in the variety and differences among their materials. From this variety of experience comes a wide range of skills.

Beginning craftsmen in jewelry should experiment with many materials before settling down to one or possibly two alternative materials. The beginner should develop a feel for the creative expressiveness of each material. Only by actually working with a material can a crafts worker appreciate its nuances and unique characteristics.

The purpose of this chapter is to introduce the basic qualities of materials useful in crafting jewelry. As a summary, Table 16A compares the relative properties of the metals most used by craftsmen for making jewelry.

## METALS

**Gold** — Long the established king of jewelry materials, gold is extremely malleable; it can be hammered into sheets as thin as 1/300,000 of an inch thick. Gold is also extremely ductile; one ounce can be drawn

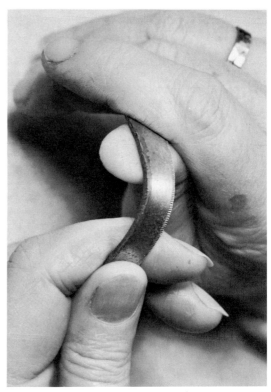

*The variety of jewelry materials is seemingly unlimited. The type of material you select and the way in which you use it will give every piece you make an interesting and unique quality.*

into a single wire thirty-five miles long and much finer than a human hair. Gold's long reign as the premium jewelry metal is partially due to its "noble" characteristics; that is, its resistance to oxidation and most common chemicals. Gold can be dissolved, however, in a mixture of hydrochloric and nitric acids.

Karat gold is alloyed gold with the number of karats representing the gold content. On the karat scale, 24-karat gold is pure — also termed "fine."

However, pure gold is relatively soft and wears away rapidly in jewelry. So alloys of gold have been developed for several reasons. First, alloys cost less. Second, alloys

## TABLE 16A—Characteristics of Jewelry Metals*

| Metal or Alloy | Melting Temperature Fahrenheit | Oxidizes | Work-Hardens | After Annealing | Heat Conductivity | Flux | Solder |
|---|---|---|---|---|---|---|---|
| Platinum | 3224 | At very elevated temp. | Very easily | Very springy | Fair | Special | Platinum |
| Gold—Fine | 1945 | Not at all | Almost none | Soft | Good | | |
| 18-karat | 1700 | With great difficulty | With difficulty | Fairly soft | Good | ↑ | Gold |
| 14-karat | 1615 | With difficulty | Easily | Springy | Fair | | |
| 10-karat | 1665 | With difficulty | Very easily | Very springy | Poor | Borax or | |
| Silver—Fine | 1762 | With difficulty | With difficulty | Dead soft | Excellent | "Self- | |
| Sterling | 1640 | Easily | Easily | Dead soft | Excellent | Pickling" | Silver |
| Coin | 1615 | Very easily | Very easily | Springy | Excellent | ↓ | |
| Brass—Hard | 1800 | Very easily | Very easily | Soft | Good | | |
| Soft | 1706 | Very easily | Easily | Dead soft | Good | Borax, heavy mix, consistency of light cream | Silver |
| Bronze | 1920 | With difficulty | Very easily | Springy | Good | | or |
| Copper | 1981 | Very easily | Easily | Dead soft | Excellent | | Brass |
| Nickel silver (nonferrous) | 2030 | Only above approx. 1000° | Very easily | Fairly soft | Fair | | |
| Monel | 2460 | Only at temp. above 1500° | Instantly | Very spring | Poor | Special | Special |
| Pewter | 475 | With difficulty | Not at all | Dead soft | Fair | Pewter | Pewter |
| Aluminum | 1232 | Very easily | Depends on alloy | Depends on alloy | Excellent | Aluminum | Aluminum |
| Steel | 2800 | Very easily | Very easily | Fairly springy | Fair | Brazing | Silver or Brass |

*Adjectives used are relative to metals listed rather than to an "absolute."

*The variety of jewelry materials is seemingly unlimited. The type of material you select and the way in which you use it will give every piece you make an interesting and unique quality.*

are harder than gold. Third, karat golds resist abrasion. The gold content of alloys is normally expressed in karats. Thus, 14-karat gold contains 14 parts of gold and 10 parts of other alloying elements. Metals alloyed with gold vary according to the purpose of the alloy. One property controlled by the alloying element is color. Gold alloyed with silver tends to be greenish in tone and is prized for antique jewelry. White golds result from nickel and zinc in the alloy. An exceptionally strong, but expensive, white gold is an alloy of gold and platinum. A gold alloy very nearly the color of fine gold contains silver, copper, and zinc plus gold. Reddish golds contain considerable copper. Melting points for the various alloys of gold are noted in Table 16B.

Fine gold jewelry is often fabricated from 18-karat gold, although this alloy tends to be soft. More popular are the 14-karat golds in various colors. Alloys with less than 10 of 24 parts cannot be stamped as gold. Even 10-karat golds are less than half gold. White gold alloyed with platinum and/or palladium is very strong and is most often used in fine, delicate mountings for diamonds where the whiteness of the metal harmonizes with the stones. One thing to remember when working with gold is its density. An 18-karat gold ring, for example, weighs 50 percent more than a similar ring crafted in sterling silver. Depending on the alloying elements, a 14-karat gold ring would be about 25 percent heavier than sterling. The price of gold relative to the price of silver, about ten to one, has varied very little over the past 2000 years.

Gold fill, or rolled gold plate, is a relatively low-cost form of gold. To make this product, a thin layer of gold is rolled on the outside of a base metal. Gold fill looks like gold because it is gold on the outside. However, designs that expose the edges must be avoided. Otherwise, the base metal shows in a contrasting color, like the filling in a sliced sandwich. When buying gold fill, two figures are important — surface thickness and karat content of the gold. For example, 1/20 — 14-K gold fill means that the surface layer is 1/20th of the weight and the gold alloy of that layer is 14 karats. Overall, the metal is .7 karat gold.

**Silver** — Probably the most popular of the precious metals for jewelry crafting is silver or one of the silver alloys. Pure silver, also known as "fine" silver, is very white in color and, like gold, very malleable and ductile. Fine silver is soft and easily formed. It is used frequently for the thin edges of bezels. To improve its hardness and durability, silver is also available in various alloys. The most popular of the alloys is sterling.

Sterling silver is an alloy of silver containing 92.5 percent silver and 7.5 percent copper. The small percentage of copper adds strength with only a minor effect on workability and color. Sterling is a term that denotes high quality and fine silverware. Particularly in England, "sterling" symbolizes quality. Sterling is also known as "925 fine" because it contains 925 parts of silver out of 1000. The relative price scale for jewelry metals (Fig. 16-1) places sterling in the popular but still expensive class of materials.

Coin silver contains 90 percent silver and 10 percent copper. The added copper increases hardness compared to sterling. Coin silver is less popular among jewelry craftsmen than the more readily available sterling silver.

Other silver alloys may contain varying percentages of silver. For centuries, Mexican and southwest Indians have worked silver. These talented craftsmen learned their techniques from the Spanish, who formerly smelted their own silver. Alloys were far from standardized. There is still no common standard for Mexican or Indian silver, but most of the work contains at least 90 percent silver.

The melting point for silver depends on the alloy. Fine silver melts at 1762° F., sterling at 1640° F., and coin silver at 1615° F.

## TABLE 16B –Characteristics of Gold Alloys

| Gold Alloy | Melting Point | | Specific Gravity |
| --- | --- | --- | --- |
| | Fahrenheit (°F) | Centigrade (°C) | |
| 24k (Fine gold) | 1945.4 | 1063 | 19.4 |
| 18k Green | 1810 | 988 | 15.9 |
| 18k Yellow | 1700 | 927 | 15.6 |
| 18k White | 1730 | 943 | 14.6 |
| 18k Red | 1655 | 902 | 15.2 |
| 14k Green | 1765 | 963 | 14.2 |
| 14k Yellow | 1615 | 879 | 13.1 |
| 14k White | 1825 | 996 | 12.6 |
| 14k Red | 1715 | 935 | 13.3 |
| 10k Green | 1580 | 860 | 11.0 |
| 10k Yellow | 1665 | 907 | 11.6 |
| 10k White | 1975 | 1079 | 11.1 |
| 10k Red | 1760 | 960 | 11.6 |

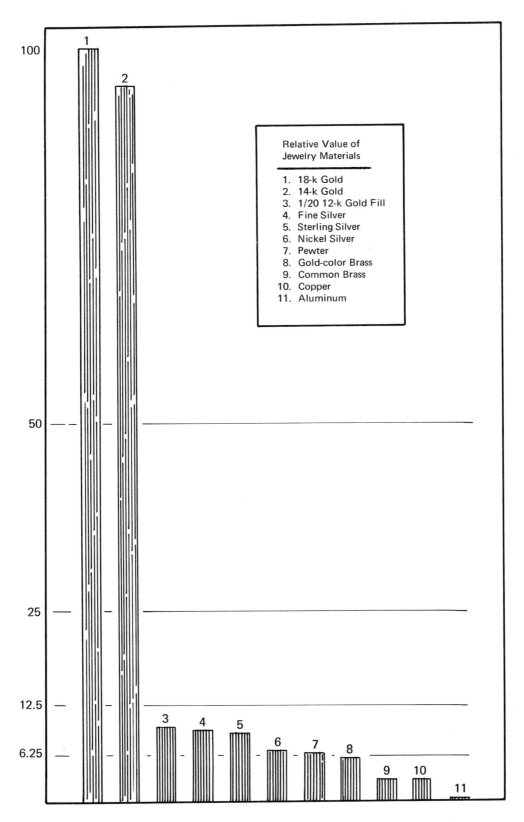

Relative Value of
Jewelry Materials

1. 18-k Gold
2. 14-k Gold
3. 1/20 12-k Gold Fill
4. Fine Silver
5. Sterling Silver
6. Nickel Silver
7. Pewter
8. Gold-color Brass
9. Common Brass
10. Copper
11. Aluminum

*Fig. 16-1. - Comparative cost of metals by unit measure. Values shown
are approximate.*

One of the main reasons for the popularity of sterling silver among jewelry craftsmen is the variety of shapes and sizes of stock materials available. Sterling wire is available in round, half-round, square, and triangular shapes. Many gauges of sheet sterling are available. Specialized shapes, such as round tubes, various depths of bezel wire, and other odd pieces simplify certain tasks. See Fig. 16-2 for a comparison of sizes, shapes, and gauges.

Most sterling findings are now rhodium plated. The coating prevents their being "antiqued." Lacquered sterling findings can be stripped of the lacquer. With the coating off, these findings can be antiqued like any sterling.

**Copper** — Low cost is a popular attribute of copper, and many popular pieces of jewelry are crafted from it. Copper melts at 1981° F. In its pure state, it is highly workable, yet sturdy. A small amount of arsenic, as little as 0.2 percent, increases copper's resistance to abrasion. Copper work hardens readily and must be annealed often if forged or hammered extensively. Copper tarnishes readily either from oxidation or from contact with sulfur. If the true reddish color of copper is desired, a clear surface coating of clear lacquer or other transparent sprays must be applied to protect the copper from tarnish. See Chapter 17.

Copper is frequently used for practicing techniques. It is a jewelry metal that is doubly useful. If the jewelry piece turns out well, it can be worn or given as a gift with confidence. However, if you muff a piece of jewelry with copper, the cost of the material is so low you can throw it away without feeling extravagant. Copper is one of the few jewelry materials that cannot be cast. One word of caution: Copper alloys containing beryllium should be avoided because they may be quite toxic when heated.

**Brass** — Another jewelry metal popular for practice and finished pieces is brass. The term brass is not definitive because, unlike gold, silver, or copper, there is no such thing as pure brass. All brasses are alloys. Most common brasses are alloys of copper and zinc in various percentages. A popular brass for jewelry crafting contains 90 percent copper and 10 percent zinc. This reddish brass closely resembles gold in color. A stronger alloy of brass contains 70 percent copper and 30 percent zinc, but this alloy is little used for jewelry.

Jewelry brass works and handles very much like silver. Melting temperature for jewelry brass is about 1912° F. Brass is not as malleable as copper and considerably less malleable than silver or gold. However, brass can be filed, cut, or stamped easily. It does not respond to "antiquing" with sulfur like sterling silver or copper. Chemical treatments to color brass or to retard discoloration are described in Chapter 17.

**Bronze** — Although seldom used for small jewelry work, bronze closely resembles brass in many of its properties. Bronze is also an alloy — copper and tin primarily. However, there are many other alloys of bronze, such as phosphor bronze, aluminum bronze, and others. Bronze is especially favored for small castings.

**Nickel alloys** — Several alloys of nickel are popular and useful for crafting jewelry. Nickel silver, sometimes termed German silver, actually contains no silver. Nickel silver has little of the fine, quality look of sterling silver, being much glossier and brighter in appearance. Common nickel silver alloys normally contain 60 percent copper, 20 percent nickel, and 20 percent zinc. Exact percentages vary among manufacturers. Nickel silver melts around 2030° F., depending on the exact alloy, and its workability, particularly its ability to be soldered, closely resembles sterling silver. Some suppliers furnish a nickel silver containing 18 percent nickel and 82 percent iron. This ferrous nickel alloy is quite different from nonferrous nickel silver and is little used for jewelry.

Monel is a grayish nickel alloy with considerably more nickel than nickel silver. Monel contains about 69 percent nickel,

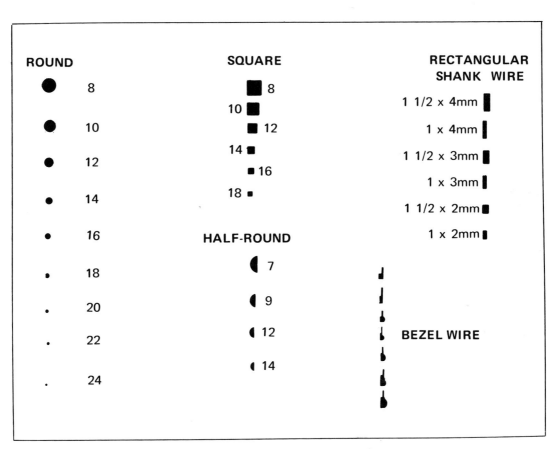

*Fig. 16-2. - Cross-section shapes of wire and various special products useful in fabricating jewelry. Numbers are gauge sizes.*

167

29 percent copper, 1 percent iron, and trace amounts of manganese, silicon, sulfur, and carbon. Monel resists oxidation and remains bright. It also work hardens readily and is difficult to form for that reason. Monel melts at 2460° F.

**Pewter** — This low-melting-point alloy of lead and tin melts as an amorphous mass at about 500° F. Pewter is quite soft and was formerly used much more than it is today. Actually, the alloy content of pewter varies widely. Modern alloys include copper and antimony in addition to the traditional lead and tin. Olden-day craftsmen were able to form pewter by *repousé* and smithing because of its soft and easily formed consistency. However, pewter lacks strength and must be soldered with low-strength soft solders that also contain lead and tin. Some pewters should not be used to hold food or drink, or lead poisoning can result.

**Platinum** — Like gold and silver, platinum is highly malleable and ductile but is more expensive than either gold or silver. Platinum is seldom used in craft jewelry because of its cost. Platinum is most often used for setting diamonds where platinum's strength, color, and workability are more important than its cost in relation to the gemstone. Platinum is also very dense with a specific gravity of 21.45, making it about 1.6 times as heavy as sterling silver. Platinum has a very high melting point, 3224° F. It can be soldered or welded with strong materials to take advantage of its own strength and hardness.

**Aluminum** — At the opposite end of the density scale from platinum there is aluminum. Though often scorned for jewelry, today aluminum has been used with some of the crown jewels of Europe. Common aluminum alloys contain small amounts of copper, silicon, magnesium, zinc, and occasionally iron. When used for rings, bracelets, and pins, the lightness of aluminum connotes a lack of substance for some wearers. Aluminum can be particularly useful where weight is a problem, such as

with earrings. Massive danglers can be fabricated from very thin aluminum sheet or wire without exceeding the weight limit for earrings.

However, aluminum presents two problems for jewelry crafters. First, it is difficult to solder. Special aluminum solders and fluxes must be used. The problem of soldering can be solved most easily by avoiding aluminum. Jewelry designs in aluminum should be joined mechanically with jump rings, figure-8 links, or chains.

The second problem with aluminum is that in pure form it bends easily, due to its low modulus of elasticity. Once bent, aluminum can be difficult to straighten, particularly with very thin sheet materials. Some alloys of aluminum will break rather than bend.

**Steel** — As an alloy of iron, steel is seldom considered as a jewelry material. Steel does not solder well without the use of special fluxes. With a melting point around 2800° F., steel is hard to work and is difficult to anneal after work hardening. Stainless steel is an alloy of iron with about 18 percent chromium and 8 percent nickel. It can be brightly polished and remain bright. It is difficult to solder without special fluxes. Stainless steel, however, is springy and resists bending or denting much more than aluminum in very thin sheets. So stainless steel can be used for large area danglers on earrings without exceeding weight limits. Stainless steel is much easier to cut with shears than with a saw. Weights of jewelry metals in sheet and wire form are detailed in Table 16C.

## GEMSTONES

Gems can be valuable, like the diamond, or simply pretty and eye-catching, like many varieties of quartz. Man's fascination with exquisite gemstones transcends recorded history. Lapidaries, from the Latin *lapis* meaning stone, earnestly search out and polish or shape an almost endless variety of gems and gemlike stones. In addition to the

## TABLE 16C-Sheet Metal Thickness and Wire Diameter

B & S (Brown and Sharpe) and American Wire Gage (AWG) are the same and are used interchangeably to measure the thickness of nonferrous alloy sheets and the diameter of wires. One gage does both.

| B & S Gage | Thickness | |
|---|---|---|
| | Inches | Millimeters |
| 0 | .325 | 8.25 |
| 2 | .258 | 6.54 |
| 4 | .204 | 5.19 |
| 6 | .162 | 4.12 |
| 8 | .128 | 3.26 |
| 10 | .102 | 2.59 |
| 12 | .081 | 2.05 |
| 14 | .064 | 1.63 |
| 16 | .051 | 1.29 |
| 18 | .040 | 1.02 |
| 20 | .032 | .81 |
| 22 | .025 | .64 |
| 24 | .020 | .51 |
| 26 | .016 | .40 |
| 28 | .013 | .32 |
| 30 | .010 | .25 |
| 32 | .008 | .20 |
| 34 | .006 | .16 |

*B & S (Browne and Sharpe) and American Wire Gauge (AWG) are the same and are used interchangeably to measure the thickness of nonferrous alloy sheets and the diameter of wires. One gauge does both.*

*materials*

## TABLE 16D–Characteristics of Gemstones

### TRANSPARENT STONES

| Color and Common Name | Hardness (Mohs No.) | Specific Gravity | Color and Common Name | Hardness (Mohs No.) | Specific Gravity |
|---|---|---|---|---|---|
| **Red** | | | **Yellow** | | |
| Alexandrite* | 8.5 | 3.5 | Beryl | 8.0 | 2.6 |
| Garnet | 7-7.5 | 3.4-4.3 | Citrine | 7.0 | 2.8 |
| Almadite | 7.5 | 3.4 | Sapphire | 9.0 | 4.0 |
| Pyrope | 7.5 | 4.0 | Topaz (true) | 8.0 | 3.5 |
| Ruby | 9.0 | 4.0 | Zircon | 7.5 | 4.4 |
| Spinel | 8.0 | 3.6 | **Pink** | | |
| Zircon | 7.5 | 4.4 | Morganite | 8.0 | 2.6 |
| **Green** | | | Rubellite | 7-7.5 | 3.1 |
| Alexandrite** | 8.5 | 3.5 | Ruby | 9.0 | 4.0 |
| Demantoid | | | Topaz (true) | 8.0 | 3.5 |
| garnet | 7.0 | 4.0 | **Purple** | | |
| Emerald | 9.0 | 4.0 | Amethyst | 7.0 | 2.8 |
| Spinel | 8.0 | 3.6 | **Clear** | | |
| Tourmaline | 7-7.5 | 3.1 | Diamond | 10.0 | 3.5 |
| Peridot | 6.5-7 | 3.4 | Fabulite | 6.5 | 5.1 |
| **Blue** | | | Quartz (crystal) | 7.0 | 2.8 |
| Aquamarine | 9.0 | 4.0 | Spinel | 8.0 | 3.6 |
| Sapphire | 9.0 | 4.0 | Zircon | 7.5 | 4.4 |
| Spinel | 8.0 | 3.6 | **Brown** | | |
| Zircon | 7.5 | 4.4 | Smoky quartz | 7.0 | 2.8 |

### TRANSLUCENT STONES

| Color and Common Name | Hardness | Specific Gravity | Color and Common Name | Hardness | Specific Gravity |
|---|---|---|---|---|---|
| **Red** | | | **Yellow** | | |
| Agate or Carnelian | 7.0 | 2.8 | Agate | 7.0 | 2.8 |
| Ruby (aster) | 9.0 | 4.0 | Chrysoberyl | 8.5 | 3.5 |
| Rubelite | | | Topaz | 8.0 | 3.5 |
| tourmaline | 7-7.5 | 2.9-3.2 | **Pink** | | |
| **Green** | | | Rose quartz | 7.0 | 2.8 |
| Agate | 7.0 | 2.8 | **Brown** | | |
| Chrysoprase | 7.0 | 2.8 | Agate | 7.0 | 2.8 |
| Jadeite & | | 3.3 | **White** | | |
| Nephrite | 6-7.0 | 2.9 | Agate or | | |
| Tourmaline | 7-7.5 | 2.9-3.2 | Chalcedony | 7.0 | 2.8 |
| **Blue** | | | Moonstone | 6.0 | 2.6 |
| Saphhire (aster) | 9.0 | 4.0 | Opal | 6.0 | 2.2 |
| Chalcedony | 7.0 | 2.8 | **Black** | | |
| | | | Obsidian | 7.0 | 2.8 |

### OPAQUE STONES

| Color and Common Name | Hardness | Specific Gravity | Color and Common Name | Hardness | Specific Gravity |
|---|---|---|---|---|---|
| **Red** | | | **Yellow** | | |
| Agate | 7.0 | 2.8 | Agate | 7.0 | 2.8 |
| Jasper | 7.0 | 2.8 | Amber | 2-2.5 | |
| **Green** | | | Beryl (golden) | 8.0 | 2.6 |
| Agate | 7.0 | 2.8 | **Brown** | | |
| Bloodstone | 7.0 | 2.8 | Agate | 7.0 | 2.8 |
| Cat's eye | 8.5 | 3.5 | Tiger's eye | 7.0 | 2.8 |
| Jadeite | 6.5-7.0 | 3.3 | **Black** | | |
| Labradorite | 6-7.0 | | Agate | 7.0 | 2.8 |
| Turquoise | 6-7.0 | 2.7 | Hematite | 6.0 | |
| **Blue** | | | Obsidian | 5.0 | |
| Lapis Lazuli | 5.5 | 2.85 | Onyx | 7.0 | 2.8 |
| Pearl | 2.5-3.5 | 2.6 | Nephrite | 6-7.0 | 2.9 |
| Turquoise | 6-7.0 | 2.7 | | | |
| **Pink** | | | | | |
| Coral | 3.5 | | | | |
| Pearl | 2.5-3.5 | 2.6 | | | |
| Rhodonite | | | | | |

*By artificial light
**By daylight

NOTE: A number of gemstones are noted under more than one color as variations of the basic mineral.

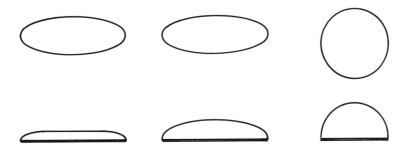

*Fig. 16-3. - Shapes of cabochon stones.*

true gems and minerals, there are many imitation gemstones made from glass or plastic.

A number of systems for classifying gemstones have developed over the years. One is the separation of precious from semiprecious stones. Another system classifies gemstones according to hardness, using Mohs' system. Color, origin (whether true minerals or from animal or vegetable beginnings), and crystalline structure are other criteria for categorizing gemstones. Regardless of their other qualities, gemstones divide into two basic classes when cut or polished — cabochon or faceted. Cabochon stones are rounded or dome-shaped on top. Faceted stones are ground with a series of flat faces, or facets. Following are several of the traditional gemstone classifications:

**Value** — The terms, precious and semiprecious, are almost meaningless today. Ordinarily, the diamond, sapphire, emerald, and ruby are considered the most important "precious" stones. Opals are sometimes included in this group of precious stones, but pearls are often erroneously referred to as precious stones even though they are not minerals. All other minerals worth cutting and/or polishing are called semiprecious stones. This list includes such worthy stones as jasper, onyx, zircon, and amethyst, among others. The most popular of these stones are classified according to color and hardness in Table 16D.

**Shape** — Gemstones are cut and polished in only two basic shapes — cabochon and faceted. Cabochon stones are rounded or dome-shaped on the top. Normally, cabochon stones are domed on only one side and have a flat bottom. Double cabochon stones, used mainly outside the United States, are dome-shaped on both top and bottom with no flat surface. Cabochon stones vary from relatively flat to high domed (Fig. 16-3). The rounded top may also begin from a flat bottom that is circular, oval-shaped, or straight-sided. Gemstone sizes are usually noted in millimeters. A stone will have two numbers to define length and width. Thus, a 16 by 8 stone would be 16 millimeters long and 8 millimeters wide.

Faceted stones are ground with a series of flat planes or facets over the surface (Fig. 16-4). Diamonds are the prime example of a faceted stone. Most of the transparent stones are faceted because the ground faces transmit, refract, and reflect light to add brilliance to the stones. Faceted stones may be ground with step or crown facets in a variety of shapes. Ordinarily, faceted stones are rigorously symmetrical and geometrical.

Free-form, or natural, gemstones are used as they are found. Many delightful pieces of jewelry are crafted from these natural stones. Some of the natural stones are mounted by wrapping them with fine wires before attaching them to an ear-screw or cementing them to tie tack pins, cuff-

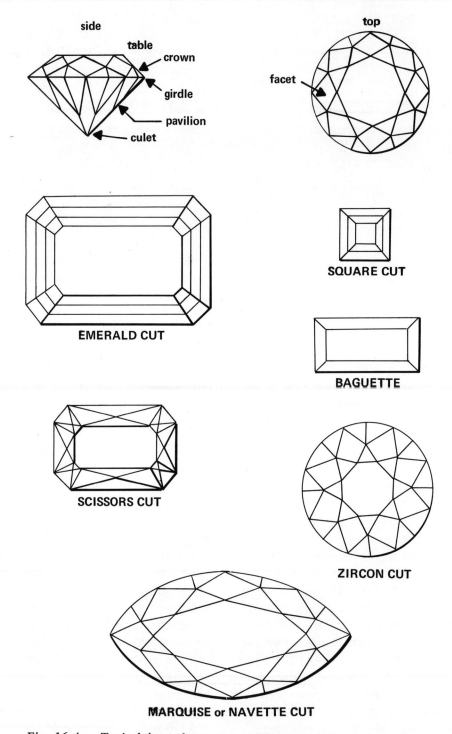

*Fig. 16-4. - Typical faceted gemstones. The arrangement of the faces
is controlled by machine devices to assure symmetrical
shapes during grinding.*

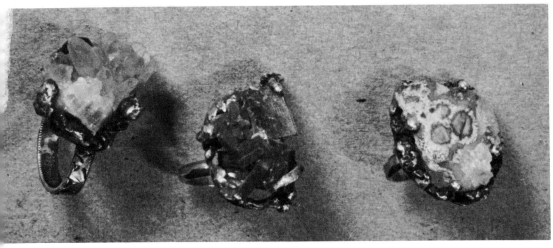

*Fig. 16-5. - Mounted natural stones.*

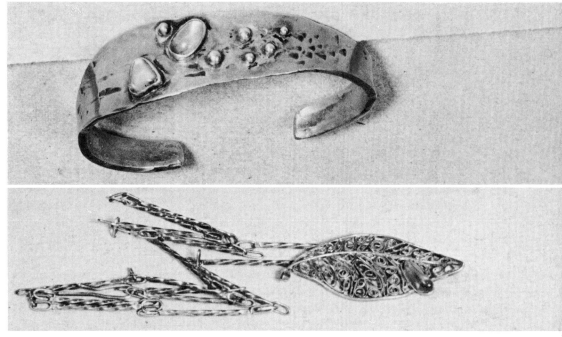

*Fig. 16-6. - Tumbled stones in handcrafted mountings.*

link backs, or other findings. Natural stones may also be used very effectively in a crafted mounting (Fig. 16-5).

Tumbled stones are one step beyond the rough, or natural stones. Tumbling stones in a container with water and a carborundum dust for many days or weeks removes the cloudy dirt and surface scum, rounds the sharp corners, and polishes the surface to highlight the natural beauty of the stones. Tumbled stones are not shaped enough to qualify for the cabochon or faceted label. Jewelry that combines a tumbled stone in a handcrafted mounting can be very handsome (Fig. 16-6).

**Hardness** — Mohs' scale, named for the

German mineralogist Friedrich Mohs, provides a means for classifying gemstones according to hardness. Scale numbers run from 1 (soft) through 10 (hard). Minerals are segregated on the basis that a mineral of one number will scratch any mineral with a lower number. Table 16E defines the 10 basic minerals in the Mohs' scale.

**Color** — Gemstones literally come in every color of the rainbow. Further, colors may be in transparent stones, such as the diamond, sapphire, emerald, or amethyst, or in translucent or opaque colors. Minerals such as quartz, appear in many colors and range from transparent to opaque stones. Table 16D lists a number of common gemstones according to color and whether they are considered transparent, translucent, or opaque.

**Specific gravity** — The specific gravity of a gemstone is the ratio of its weight to an equal volume of water. A gemstone with a specific gravity of 3 is, then, three times as heavy as water. Opals, for example, are relatively light with a specific gravity of 2.15 compared to fabulite (a man-made gem) with a specific gravity of 5.13 — more than double that of the opal. Diamond has a specific gravity of 3.51. Table 16D also includes the specific gravity for a number of the stones listed.

**Other characteristics** — Gemstones exhibit other characteristics, such as varied indexes of refraction, toughness, and chromatic dispersion. However, further discussion of these gemstone characteristics is beyond the scope of this chapter.

## NONMINERAL MATERIALS

Not all of the "pretties" and baubles used in decorative jewelry are of mineral origin. Some of the most unique possibilities for one-of-a-kind jewelry involve the use of exotic and unusual materials or valuable "found" objects. When used imaginatively and creatively, truly striking jewelry can be crafted from many of the following non-metallic materials:

174

**Ivory and bone** — These basically white materials are of organic origin. Either ivory or bone can be selected for its grain or variegated color characteristics. Depending on the size of the pieces, you can make pendants, pins, or tiny earrings from ivory and bone. True ivory, of course, is obtained from the tusks of elephants, walrus, and other tusk-bearing animals. In addition to bleached bones, some with odd-shaped joints, there are the teeth of elk, wolves, and many other animals that can be fabricated into fascinating jewelry items. Petrified ivory is quite abundant in Alaska.

**Wood** — Exotic varieties of wood offer a great change of pace from minerals. Wood can be cut, carved, polished, and mounted with the same tools used for shaping gemstones. Ebony is a classic material used for rings and tie bars. Zebrawood, rosewood, and many other varieties can be worked into jewelry items imaginatively with striking results. End-grain slices of rare woods are relatively inexpensive and are engaging conversation starters. Creative use of the grain patterns in wood offers another effective design element.

**Horn, shells, seeds, and other organic materials** — Although of organic origin, shells are actually mineral in content. However, they fit naturally among the many materials associated with plants and animals. Varieties of hard seeds, carved or sawed pieces of horn, chunks of bamboo or other reeds, and combinations of these elements offer jewelry crafters a whole new pallet of design possibilities.

Amber and coral are often used in jewelry, although they are relatively soft. Insects, particularly the brilliantly colored small butterflies, or the fish-food flies of interest to fishermen, may be cast in clear plastic before making them into key chain fobs or other jewelry. Fossils are unique conversation starters, particularly if the wearer found them.

**Plastics** — Brightly colored in transparent, translucent, or opaque material,

| TABLE 16E—Mohs' Scale of Mineral Hardness | |
| --- | --- |
| **Mohs No.** | **Mineral** |
| 1 | Talc |
| 2 | Gypsum |
| 3 | Calc spar |
| 4 | Fluor spar |
| 5 | Apatite |
| 6 | Feldspar |
| 7 | Quartz |
| 8 | Topaz |
| 9 | Sapphire |
| 10 | Diamond |

*In the Mohs' scale of hardness, minerals with a higher number can scratch minerals with a lower number. The scale relation from 1 through 9 is a relatively straight line, but if the scale was a straight line through diamond, it would be "sapphire 9, diamond 50." Minerals with a Mohs' number of 7 or higher are usually considered hard enough to wear well for jewelry.*

plastics are ideal for large, inexpensive jewelry. Plastics are not really suitable for positioning in metal mounts and settings. Tiny plastic beads or baubles are ideal, however, for decorating loop earrings (see Chapter 2).

## FOUND OBJECTS

The sky is really the limit when it comes to making jewelry out of what many people may term "junk" — antiques, curios, or just plain odd pieces of "stuff." Old coins are favorites for earrings or cuff links if available in pairs. Antique buttons, hammered metal pieces, chunks of ceramics, nails, rope, felt, and many other objects when combined with imagination can be eye-catching, even sophisticated, jewelry pieces.

## SUPPLIES AND ACCESSORIES

Relatively few supplies and materials are required for jewelry metalcrafting other than the metals and gemstones themselves. Most important are solder, flux, cleaning materials, and polishing agents. This section considers each of these materials in turn.

Only the major groups and the most common materials within each group are noted in the following sections. Many variations of the materials are available. The practicing professional will appreciate knowing the subtle differences between the properties of certain materials.

### Solder

Solders used in jewelry metalcrafting fall into either of two major categories — hard solder and soft solder. The distinction between these groups is based on melting temperature. Solder, as noted in the Glossary in Chapter 18, is an "...alloy of metals that melts at a lower temperature than the materials to be joined."

**Silver solder** — Most of the soldering for jewelry metalcrafting is accomplished with silver solder. It is the most popular and

most used of the "hard" solders. Silver solder is a mixture of several metals, mainly silver, copper, and zinc. Variations in the composition of silver solders yield a range of melting temperatures from "very hard" to "very easy." The melting temperatures of the five common silver solders are noted in Fig. 16-7. Differences in the melting temperature of silver solder are often referred to as "melts." Using this terminology, a high-melt solder would be a very hard or hard solder. Different melts are useful in jewelry metalcrafting when several joints are soldered in sequence. By soldering the first joint with very hard silver solder, it is less likely to melt at the temperature used to join the succeeding joints made with easy or very easy solders, because the metal need not be so hot to effect a joint with the lower-melt solders.

**Gold solder** — Many varieties of gold solder are available to assure good color match when joining karat golds. Gold solders are not only classified according to melting temperature, as is common with silver solder, but are also distinguished by karat designation and color, with several melts available for each. For example, when ordering gold solder, one should specify the karat content and the color, for example, 12-karat, white, and the melt desired.

**Brass solder** — The third major group of hard solders is compounded to match the color of brass. These solders are specialty items and are not often used. However, the use of brass solders will minimize joint distinction.

**Soft solder** — Various combinations of lead and tin make up the alloys for most soft solders. Bismuth and antimony are additives used in special solders. The melting temperatures of the various alloys are noted in Fig. 16-7. Several deficiencies in soft solder render it unsuitable for most work with jewelry materials:

1. Soft-soldered joints are very weak compared to joints soldered with one of the hard solders.

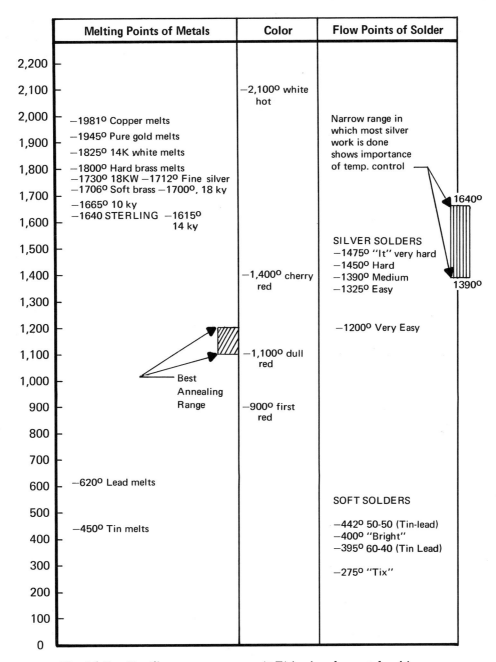

*Fig. 16-7. - Significant temperatures ( °F) for jewelry metalcrafting.*

2. Soft solder requires considerably more bulk, and the color contrasts with all jewelry materials except pewter. Therefore, soft-soldered joints are easily visible unless plated or gilded.

3. Soft solder will burn holes in jewelry metals if these metals are annealed for any purpose after soldering with one of the lead-tin solders.

One of the main uses for soft solder is to join cuff link and other spring-operated findings to designed jewelry. The low melting temperature of soft solder permits joining these findings to jewelry pieces without affecting the temper of the springs in the findings. If these joints were soldered with one of the hard solders, the spring in the findings would be annealed and made useless unless special techniques were used. If the joint with spring-operated findings must be soldered with one of the hard solders, the spring should normally be removed from the finding before soldering.

A soft solder that has some silver content is especially useful for jewelry since it stays bright and can be plated. The tin-lead solder quickly dulls and cannot be plated.

## Flux

Flux is a nonmetallic compound or material that protects metals from oxidation during heating.

**Borax flux** — Most common of the fluxes used with copper, brass, silver, and gold is plain borax. It may be supplied as a paste, liquid, or powder, the only difference being the amount of water in the mixture. Paste flux may be applied more thickly than one of the thin slurries. Either paste or liquid flux dries out during the heating in preparation for soldering. Powdered flux is melted so that it flows onto the work. Borax flux resists heating and continues to protect metallic surfaces even when they reach normal hard-soldering temperatures. However, plain borax flux provides little or no cleaning action; therefore, metals must be clean and free of oxidation before the flux is applied.

**Self-pickling flux** — Mixtures of borax and a cleaning (pickling) material are sold under various trade names. A self-pickling flux actually removes minor surface contaminants and oxidation from a joint during the heating in preparation for soldering. Although the metal surface may be soldered when dirtier than if plain borax flux is used, considerable judgment and skill are required to assess the resulting surface conditions.

**Special fluxes** — Certain metals used in the crafting of jewelry require their own unique flux. Metals, such as stainless steel, aluminum, and pewter, cannot be soldered without the use of specially compounded fluxes.

### Pickling — Cleaning agents

Oxidation and fire scale are far more easily removed by chemical means than mechanically with abrasives.

**Acid pickle baths** — Old-time methods call for the use of dilute sulfuric or nitric acids to remove oxidation and other contaminants from jewelry metals. Both of these acids are potentially hazardous, although either is safe enough if the proper precautions are observed and reasonable care is exercised in handling them. A sulfuric acid pickle bath can be made by pouring 1 part acid into 9 parts water — and be sure to *pour the acid into the water*. Do not pour water into the acid or a violent chemical reaction will result. The 10 percent pickle will eat holes in clothing and will affect the skin seriously unless it is washed off immediately and neutralized with a paste of common baking soda and water.

**Nonacid pickle baths** — Proprietary substitutes for acid pickle baths are safer, and they clean metals satisfactorily. *Sparex* is one line of these materials. *Sparex* materials are supplied in bulk as a dry powder, which is mixed with water to make a pickle solution. *Sparex* comes in two types — No. 1 for cleaning ferrous alloys and No. 2 for cleaning nonferrous metals. *Sparex No. 2* is nonflammable and nonexplosive. To

*Fig. 16-8. - Tripoli in chunk form.*

speed the removal of oxidation and fire scale from jewelry materials, *Sparex No. 2* may be boiled on a heating stand with the propane torch. Although *Sparex No. 2* is not an acid, it will affect clothing and may affect sensitive skin, so contact should be avoided.

### Abrasives

Most abrasive materials, whether in the form of coated paper, loose powder, or in solid sticks or wheels, are either aluminum oxide or silicon carbide. These man-made materials are sintered in an electric furnace, forming huge chunks. When cool, they are broken into pieces and ground to specific sizes. Grit sizes vary from 60 (coarse) to 600 (finest). See Table 16F for a complete range of grit numbers. A silicon carbide board may be constructed by cementing silicon carbide paper of 240 grit to one side and 400-grit paper to the opposite side. The silicon carbide board should be moistened before each use; otherwise, it will wear away rapidly. The paper should be cemented to the board with a waterproof contact cement to permit using the board wet. A piece of both grit papers is also handy for off-hand cutting.

### Polishing Compounds

Closely related to abrasive materials are the polishing compounds. These compounds cut very little. Their job is to bring a piece of jewelry to a lustrous finish. Although there are many compounds formulated for use on specific materials, most jewelry metalcrafters use one type of tripoli and one type of rouge.

**Tripoli** — Relatively coarse compared to the final polishing rouges, tripoli is a "next-to-last" compound. Tripoli is coarse enough to cut metal and is used mainly to remove scratches and oxidation from the surface. Excessive polishing will round corners and may remove some of the design detail that has been cut, stamped, or engraved into jewelry pieces. Tripoli is supplied in a chunk, mixed in a cakelike block of waxy material (Fig. 16-8). In use, the tripoli is transferred to a felt or muslin buff by rubbing the buff against the cake.

179

### TABLE 16F—Silicon-Carbide Abrasive Paper

| Grit No. | Roughness |
|----------|-----------|
| 60 | Coarsest |
| 80 | Coarse |
| 100 | Medium |
| 120 | Medium |
| 150 | Medium |
| 180 | Medium |
| 220 | Fine |
| 240 | Fine |
| 280 | Fine |
| 320 | Fine |
| 400 | Very Fine |
| 500 | Very Fine |
| 600 | Finest |

The felt buff is then used to polish the work piece. A buff used with tripoli should be used for that purpose only and not used with rouge. Tripoli will contaminate the buff reserved for rouge alone.

**Rouge** — Final polishing with one of the rouges brings metal portions of jewelry to a brilliant luster. Rouge is not a cutting compound; it is strictly a polishing agent for developing the luster of the metallic surfaces. Rouge will not eliminate surface scratches. Red rouge made with iron oxide in a cake of wax is the most common type.

**Chemical polishing agents** — Various chapters call for the use of a liquid metal polishing material like those used for polishing the chrome or stainless steel trim on automobiles. These polishing liquids remove surface layers of dirt and some oxide films and impart a high luster to some metals. These polishing liquids are readily available at automobile service stations, auto parts stores, or local hardware stores.

### Cement

Cements are used in metalcrafted jewelry for specific purposes, such as to hold a pearl in place on a peg. Cements are also used occasionally to help secure a stone in a mount. Ordinarily, however, if the mount is designed and fabricated correctly, there is little need for cement to hold a stone in place.

Ordinary household cements are not desirable for jewelry use because they depend on air contact to dry or set up. When such cements are used in places not open to the air, as in the hole for a peg, the cement might take weeks or months to set up firmly. Special cements compounded for jewelry use include, but are not limited to, the following:

**Epoxy cements** — These effective cements are probably the best for all-around use in jewelry. Epoxy cements do not depend on air-drying to set up. Instead, an accelerator is mixed with the cement before use, and the cement hardens chemically. Epoxy cements come in two tubes to keep the chemicals separate until they are mixed for use. Epoxy cements may be "regular" setting, which requires about 24 hours to harden, or "fast" epoxy cement, which begins to thicken and set up in 15 to 30 minutes.

Thorough mixing is essential when using epoxy cements. Since small amounts are usually mixed, a regular spatula would use up all the cement necessary just to cover the surface. Instead, flatten the end of a coat hanger wire for use as a small spatula when mixing the two parts of the cement. A broken jewelry saw blade is an excellent tool for placing droplets of epoxy cement, particularly when pushing the cement into the hole in a pearl for pegging. As part of the chemical action in setting up, epoxy cements become thin and fluid, even though the freshly mixed compound was thick. Therefore, parts being cemented must be held in place until the epoxy sets up firmly. Wires or clamps should be used to make sure the pieces remain together through the full setting-up cycle.

**Liquid cements** — Fast-setting contact cements are available under various trade names. This type cement is particularly good for pegging pearls, because it is liquid enough to pull itself into the hole in a pearl by capillary attraction. It sets up in 15 to 30 seconds.

**Hard cements** — Older "pearl cements" on the market require heating to melt or remelt the material. These materials are temperature sensitive and set up hard as they cool. However, since pearls are quite sensitive to heat, the hard cements must be used with some caution. Ordinary stick shellac or lapidary dopping wax may also be used when heated to the fluid stage as a hard cement.

### Findings

Accessories useful in crafting jewelry include a wide variety of "findings." These accessories are usually some form of support for a jewelry piece and are usually hidden, at least partially. Such findings as ear-screws for attaching crafted earrings onto the ear lobes are difficult to make because of the screw thread. They form an insignificant part of the total earring because so little of the ear-screw can be seen while it is being worn. Findings are manufactured by production machinery and are quite inexpensive compared to hand-produced pieces.

# coloring and coating

JEWELRY METALS are frequently colored, chemically or by painting, antiqued to add a look of depth and a simulated patina of age, or simply sprayed or dipped with a clear coating to prevent oxidation or tarnish. Some of these methods are simple; others require chemical treatments that can be hazardous unless precautions are observed.

## ANTIQUING

Tarnish that forms on silver or copper, particularly if utensils are exposed to eggs, is a natural form of antiquing. Antiquing is the term given to this chemical action because silver tarnishes in air. Rather than wait, you can quickly antique the various jewelry materials as follows:

**Sterling silver** — One of the easiest of the jewelry materials to antique, sterling silver is simply exposed to liver of sulfur in water and allowed to dry in air or heated. Exposure to the sulfur gives sterling silver a variety of color tones from gray to black, depending on the strength of the liver of sulfur solution and exposure time. This gray to black coating is not oxidation and is not removed by *Sparex No. 2*. The antique coating on sterling can be easily removed with silver polish — the kind sold for polishing silver flatware or hollowware. Heating also removes the antiqued silver coating.

For a uniform antique finish, first clean the work piece in *Sparex No. 2* or other pickle bath. Any of the following three methods of antiquing silver can be used to impart the desired gray or black look:

1. Prepare a solution of liver of sulfur in water by dropping a piece of sulfur about the size of a pea into one cup of water. Use a *Pyrex* glass beaker or cooking utensil in preference to a metal pan. Liver of sulfur is also known as sulfurated potash. The strength of the solution is not critical, although you may find it easier to control the depth of the antiquing if the solution is weaker than noted above. For a light gray, allow the sterling to remain in the solution only a few seconds. Check for the

*There are various ways of antiquing metals so they have a more interesting aged patina. Some methods are simple; others involve the use of chemicals that can be hazardous unless used cautiously.*

depth of gray desired by removing it from the solution at intervals. For a deep black, boil the piece in the liver-of-sulfur solution. However, if you leave the work piece in the solution too long, the black coating builds up and tends to flake off. Wash the piece in plain water to stop the chemical action and allow the piece to dry in air.

2. The second technique for antiquing silver is really a variation of the first. Instead of allowing the sterling work piece to remain in the liver-of-sulfur solution at room temperature, plunge the hot work piece, cleaned in a pickle bath, into the warm liver-of-sulfur solution and immediately remove it. The hot metal and the warm

solution react almost instantly. Therefore, to prevent varying shades of gray, plunge the work piece quickly into the solution. Do not lower it gradually.

3. No solution of liver of sulfur in water as a bath is used for this third technique. Instead, a double-strength solution of liver of sulfur in water is painted onto a cool, cleaned sterling piece. The piece is then heated with the torch to quicken the chemical reaction of the sulfur with the copper in the sterling alloy. With this system, you need not antique all surfaces. You can control the areas to be blackened by brushing the liver-of-sulfur solution only on those areas.

**Copper** — The liver-of-sulfur solution used for antiquing sterling silver actually reacts with the copper in the alloy. Therefore, when treating pure copper, plan to use an even weaker solution of the liver of sulfur than for treating sterling. Copper reacts quickly with the liver-of-sulfur solution. Follow generally the same steps with copper as for sterling silver.

**Brass** — Many chemical formulas exist for coloring brass, but they are quite complex and some are hazardous. The best all-around solution for blackening brass is a simple solution of cupric nitrate in water. A precise formula is not necessary, but a solution of one ounce of cupric nitrate in one cup of water works best. You can buy cupric nitrate from a local druggist. Add a teaspoonful of ordinary rubbing alcohol to assist in wetting. If available, a few drops of silver nitrate can be added to the cupric nitrate solution to speed the chemical reaction. (In many areas silver nitrate is a controlled chemical that is not readily available. Also, silver nitrate will burn the skin and turn it black wherever it touches — so handle it very carefully.) Dip the clean brass work pieces into the solution for only a few minutes and allow them to dry in air; then heat with a low flame until the work turns black. For a faster reaction, warm the brass to a temperature no higher than 200 to 300°F. before dipping the work piece into the solution. A green fungus-type growth appears on the warm brass. The growth then turns black as it is heated. A small amount of somewhat toxic fumes may be given off during the process. Therefore, make sure you work at this in a place with plenty of ventilation — like outdoors. The black coating produced on brass with the cupric nitrate solution is long lasting and resists abrasion and wear very well.

**Nickel silver (nonferrous type)** — Nickel (German) silver reacts and responds to the same chemical treatment detailed for brass.

**Karat gold and gold fill** — Pure gold is difficult to change because it resists oxidation and other chemical attacks. Alloys of gold, the karat golds, however, will change color depending on the type of treatment, because the alloying elements in karat golds are less noble than pure or fine gold. Two ways to change karat gold colors are tincture of iodine and heat.

Tincture of iodine in water will change the color of karat golds permanently. But the change in color is not a blackening. Instead, the color is a rich brown. A bit of iodine right from the bottle will produce this color.

Permanent gray-black can be produced by heating karat gold to a dull red and allowing it to air cool. As the gold approaches red heat, move the torch back from the gold, allowing more oxygen to reach the hot surface. Highlights may be produced by polishing, but the surface discoloration is quite tenacious and requires considerable effort to remove.

## COATING

Metals are simple to coat with a pigmented chemical, such as paint, or with a clear material to protect the surface from tarnish and oxidation.

**Felt-marker coating** — Probably the simplest way to add color or to simulate an antique finish is to use one of the felt markers. The ink in the felt markers varies considerably, and some are more permanent

183

than others. Experiment to find the one best suited to your craft. A black felt marker, for example, can be used to produce a pseudo-antique finish by simply filling any cuts or marks with the ink. Polishing the surface around the marks leaves them in dark relief to highlight a design. Make sure the surface of the metal is clean and dry before applying the marker. Felt markers also come in a rainbow of colors that permit the creative jewelry craftsman to use color liberally. The felt marker tip permits colors to be mixed with a minimum of fuss because the area to be coated can be closely controlled. Multicolor earrings, for example, are possible and practical from the pallet of felt marker colors.

**Spray painting** — Everything from wood beads to metal disks and wire can be colorfully coated with any of the several quick-drying lacquers or enamels packaged in aerosol spray cans. Hues available from spray cans are almost unlimited, and the aerosol propellant system is ideal for the small areas to be spray painted. Just make certain that the spray paint you buy is formulated for application to metal.

When spraying sheet metal or wire, make certain the surface is chemically clean. Most paint failures stem from dirt or grease on the surface, which acts as a release agent. Clean the metal in a pickle to remove oxidation or wash thoroughly in a 1:1 mixture of ammonia and warm water. Allow the piece to dry in air before painting.

Lay the articles to be spray painted on old newspaper. Work only in an area with no draft. Very few opportunities are available for spraying outside, although the ventilation outside is preferable. Since most jewelry spraying is quite small, you can spray inside in a basement or laundry area where the possibility of overspray is slight. Follow directions on the can for the specific type of paint and nozzle you are using. Pay close attention to the distance from nozzle to work. Most sprays are mixed with quick-drying solvents that allow you to paint both sides within minutes. Lacquers tend to dry more quickly than enamels, but either may be used successfully on metals.

**Brush painting** — A small artist's brush and one of the many and readily available model enamels can be extremely useful in adding color to jewelry designs. A small brush is ideal where only a part of the area is to be painted. To be sure, parts of a design can be masked out with pressure-sensitive masking tape and spray painted, but small areas are more easily colored with a brush. The model enamels are also quick drying and available in a myriad of colors. For close control, spend a few cents more and buy a good quality artist's brush that forms a point when wet.

**Clear coating** — Lacquers and a new selection of clear plastic coatings are available in aerosol cans for spraying finished work. Clear coatings may add a certain gloss (desirable or undesirable), but their main purpose is to protect a bright metal surface from tarnish and oxidation. Follow the same directions for spraying clear coatings as for spray painting. Generally, clear coatings applied with a brush are less satisfactory than those applied with a spray.

# glossary and tables

## GLOSSARY

**Abrasive** — Any of many hard materials for grinding or polishing. Abrasives vary from very rough grinding wheels to rough powders used only for final polishing. Abrasives are often glued to paper or cloth to simplify their use. Most modern abrasives are metallic oxides.

**Alloy** — Basically a union of two or more metals, sometimes in combination with small amounts of nonmetals. Alloys are not simple mixtures — each alloying element is dissolved in the others when the whole is molten. As an alloy cools to a solid state, some of the elements may separate out. Most jewelry materials exist as alloys. Sterling silver, for example, is an alloy containing 92.5 percent pure silver and 7.5 percent copper. Alloying elements are added to enhance specific properties of the base metal. Copper in sterling increases the strength and hardness of the silver alloy with little effect on its ductility or malleability.

**Amalgamation** — A combination, mixing, or blending of metals that occurs at temperatures below the melting temperature of either metal.

**Annealing** — The process of heating a metal to the proper temperature and cooling it. Annealing accomplishes three effects:
1. Relieves internal strains, usually from previous cooling.
2. Reduces or changes character of metallic grain structure.
3. Softens the metal to remove effects of work hardening.

**Avoirdupois** — Standard system of weights most commonly used in the United States, Canada, and England. See Table 18D for conversion of avoirdupois units to troy units.

**Bezel** — An edge of thin metal that extends around the perimeter of a stone to retain it in a base or mounting. The bezel may or may not have an inner "seat."

**Bezeling** — Procedure for forming the bezel around the stone's perimeter. Various tools are used to shape the edge, or bezel, to a stone's rounded edge.

**Cabochon** — One of two basic shapes for gemstones that is characterized by a rounded or semiflat top. Cabochon stones may be circular, oval, straight-sided, or a combination of shapes as long as the upper surface is somewhat rounded. A double cabochon is a stone that is rounded on both top and bottom.

**Carat** — Unit of weight measure for gemstones. A carat is equivalent to 3.086 grains, or 0.200 gram. (Not to be confused with karat, a means for noting alloys of gold. See *Karat*.) In weighing gemstones, the carat is divided into 100 points. A "ten point" stone is .10 carat, for example.

**Chasing** — Technique for indenting or forming the surface of metal without cutting. Chasing requires special hammers and other tools to achieve a variety of shapes and is generally little practiced today in the United States because of the time required.

**Chuck** — Device for holding twist drills mainly, but sometimes applied to other elements, such as grinding bits, small grinding wheels, or polishing heads.

**Crystallization** — A change in metal structure indicated by grainy, rough structure. Crystallization occurs with some metals as a result of certain heating that separates alloys or affects lattice structure of individual crystals. Crystallization weakens a metal or alloy and can generally be corrected only by remelting the metal and cooling.

**Cupping** — A forging technique, mainly with the peen of a ball-peen hammer, to

185

form a cup-shaped depression in metal. Cupping usually stretches the metal to leave the bottom of the cup thinner than the surrounding metal. Dapping is a more precise form of cupping (see *Dapping*).

**Dapping** — A technique for forming metal into dome or cup shapes with the aid of a dapping block (also called a die) and punches. The dapping block includes many sizes of hollowed-out spheres, and a punch fits each size of dome. Dapping is a precise form of cupping or drawing metal.

**Drawing-in** — A forging technique for thinning edges of a metal surface by forcing metal toward center — hence the term "drawing-in," or forcing. Drawing-in is the opposite of cupping, but both techniques result in variable metal thickness around and through forged areas.

**Ductility** — A metal's ability to suffer a large amount of plastic deformation without breaking. Usually the term *ductility* represents a metal's ability to be drawn into wire. *Malleability* is a related term that expresses a metal's reaction to compressive plastic deformation — such as hammering or forging.

**Emery paper** — An abrasive-coated paper used for smoothing and polishing. Emery is not as hard as silicon carbide and wears away faster. In its natural state emery, corrundum, was the hardest abrasive known before present man-made materials were developed.

**Facet** — A flat surface cut on a stone. Generally only transparent stones are faceted, because the facets highlight the sparkle of reflected or refracted light.

**Finding** — A support, or attachment, for decorative parts of jewelry. Ear-screws and ear-wires, cuff-link backs, brooch or pin backs, necklace and bracelet latches, and clutches for tie tacks are typical findings. Findings include elements, such as screw threads, that are difficult to make by hand. Since they are usually hidden or only partially visible, findings are usually mass produced by machinery and purchased for

attachment to handcrafted jewelry items.

**Fire-scale** — A hard surface oxidation caused by heating at high temperatures. Fire-scale, except for special effects, should be removed during finishing or polishing. Fire-scale may be removed mechanically by abrasives or chemically.

**Flux** — A nonmetallic chemical compound that resists heat and prevents surface oxidation, enabling solder to bond. Two common fluxes are used in jewelry metalcrafting for hard soldering (1) borax flux — a thick slurry, or paste, of borax and water, and (2) self-pickling flux — a mixture of borax and a deoxidant that protects joint areas from further oxidation during heat. In addition to paste application, fluxes may also be applied as a dry powder. Soft solder fluxes are usually adapted to the particular alloy with which they are used and will vary greatly in chemical content.

**Forge** — Technique for forming metal by hammering or beating. Forging may mean only to flatten wire, or it can include curving or cupping metal over a form of some kind. Forging of jewelry metals usually occurs at room temperature in contrast to the forging of steel or wrought iron, which requires considerable heat.

**Fusion** — Technique for joining similar materials by a form of welding that uses no other material. Fusion occurs when the surface metal of joining pieces melts and "fuses" together to form a solid joint after cooling.

**Gallery** — Shoulder around inside of mounting rim that supports perimeter of stone.

**Gauge — Also gage —** Thickness of sheet metal or diameter of wire. See Table 16C for specific gauge numbers and thicknesses. Browne and Sharpe (B&S) gauge is now also known as the American Wire Gauge (AWG). Although called "wire gauge," the same dimensions apply to metal thickness or wire diameter. Numbers are reversed — that is, small gauge numbers mean thick metal or wire diameter. As gauge numbers increase, thickness decreases. AWG is not to be confused with the "U. S. Standard" gauge, which is for iron and steel.

**Gold fill** — Combination jewelry metal manufactured by bonding a layer of karat gold alloy to one or both sides of a base metal and rolling the sandwich to the desired thickness. This process provides jewelry metal with the true look of gold at a greatly reduced price, since all of the gold is on the outside of the piece.

**Gold, rolled** — Rolled gold is similar to gold fill and consists of an outer layer of gold alloy on a low-cost base. However, the outer layer of gold alloy is thinner than gold fill. Therefore, rolled gold is lower in price.

**Grain** — Basic unit of weight that is common for both Troy and avoirdupois systems. See Tables 18A and 18B for conversion of grains to other units.

**Graver** — Cutting tool for removing metal from surface in engraving. Various gravers are ground to shapes for making specific cuts. Also called *burin*.

**Heat conductivity** — The rate at which heat flows through a metal. Metals are, as a group, good heat conductors. Nonmetallic substances, such as asbestos, are such poor conductors of heat that they are used as insulators.

**Karat** — Unit for measuring gold based on pure gold being 24 karats. Thus, 14K (for karat) gold is 14 parts gold and 10 parts of other metal by weight. Not to be confused with *carat*, which is a unit for measuring gemstones (see *Carat*). It is improper to use the term "karat gold" for any alloy below 10K.

**Malleability** — A metal's ability to suffer large amounts of plastic deformation, mainly from hammering or forging, without breaking (see *Ductility*). A metal that is malleable is not brittle and can be shaped with little fear of breaking.

**Mandrel** — A steel tool device over which metals are forged or shaped. Man-

drels may be various shapes. The most important shape is the tapered ring mandrel for shaping rings (see Chapter 15). Mandrel is also the term for the cone or screw device for attaching polishing or grinding wheels to a motor shaft.

**Matting** — Technique for texturing the surface of a metal instead of polishing. Matting is accomplished with the aid of stamps that have a variety of surface textures on the end surface.

**Oxidation** — Combination of oxygen with the base metal to form a metal oxide. Rust or iron oxide is a familiar form of oxidation, which occurs on the surface and prevents solder from bonding to metals being joined. Jewelry metals oxidize to varying degrees when heated.

**Passivate** — Chemical treatment of metallic surface to prevent further chemical reaction. Copper and brass are metals that are often passivated to prevent them from leaving greenish marks on the skin. Some form of a dichromate-based solution is common treatment for copper and brass.

**Pickle** — A chemical method for removing surface oxidation. *Sparex No. 2* is a pickling solution for use with nonferrous metals and is noted in these chapters in preference to traditional pickling solutions, such as mixtures of sulfuric acid and water.

**Planishing** — A technique for smoothing and hardening the surface of metal with a smooth-faced hammer specifically designed for this task. Planishing is usually accomplished over an anvil or steel block of some sort.

**Plating** — Electrodeposition of a metal onto a base. Plating occurs in a chemical bath with a cathode and anode forming an electrical cell. Gold plating must be at least 10K alloy and must be deposited with the equivalent of 0.000,007 inches of 24K gold. Plating thicknesses less than this are called "gold colored" or "gold washed." Silver may also be electroplated.

**Polishing** — A technique for achieving

high luster on metallic surfaces by rubbing with successively finer abrasive polishing materials. Polishing involves the removal of fine surface scratches as well as chemical blemishes.

**Prong** — Small, usually tapered, metal extensions for holding a stone in a mount. Prongs include only those elements bent into position after the stone is in place. Prongs may be built up with fusion or shaped and attached at the base by fusion welding. Prongs are usually of different lengths with only the minimum required to restrain a stone in its mount.

**Quenching** — Quick cooling, usually after annealing, but also after soldering or fusing. Quenching simply means to pick up a piece of metal and drop it in plain water at room temperature.

**Rouge** — A final polishing compound with no cutting action. Rouge is the last step in polishing and is mainly used to bring out and highlight the surface luster of metals. Rouge comes in a cake of waxy material. While red rouge (also called jeweler's rouge) is the most common form, rouge is also available in white, yellow, green, and black for special purposes.

**Shank** — That part of a ring which encircles a finger. Shank or ring sizes vary according to a standard scale. (See Table 18E.)

**Silicon carbide** — A very hard abrasive manufactured by sintering silicon and carbon in a high-temperature furnace and breaking crystals into graded sizes. Silicon carbide paper comes in a variety of grits. The two most frequently used are the 240 grit, a cutting grit for removing scratches and coarse fire-scale or oxidation, and the 400 grit for semipolishing and bringing out the luster of jewelry metals.

**Solder** — An alloy of metals that melts at a lower temperature than the materials to be joined. Solder falls into two basic classes — hard solder and soft solder. Hard solders have a variety of melting temperatures depending on the alloying percentages.

Soft solders are mainly alloys of tin and lead. See Fig. 16-7 for melting temperatures of hard and soft solders.

**Soldering** — A method of joining similar or dissimilar metals together with an alloy of other metals. Solder is melted in the process of heating the metal and flows to the surfaces to be joined forming a metal-to-metal bond. The term "hard soldering" refers to soldering done at temperatures above 1000° F., while "soft soldering" refers to soldering done at temperatures below 1000° F.

*Sparex* — Trade name for a pickling material that is supplied in dry powder form (see Chapter 19 for source). *Sparex* dissolves in water to form a solution that can be used over and over again. *Sparex No. 1* is used for removing scale and oxidation from ferrous or iron-bearing materials. *Sparex No. 2* is used for removing oxidation from nonferrous metals, such as copper, silver, and brass among others. About 1 teaspoon of *Sparex No. 2* to 1 pint of water is used for pickling. If pickle is too strong, sterling will turn a dark gray.

**Stake** — A metal forging tool with a form that assists in shaping, usually cupped objects. A stake fits into a hole in an anvil or in a wood stump, hence the name. A great many shapes and sizes of stakes are available. For example, stakes shaped like the bowl of a teaspoon aid in forming cupped objects quickly and uniformly.

**Tempering** — Relief of brittleness, usually in steels previously hardened by heating and quenching. Steels are tempered by reheating followed by air cooling.

**Tripoli** — A fast-cutting buffing compound that usually is the next-to-last step in final polishing.

**Troy** — System of weights used for precious metals. See Table 18C for conversion of troy units to avoirdupois units.

**Work hardening** — Also called cold working, is the stiffening or hardening of metals due to bending, hammering, or stretching.

## TABLE 18A-Commonly Used Weights and Measures

*Jewelry metals are described, sold, and used on the basis of the Troy system. The basic unit of weight is the Troy ounce — with equivalents as noted below.*

|  |  |  |
|---|---|---|
| 24 Grains | = 1 Pennyweight (dwt) | |
| 20 Pennyweights | = 1 Ounce (Troy) = 480 Grains | |
| 12 Ounces (Troy) | = 1 Pound = 5760 Grains | |
| 1 Pound (Troy) | = .8229 Pound (Avoirdupois) | |
| 1 Pound (Avoirdupois) | = 1.2153 Pound (Troy) | |
| 1 Gram (Metric) | = 15.43 Grains (Troy or Avoirdupois) | |
| 1 Gram | = 0.03527 Ounces (Avoirdupois) | |
|  | = 0.03215 Ounces (Troy) | |
| 1 Carat | = 3.086 Grains = 0.200 Gram | |

### TABLE 18B–Decimal Equivalents—Troy System

| Pennyweight | Troy Ounce | Grains* |
|:---:|:---:|:---:|
| 1/4 | .0125 | 6 |
| 1/2 | .025 | 12 |
| 3/4 | .0375 | 18 |
| 1 | .050 | 24 |
| 2 | .100 | 48 |
| 3 | .150 | 72 |
| 4 | .200 | 96 |
| 5 | .250 | 120 |
| 6 | .300 | 144 |
| 7 | .350 | 168 |
| 8 | .400 | 192 |
| 9 | .450 | 216 |
| 10 | .500 | 240 |
| 11 | .550 | 264 |
| 12 | .600 | 288 |
| 13 | .650 | 312 |
| 14 | .700 | 336 |
| 15 | .750 | 360 |
| 16 | .800 | 384 |
| 17 | .850 | 408 |
| 18 | .900 | 432 |
| 19 | .950 | 456 |
| 20 | 1.000 | 480 |

*The grain is the same in either the Troy or Avoirdupois system.

1 Ounce Troy = 480 Grains = 31.10348 Grams (Metric)

1 Ounce Avoirdupois = 437.5 Grains = 28.3495 Grams (Metric)

# TABLE 18C-Ounces Troy to Pounds and Ounces Avoirdupois

| Ounces Troy | Lbs. & Ozs. Avoir. | Ounces Troy | Lbs. & Ozs. Avoir. | Ounces Troy | Lbs. & Ozs. Avoir. |
|---|---|---|---|---|---|
| 1 | 1.1 | 11 | 12.1 | 21 | 1-7.1 |
| 2 | 2.2 | 12 | 13.2 | 22 | 1-8.2 |
| 3 | 3.3 | 13 | 14.3 | 23 | 1-9.3 |
| 4 | 4.4 | 14 | 15.4 | 24 | 1-10.4 |
| 5 | 5.5 | 15 | 1-0.5 | 25 | 1-11.5 |
| 6 | 6.6 | 16 | 1-1.6 | 26 | 1-12.6 |
| 7 | 7.7 | 17 | 1-2.7 | 27 | 1-13.7 |
| 8 | 8.8 | 18 | 1-3.8 | 28 | 1-14.8 |
| 9 | 9.9 | 19 | 1-4.9 | 29 | 1-15.9 |
| 10 | 11.0 | 20 | 1-6.0 | 30 | 2-1.0 |
| 31 | 2-2.1 | 59 | 4-0.8 | 87 | 5-15.5 |
| 32 | 2-3.2 | 60 | 4-1.9 | 88 | 6-0.6 |
| 33 | 2-4.3 | 61 | 4-3.0 | 89 | 6-1.7 |
| 34 | 2-5.4 | 62 | 4-4.1 | 90 | 6-2.8 |
| 35 | 2-6.4 | 63 | 4-5.2 | 91 | 6-3.9 |
| 36 | 2-7.5 | 64 | 4-6.3 | 92 | 6-5.0 |
| 37 | 2-8.6 | 65 | 4-7.4 | 93 | 6-6.1 |
| 38 | 2-9.7 | 66 | 4-8.5 | 94 | 6-7.2 |
| 39 | 2-10.8 | 67 | 4-9.6 | 95 | 6-8.3 |
| 40 | 2-11.9 | 68 | 4-10.7 | 96 | 6-9.4 |
| 41 | 2-13.0 | 69 | 4-11.8 | 97 | 6-10.5 |
| 42 | 2-14.1 | 70 | 4-12.8 | 98 | 6-11.6 |
| 43 | 2-15.2 | 71 | 4-13.9 | 99 | 6-12.7 |
| 44 | 3-0.3 | 72 | 4-15.0 | 100 | 6-13.8 |
| 45 | 3-1.4 | 73 | 5-0.1 | 200 | 13-11.5 |
| 46 | 3-2.5 | 74 | 5-1.2 | 300 | 20-9.2 |
| 47 | 3-3.6 | 75 | 5-2.3 | 400 | 27-6.9 |
| 48 | 3-4.7 | 76 | 5-3.4 | 500 | 34-4.6 |
| 49 | 3-5.8 | 77 | 5-4.5 | 600 | 41-2.3 |
| 50 | 3-6.9 | 78 | 5-5.6 | 700 | 48-0.0 |
| 51 | 3-8.0 | 79 | 5-6.7 | 800 | 54-13.8 |
| 52 | 3-9.1 | 80 | 5-7.8 | 900 | 61-11.5 |
| 53 | 3-10.2 | 81 | 5-8.9 | 1000 | 68-9.2 |
| 54 | 3-11.3 | 82 | 5-10.0 | 2000 | 137-2.3 |
| 55 | 3-12.4 | 83 | 5-11.1 | 3000 | 205-11.5 |
| 56 | 3-13.5 | 84 | 5-12.2 | 4000 | 274-4.7 |
| 57 | 3-14.6 | 85 | 5-13.3 | 5000 | 342-13.8 |
| 58 | 3-15.7 | 86 | 5-14.4 | | |

**TABLE 18D – Ounces and Pounds Avoirdupois to Ounces Troy**

| Avoir. Ounces | Troy Ounces | Avoir. Ounces | Troy Ounces | Avoir. Ounces | Troy Ounces |
|---|---|---|---|---|---|
| 1 | .9115 | 6 | 5.469 | 11 | 10.026 |
| 2 | 1.823 | 7 | 6.380 | 12 | 10.937 |
| 3 | 2.734 | 8 | 7.292 | 13 | 11.849 |
| 4 | 3.646 | 9 | 8.203 | 14 | 12.760 |
| 5 | 4.557 | 10 | 9.115 | 15 | 13.672 |
| 1 | 14.583 | 11 | 160.417 | 26 | 379.167 |
| 2 | 29.167 | 12 | 175.000 | 27 | 393.750 |
| 3 | 43.750 | 13 | 189.583 | 28 | 408.333 |
| 4 | 58.333 | 14 | 204.167 | 29 | 422.917 |
| 5 | 72.917 | 15 | 218.750 | 30 | 437.500 |
| 6 | 87.500 | 16 | 233.333 | 31 | 452.083 |
| 7 | 102.083 | 17 | 247.917 | 32 | 466.667 |
| 8 | 116.667 | 18 | 262.500 | 33 | 481.250 |
| 9 | 131.250 | 19 | 277.083 | 34 | 495.833 |
| 10 | 145.833 | 20 | 291.667 | 35 | 510.417 |
| | | 21 | 306.250 | | |
| | | 22 | 320.883 | | |
| | | 23 | 335.417 | | |
| | | 24 | 350.000 | | |
| | | 25 | 364.583 | | |

## TABLE 18E

| Ring Size | Band Length Decimal | Band Length MM | Band Length English | Inside Diameter |
|-----------|---------------------|----------------|---------------------|-----------------|
| 2½ | 1.80 | 45.8 | 1 51/64 | .538 |
| 3 | 1.85 | 47.0 | 1 27/32 | .554 |
| 3½ | 1.90 | 48.3 | 1 57/64 | .570 |
| 4 | 1.95 | 49.6 | 1 61/64 | .586 |
| 4½ | 2.00 | 50.8 | 2 | .602 |
| 5 | 2.05 | 52.1 | 2 3/64 | .618 |
| 5½ | 2.10 | 53.4 | 2 3/32 | .634 |
| 6 | 2.15 | 54.7 | 2 9/64 | .650 |
| 6½ | 2.20 | 55.9 | 2 13/64 | .666 |
| 7 | 2.25 | 57.2 | 2 1/4 | .682 |
| 7½ | 2.30 | 58.5 | 2 19/64 | .698 |
| 8 | 2.35 | 59.8 | 2 11/32 | .714 |
| 8½ | 2.40 | 61.0 | 2 13/32 | .730 |
| 9 | 2.45 | 62.3 | 2 29/64 | .746 |
| 9½ | 2.50 | 63.6 | 2 1/2 | .762 |
| 10 | 2.55 | 64.8 | 2 35/64 | .778 |
| 10½ | 2.60 | 66.0 | 2 19/32 | .794 |
| 11 | 2.65 | 67.3 | 2 21/32 | .810 |
| 11½ | 2.70 | 68.6 | 2 45/64 | .826 |
| 12 | 2.76 | 70.1 | 2 3/4 | .842 |
| 12½ | 2.81 | 71.5 | 2 13/16 | .858 |
| 13 | 2.86 | 72.7 | 2 55/64 | .874 |
| 13½ | 2.91 | 74.0 | 2 29/32 | .890 |

*For 16-gauge sheet metal. Thicker metals will be slightly more—thinner metals will be slightly less. As an example, for 12-gauge metal, add 1/16 inch to noted dimensions of blank length. For 20-gauge metal, subtract 1/32 inch from indicated blank length.*

**TABLE 18F—Wire Blank Lengths for Large Loops**

| Loop Diameter | Blank Length | Loop Diameter | Blank Length |
|---|---|---|---|
| 1-1/16 | 3-1/2 | 2-1/8 | 6-7/8 |
| 1-1/8 | 3-3/4 | 2-1/4 | 7-1/4 |
| 1-3/16 | 3-15/16 | 2-3/8 | 7-11/16 |
| 1-1/4 | 4-1/8 | 2-1/2 | 8-1/16 |
| 1-5/16 | 4-5/16 | 2-5/8 | 8-7/16 |
| 1-3/8 | 4-1/2 | 2-3/4 | 8-13/16 |
| 1-7/16 | 4-3/4 | 2-7/8 | 9-1/4 |
| 1-1/2 | 4-15/16 | 3 | 9-5/8 |
| 1-9/16 | 5-1/8 | 3-1/8 | 10 |
| 1-5/8 | 5-5/32 | 3-1/4 | 10-3/8 |
| 1-11/16 | 5-1/2 | 3-3/8 | 10-13/16 |
| 1-3/4 | 5-11/16 | 3-1/2 | 11-3/16 |
| 1-13/16 | 5-29/32 | 3-5/8 | 11-9/16 |
| 1-7/8 | 6-1/16 | 3-3/4 | 11-15/16 |
| 1-15/16 | 6-9/32 | 3-7/8 | 12-3/8 |
| 2 | 6-1/2 | 4 | 12-3/4 |

## TABLE 18G–Common Soft Solder Compositions and Melting Temperatures

| Grade or Metal | Composition (Percent) | | | Melting Temperature (F) | |
|---|---|---|---|---|---|
| | Tin | Lead | Antimony* | Initial Melt | Completely Molten |
| 100% Tin | 100 | | | 450 | 450 |
| 0 | 63 | 37 | 0.12 | 360 | 360 |
| 1 | 50 | 50 | 0.12 | 360 | 415 |
| 2 | 45 | 55 | 0.12 | 360 | 435 |
| 3 | 40 | 60 | 0.12 | 360 | 459 |
| 4 | 37.5 | 62.5 | 0.12 | 360 | 468 |
| 5 | 33 | 67 | 0.12 | 360 | 486 |
| 100% Lead | | 100 | | 621 | 621 |

*Maximum permitted

## TABLE 18H–Fraction and Decimal Inches plus Millimeter Equivalents

| Fractions | | | | Decimal | Millimeters |
|---|---|---|---|---|---|
| 1/64 | | | | .0156 | 0.397 |
| | 1/32 | | | .0313 | 0.794 |
| 3/64 | | | | .0469 | 1.191 |
| | | 1/16 | | .0625 | 1.588 |
| 5/64 | | | | .0781 | 1.984 |
| | 3/32 | | | .0937 | 2.381 |
| 7/64 | | | | .1094 | 2.778 |
| | | | 1/8 | .1250 | 3.175 |
| 9/64 | | | | .1406 | 3.572 |
| | 5/32 | | | .1562 | 3.969 |
| 11/64 | | | | .1719 | 4.366 |
| | | 3/16 | | .1875 | 4.762 |
| 13/64 | | | | .2031 | 5.159 |
| | 7/32 | | | .2187 | 5.556 |
| 15/64 | | | | .2344 | 5.953 |
| | | | 1/4 | .2500 | 6.350 |
| 17/64 | | | | .2656 | 6.747 |
| | 9/32 | | | .2812 | 7.144 |
| 19/64 | | | | .2969 | 7.541 |
| | | 5/16 | | .3125 | 7.937 |
| 21/64 | | | | .3281 | 8.334 |
| | 11/32 | | | .3438 | 8.731 |
| 23/64 | | | | .3594 | 9.128 |
| | | | 3/8 | .3750 | 9.525 |
| 25/64 | | | | .3906 | 9.922 |
| | 13/32 | | | .4062 | 10.319 |
| 27/64 | | | | .4219 | 10.716 |
| | | 7/16 | | .4375 | 11.112 |
| 29/64 | | | | .4531 | 11.509 |
| | 15/32 | | | .4687 | 11.906 |
| 31/64 | | | | .4844 | 12.303 |
| | | | 1/2 | .5000 | 12.700 |

## TABLE 18H (Cont.)

| Fractions | | | | Decimals | Millimeters |
|---|---|---|---|---|---|
| 33/64 | | | | .5156 | 13.097 |
| | 17/32 | | | .5313 | 13.494 |
| 35/64 | | | | .5469 | 13.891 |
| | | 9/16 | | .5625 | 14.288 |
| 37/64 | | | | .5781 | 14.684 |
| | 19/32 | | | .5938 | 15.081 |
| 39/64 | | | | .6094 | 15.487 |
| | | | 5/8 | .6250 | 15.875 |
| 41/64 | | | | .6406 | 16.272 |
| | 21/32 | | | .6563 | 16.669 |
| 43/64 | | | | .6719 | 17.066 |
| | | 11/16 | | .6875 | 17.462 |
| 45/64 | | | | .7031 | 17.859 |
| | 23/32 | | | .7188 | 18.256 |
| 47/64 | | | | .7344 | 18.653 |
| | | | 3/4 | .7500 | 19.050 |
| 49/64 | | | | .7656 | 19.447 |
| | 25/32 | | | .7813 | 19.844 |
| 51/64 | | | | .7969 | 20.241 |
| | | 13/16 | | .8125 | 20.637 |
| 53/64 | | | | .8281 | 21.034 |
| | 27/32 | | | .8438 | 21.431 |
| 55/64 | | | | .8594 | 21.828 |
| | | | 7/8 | .8750 | 22.225 |
| 57/64 | | | | .8906 | 22.622 |
| | 29/32 | | | .9063 | 23.019 |
| 59/64 | | | | .9219 | 23.416 |
| | | 15/16 | | .9375 | 23.812 |
| 61/64 | | | | .9531 | 24.209 |
| | 31/32 | | | .9688 | 24.606 |
| 63/64 | | | | .9844 | 25.003 |
| | | | 1 | 1.000 | 25.400 |

# sources of supplies

OBTAINING THE RIGHT TYPE of supplies along with tools designed specifically for jewelry handcrafting can be a time-consuming and frustrating experience. The average craftsman may experience considerable difficulty in locating sources of materials and tools whether he or she lives in a metropolitan area or in an outlying location. Two general types of difficulties arise — first, finding the right supplier who has the desired goods and who will respond within a reasonable time, and second, finding a supplier who will accept small orders.

Generally, most jewelry craftsmen do better shopping by mail from specialty suppliers. The accompanying list of suppliers is by no means exhaustive, but those listed are known to respond with fast service and will accept small orders. While most of the listed suppliers operate retail sales establishments, most of their activity is by mail. The suppliers are grouped according to the type of materials, tools, or equipment supplied.

## MAIL ORDER HOUSES

The following mail order houses supply findings, gemstones, some metals, hand and power tools, and some casting equipment. In most cases, these suppliers issue thick catalogs replete with color illustrations at a cost of $1.00 and up. Ordinarily, the catalog fee is refunded or credited on the first purchase. Some of the suppliers have established minimum order amounts.

Gemex Company
Highway 395
Pala, California 92059

J. J. Jewelcraft
4959 York Boulevard
Los Angeles, California 90050

Weidinger, Inc.
P. O. Box 39
Matteson, Illinois 60443

T. L. Baskin
732 Union Avenue
Middlesex, New Jersey 08846

C. R. Hill Co.
35 West Grand River
Detroit, Michigan 48208

Griegers, Inc.
1633 E. Walnut Street
Pasadena, California 91109

**General Arts and Crafts**

Bergen Arts and Crafts
Box 689
Salem, Massachusetts 01970

**Enamels**

Thomas C. Thompson Co.
P. O. Box 127
Highland Park, Illinois 60035

**Precious Metals**

Southwest Smelting and Refining Co.
P. O. Box 2010
Dallas, Texas 75221

T. B. Hagstoz & Son
709 Sansom Street
Philadelphia, Pennsylvania 19106

Parker Industries, Inc.
2217 Fourth Avenue
Seattle, Washington 98121

**Casting Equipment**

Southwest Smelting and Refining Co.
P. O. Box 2010
Dallas, Texas 75221

Casting Supply House, Inc.
62 West 47th Street
New York, New York 10036

Gesswein
235 Park Avenue S.
New York, New York 10003

Romanoff Rubber Co.
153-159 W. 27th Street
New York, New York 10001

Technical Specialties International Inc.
487 Elliott Ave. West
Seattle, Washington 98119

## CUSTOM CASTING SERVICES

There are numerous small casting operations in almost all metropolitan areas. But there are relatively few who advertise and solicit custom work over a large geographic area. However, pertinent information concerning known organizations is as follows:

Ala Casting Company
71 Fifth Avenue
New York, New York 10003

Avnet Shaw Art Foundry
91 Commercial Street
Plainview, New York 11803
  Specializing in fine sculpture casting in bronze, stainless steel, and other metals for professional and amateur artists.

Billanti Casting Company
64 W. 48th Street
New York, New York 10010
  Custom casting in lost wax process, precious metals only; each item priced individually.

Magic Circle Corporation
P. O. Box 22027
Seattle, Washington 98122
  Custom casting in precious metals, brass, and bronze. In most cases, castings are done on a fixed fee basis plus cost of metal. They also have special jewelry craft products, metals, tools, and hard-to-find items.

## LOCAL SOURCES

Some of the best local sources may be acquired from teachers of craft classes in the adult education program at your local high school or community college. These teachers may even operate a craft shop of their own that sells finished jewelry along with instruction. Look in the classified section of your telephone directory under such headings as Jewelers — Manufacturing, Jewelers' Supplies & Findings, Jewelry Designers, Jewelry Enamelers, Jewelry Mountings, and Jewelry — Repairing. A telephone call or a personal visit to the shops or studios listed may turn up a local source of supplies that is handier than ordering by mail. Usually, local shops will have a limited selection of most materials.

# index